SIGNS OF AGNI YOGA
SUPERMUNDANE
Vol. III

SUPERMUNDANE

THE INNER LIFE

III

1938

Agni Yoga Society
319 West 107th Street
New York NY 10025
www.agniyoga.org

© 1994 by the Agni Yoga Society.
Published 1994.

Reprinted 2017. Updated July 2020.
Translated from Russian by the Agni Yoga Society.

SUPERMUNDANE

The Inner Life

590. Urusvati knows that refinement is a quality that is gained through the experiences of many lives. Its components are a real understanding of cooperation, fieriness of thinking, loftiness of activity, a high degree of sensitivity, love for beauty. Each of these qualities can be developed only by persistent striving. People should not think that instantaneous illumination will at once create a refined nature. Illumination can open the treasure chest, but if the container is empty, nothing will come of it.

You know that it is easy for people to be in harmony when there is no task in sight, but when a difficult time approaches, reasons are always found for quarreling. It is amazing that although people read many instructive books, when the first opportunity appears to apply what was read they sink into a deep gloom, and nothing uplifting is of interest to them. People have heard much about Armageddon, but now that it is upon us, they see it as a chance misfortune that could have been avoided.

It is understandable when the ignorant ones think this way, but why should sensible people also fall so easily into such confusion? They do not realize how much harm they inflict upon themselves and upon others.

Is it possible that people are so afraid that even one sign of approaching difficulty turns them into cowards, and in their flight they discard the best that they have created? Truly, during sweet times of ease, man shows a beautiful face, but in times of danger he reveals a disgusting one. Yet, dear people, you all live in constant danger, from both above and below. At every hour your well-being can be destroyed.

The Thinker used to say, "Humanity is divided into two types. In one the Divine Principle is dominant, but the other is immersed in the earthly. We do not know what people will call the Divine Principle in the future, but this division of mankind will be with us forever."

591. Urusvati knows that to comprehend the Supermundane one must first understand the patterns of relationship in nature. People tend to go repeatedly from the one extreme, blind faith, to the other, blind denial. This confusion is caused by an equally blind fear of the Unknown. Like children afraid to face something, they cover their eyes so as not to see reality. Adults, too, will insist that it is wrong to explore beyond established boundaries. But who can forbid the gaining of knowledge?

Let us accept that on the one hand there are unenlightened cults that worship imagined deities, and on the other hand more "modern" people who deny the existence of everything beyond their understanding. Who of these are more right? One thing is clear–in both cases fear is dominant. One carves for himself terrifying idols and fears their cruelty, and the other is equally afraid of the unknown but will not admit it. Let us recall an ancient tale to illustrate this.

Once a hermit came to a raucous, quarrelsome household, bringing two caskets. He put them carefully in a corner and said, "One of these contains a healing remedy, but the other is full of a most deadly poison. Watch over them until I return, but remember that the slightest noise can provoke terrible destruction." The hermit left, and thereafter peace and quiet ruled the household. I ask, Because of which casket did this family transform itself? With a knowledge of human nature one can easily answer. The very same fears exist today.

The end of this story is that when the others were away, a little child opened both caskets and found them empty. But, also out of fear, the child did not speak of his discovery. However, do not come to any premature conclusions about this story; it is possible that the child failed to see something that was of great importance. Thus science should fearlessly investigate the unseen.

The Thinker said, "I do not know what the Divine Science will be called in the future, but it will exist. The Supermundane will become visible to us, but then, earthly life too will become Supermundane."

592. Urusvati knows that the darkest superstition in earthly life is the superstition of negators. They reject learning. They impose their will on science, and thus limit it. They act without reason, and the justifications for their actions are unfounded. They call themselves scientists, forgetting the true meaning of science. They call others fanatics, but they themselves stagnate in their own dogmatism. They insist that other worlds are not populated, but cannot prove it by their deductions. Science, when under the influence of dogma, enters upon a false way.

Such people refuse to acknowledge that true scientists contribute to the development of human consciousness. The science of energies is hated by the superstitious ones, for only by this path can people approach an understanding of the Supermundane. The superstitious ones fear the undeniable evidence provided by this science. They prefer to see space as empty, and continue to spew out their wholesale denials.

The discovery of psychic energy is inadmissible to them. Energy of thought is for them an empty phrase. In their obstinacy they do not realize that they have become malicious reactionaries. Do these madmen think that they can prevent man from thinking in unlimited freedom?

The only thing for which we can thank those superstitious dogmatists is that they act as an anvil, on which the fiery hammer of free thought forges the blade of Truth. The superstitious ones will be insulted by this comparison to an anvil. They would much prefer to be the hammer–but this hammer forges evolution, which is based upon the free pursuit of knowledge.

Superstition is the great shame of humanity. Even worse, the superstitious negators consider themselves to be superior; this is an attitude characteristic of ignorance.

We speak about the Supermundane because humanity desperately needs to know about it. We want the Supermundane to be cognized in a scientific way, through research and observation. For this man must deepen his consciousness and elevate his thought. The deniers are no real threat to this process, but we must not underestimate their malicious efforts. They will say to the free pursuit of knowledge, "Your life is my death."

The Thinker used to say, "Who can limit thinking? The one who attempts it is not just ignorant, he is insane!"

593. Urusvati knows other enemies of evolution–those who are indifferent. If We compare the negators to an anvil, to what, then, can we compare the indifferent ones? To corpses, perhaps? One philosopher taught that indifference is equal to heartlessness. He was right, because the consciousness of the indifferent one is so low that it cannot serve evolution.

Unfortunately, the number of the indifferent ones is great. They not only foster the destruction of the planet but also are the greatest burden to the Subtle World. They arrive there without spiritual striving and are unable to adapt to the conditions. They need special attention, but even the best guidance is deflected by their indifference. They bring with them the narrow limitations of earthly routine, which are an unacceptable burden to the lofty sphere of the Subtle World. They are devoid of striving and have no idea about the significance of the power of thought. They bring their dull, impoverished nature with them into the Beautiful Realms. They cannot apply themselves to their designated tasks.

One cannot imagine what an ugly spectacle these individuals are! They do not care about their garments. They have no affinity to their Guides and wander aimlessly in the gloom. On Earth they are a major affliction, a womb of calamities. Just as decomposing corpses swarm with worms, so do these people carry within themselves the germs of universal calamity.

The Thinker knew them and suffered greatly, precisely because of them. He used to say, "It is unbearable to remain amidst these decaying corpses."

594. Urusvati knows the deep meaning of silence. It has been noted that some great army leaders, rulers of nations, and spiritual leaders, after proclaiming important decisions, became immersed in silence. People usually attributed this to fatigue or depression, but in reality an important mental process was taking place. The ruler was following his order with mental reinforcement.

It should be understood that a mental order can be strengthened by concentration of the will, but even the best orders can be weakened by obstruction of the energy. One can cite many examples in history when decisions were undermined by surrounding mediocrity.

The wisdom of silence was valued by people from ancient times. The most important actions were performed in silence, and not amidst the uncontrolled shouting of the crowds. We already pointed out how difficult it is to achieve harmony. Its power is weakened by the disorderly currents generated by undisciplined wills, a condition that at present is epidemic, afflicting the world even more than war.

People do not recognize this, for they do not see the abyss of hypocrisy and falsehood. They do not want to hear about psychic achievement. They battle against all ideas of true peace. Thus, we can understand the vows of silence taken by great people.

Our co-workers learn to know when their thoughts of good can bear fruit. Only an expanded consciousness can indicate the appropriate date. Invisible friends often try to send helpful thoughts, but because of the clamor of the crowds, these currents cannot be received properly.

The Thinker often said, "Who is calling me? The speech of my friend is not understandable. Who is the obstructor?"

595. Urusvati knows that rejoicing in the misfortunes of others is a malevolent trait. One can feel sadness or indignation, but to feel satisfaction is beneath human dignity. Besides, such rejoicing transfers to the one who feels joy a part of the karma of the one who is suffering the misfortunes. This should be remembered. There is little difference between taking joy in another's suffering and slandering him. Everyone who does this will sooner or later experience the same attitude from others. People may err, or they may commit crimes, and thus deserve criticism or punishment, but one should not rejoice over their troubles.

Learning to understand human qualities is a part of the path of yoga. The contemplation of good and bad in man brings one closer to the gates of progress. We regularly point out those qualities that are worthy, and in this way We provide hints about Our Inner Life. One should not think that, having reached a certain level of spiritual development, one no longer needs to continue striving to improve one's qualities. Each level requires further refinement of one's nature. One should test oneself untiringly, and learn to love such tests. The testing of one's armor is a sign of readiness for battle. The symbol of the battle is pointed out in all the ancient Teachings. The words of wisdom are uttered in the midst of battle. Let us not forget that the synthesis of wisdom and courage is a strong guarantee of success.

It is in the stream of life that one's spiritual strivings and battles are merged.

The Thinker taught, "Look at the currents. Their design is complex, yet they rush onward. Nothing can stop them. And so, let the soul of man strive forward similarly."

596. Urusvati knows that every human contact affects all participants. This fact should be repeated, because most people do not understand what it means. Even enlightened people, when hearing this, tend to think that only important events are meant, and that the contacts of everyday life are not included. It should be stressed that We are speaking of all actions, whatever their importance.

One may wonder how petty household routine could have any profound significance. It truly can. Much talk is heard about those unfortunates who suffer for no apparent reason, but if we look at the very root of their daily routines, we can find many causes for their misfortunes. These causes can be direct or indirect. When a person experiences suffering caused by another, some link between them, resulting from past actions, must exist.

The simplest activities of family life can have strong effects on all. The family is often a malevolent breeding ground of hatred and animosity. Can such influences pass without effect? The influences may be unique to each particular family, where they are nurtured and strengthened. Such fetid soil produces dangerous enemies of human happiness. Let us also not forget the crowded workplaces in which an atmosphere of distrust and hatred can prevail. People must remember their duty not to pollute space. We have apparatuses that measure the pollution of space.

The world-leaders call attention to the great problems of the world, but the true source of discord is not so much in these, but in the daily life of the people.

The Thinker used to say, "It is not the archons who start wars, but those citizens who hide the wars that persist in their own homes."

597. Urusvati knows that the work in the depth of one's consciousness is continuous, and that people do not sense it. A sensitive person can perceive those inner calls that provide help when needed. Scientists may call it intuition or the sub-conscious. They fear to call this process the work of the consciousness. If boundaries are placed between the super-consciousness and the sub-consciousness, where then is the consciousness? Truly, it is all one. Like the heart, the consciousness works day and night, but the physical heart is an earthly organ, whereas the consciousness is an organ of the three worlds. The accumulations of consciousness take place on all levels.

We call the consciousness the subterranean fire. There are many analogies between them. The fire is needed for the balance of the planet, but besides benevolent manifestations, the very same fire can also be destructive.

Cannot the very same be said about the consciousness? It propels man toward perfectment, but it can also, if not disciplined, be explosively destructive. An obscured consciousness is ready for any crime when its balance has been lost and, its fiery nature has become explosive.

After misdeeds caused by the loss of balance, a person may try in vain to regain the dispersed particles of consciousness, but sometimes one must start all over again to build new accumulations. What a burdensome, black cargo is that slag of charred consciousness in the Subtle World! Thus one could metaphorically describe the heavy load carried by those travelers, struggling to ascend the mountain. They all think, "Why did I burden myself with such a load?" But if each of them knew how to listen to the voice of the consciousness the load would have been made light, and it would be easier for Us to help them.

We feel great joy in helping everyone in his own circumstance. But often the best sending returns, unaccepted. We have huge archives of unaccepted messages, in the same way that the post office collects undeliverable letters. Yet, some of our correspondents could have been more receptive. Why hide oneself behind doubt and irritation? When We speak about the Supermundane, it would seem that every word should be hearkened to with care.

Our Inner Life is full of touching moments when a sensitive receptivity to Us evokes Our gratitude. Many times has Urusvati heard these words of gratitude. When We summon everyone to a still greater calmness, it means that We foresee times of increased tension that must be lived through with care. It is easy to lose one's balance at such times, but no good can come of this. One must strain one's mind to its limits, and also harken to the voice of the consciousness.

The Thinker used to say, "My poor mind, where can you go without your beautiful guide, your soul?"

598. Urusvati knows why some of Our communications must be withheld until the time is right for them to be given out. People think only about effects, and do not want to think about causes. Furthermore, they grow angry when causes are pointed out to them. They do not understand that a cause indicated by a message from Us can produce the very results that they are experiencing.

They say, "What can there be in common between events that bring suffering to us, and those causes that You point out, which have no evident link to the events?" Thus speak those who have not developed their imagination and therefore did not broaden their consciousness or perceptivity. Such people can maliciously interpret true causes and, in their anger, engender only evil.

One should avoid all attitudes that can increase evil. Even without this effort, much evil can grow in every home. Therefore, a great deal of foreknowledge must be carefully withheld so as not to provoke distrust or abuse. Teachings from unknown sources also must be given out guardedly. At the beginning, their words may appear beneficent, but later they can provoke destructive consequences. One who is of steady mind can investigate all phenomena, but the wavering one can be harmed. Again we arrive at the weighing of cause and effect.

It is not so easy to grasp the idea that a seemingly insignificant cause can be the source of great calamities. Therefore one should learn to imagine how a small brooklet can become a powerful current.

The Thinker used to say, "Let the gods of Olympus teach me to discern the true causes of events."

599. Urusvati knows about those who turn away from the Teaching. Every teaching has its apostates. It is amazing to see what base motives prompt their betrayals, demeaning for mankind. History provides enough known examples, but in reality there have been many more.

We discuss this shameful behavior only because of Our desire to establish a right attitude toward it. Some people grow too upset when they learn about them. Their harmfulness should not be overestimated. They actually act as a kind of resonator, and with their energy add a special tension to the life of the Teaching. It is difficult to increase energy without opposition. This is what We meant when We spoke about the anvil.

Yet, apostates are worse than those who have always denied. One should trace the complex development of apostasy, in order to understand how the great teachings can be betrayed by the low consciousness. The best that those who repudiate the Teaching can do is to hasten their act of treason. The fate of an apostate is not to be envied. History demonstrates this. But others should not waste their time in trying to dissuade the apostate. His action is an abscess that must come to a head without interference. Therefore, let us respond calmly to this dreadful act of betrayal.

The Thinker knew the apostates among His disciples. He advised them to depart quickly.

600. Urusvati knows the qualities needed by those who desire to cognize the Supermundane World. They must understand its reality. They know that they must continue forever to learn. They realize that each human action attracts dwellers from the Supermundane World who are consonant with it. Some who think of themselves as seekers do not understand how deeply these qualities must become rooted in their nature. They are ready to chatter about the reality of the invisible worlds, but do not even trouble themselves to think about and imagine the grandeur of the Infinite. They do not desire to constantly learn, and the honor of being a disciple is not recognized by them. They will not accept as true that each of their thoughts evokes a multitude of invisible entities that can be helpful sometimes, but are more often harmful.

Such people do not accept scientific analogies. To them the statement that space is full of life means nothing. They deduce nothing from the fact that every day science brings new discoveries. One should not respond to these discoveries with denial, but rather with positive enthusiasm. People who do not accept reality deprive themselves of the most enlightened joy.

The Thinker used to say, "Where is the school that can teach people joy?"

601. Urusvati knows how We cherish and assist all acts of self-denial. But Our care also extends to all similar activities. This is not often recognized, and it may puzzle those who see that certain activities that are not directly related to Us are nevertheless under Our protection. However, close examination would reveal that these activities involve self-sacrificing people.

The quality of self-denial is important in the Subtle World too. It is developed during one's earthly life, but bears fruit in the Supermundane World. In this achievement those who strive in their earthly life learn detachment from their own creations. Attachment to one's creations is a great burden when one is in the Subtle World, where those who are absorbed with their old creations are unable to concentrate on their new work of learning.

If a dweller of the Subtle World is bound to the mentality of the previous life, he will hinder the development of new ways of thinking. In the exaltation of self-denial people can more easily free themselves from the fetters of earthly life. We value such soaring of the spirit.

Also, pay attention to those who fight against injustice. In the Supermundane World they find many new possibilities. Hypocrites will contend that the borderline between justice and injustice is a relative one. Answer firmly that in every instance injustice is clearly evident, and a person with a sensitive heart can discern clearly the borderline.

The battle against injustice is a pure one, devoid of self-interest, and you, Our friends, should help those who join in this battle. By doing this, you act with Us, and all such harmonized action increases the power of Good.

What We say today reveals another page of Our Inner Life. We apply Ourselves to caring for self-sacrificing co-workers and helping those who fight against injustice. These two kinds of workers attract furious attacks by the forces of darkness. Many of them cannot endure such attacks, because, unfortunately, they possess habits that weaken them.

At times We ask for the highest degree of trust, which will provide a salutary calmness. Our warriors must be calm, for they know that the goal is pure. They know about the evil designs of the dark ones, and know that the battle is inevitable. But they must also know that they have supportive Friends. They must know this unwaveringly. Vacillation inflicts pain on their Friends. Think about this pain and remember what has been said about the drops of perspiration.

The Thinker said, "Learn to unite your thoughts with the Supermundane Worlds."

602. Urusvati knows that rest is achieved by change of labor. Among those labors to which one can turn, let us not forget the mental work that develops the imagination. We continually perform mental exercises. A superficial observer at times may think that We are asleep, when in the midst of Our work We close Our eyes and send out thoughts to wander in the kingdom of imagination. These moments have great significance, for such imagined images become real. We cannot judge when this realization occurs, but it does take place and is of help to mankind.

Do not think that such mental work is available only to special beings. Everyone can develop the imagination, but certain conditions must be observed. It is good when one imagines the beautiful, but if ugliness is evoked, incalculable harm will result. Therefore one must think beautifully. For this excellent images are offered by nature, but if someone is incapable of contemplating the beauties of nature, he can immerse himself in beautiful works of art, in which the creators have expressed a synthesis of all their observations of nature.

Learn to concentrate on the most beautiful works, otherwise you will be exposed to ugliness.

One of Our concerns is to help artists. Frequently they succumb to the influence of invisible entities that scoff at beauty and rejoice at all manifestations of ugliness. Learn about the art of various eras. Learn about the synthesizing nature of art during periods of renewal.

The Thinker expressed admiration for the geniuses of sculpture. He said, "In earthly life, one does not encounter such perfection; the sculptor imagined it and embodied it for the future."

603. Urusvati knows that preventive medicine is the best medicine. One could wonder why, until now, preventive measures have dealt only with physical well-being, while ignoring the mental condition. But it is precisely this aspect that is of greatest importance for the preservation of health. There are known hereditary, infectious, and occupational ailments, and in all these the psychic influence plays a role, because of its ability to arrest the development of illness.

Timely help by means of suggestion can hold back or even eliminate the onset of illness. It is too much to expect that most people could master auto-suggestion. Only extraordinarily sensitive organisms are able to feel the very first symptoms of an illness and obstruct it by the power of their will. For the majority, suggestions from without are needed. But such "inoculations" will be most effective only if administered on a national scale.

Institutes will be needed in which armies of physicians are taught the methods of salutary suggestion. Supervision will of course be necessary to maintain an ethical standard, otherwise the power of suggestion could be used for criminal purposes. Such institutions will become reality. People will understand that even the healthiest conditions of physical life cannot alone solve the problem of restoration of humanity's health. The worst epidemic that threatens is from the mental side.

You know how criminality is growing. It cannot be conquered by pills and injections. Suggestion by the will, on a scientific basis, is needed. Even certain scourges of mankind, like cancer, require timely mental prophylaxis.

The Thinker taught, "Revere Hygeia, she can teach you how to improve the health of the people."

604. Urusvati knows Our joy when it is possible to help and give good advice to a worthy co-worker. But two obstacles often appear. First, people like to interpret advice in their own personal way. Notice that even the clearest advice is interpreted according to the level of understanding of the one who receives it. It is often said that one should speak in accordance with the level of the listener's consciousness, but that is not easy. The level of consciousness of the listener will determine which portion of the advice will be assimilated, and which will not. Thus what people, in their individual ways, do with the advice given to them will reveal their level of consciousness. That is why so many people cannot follow a law, even when it has been clearly explained to them.

The second obstacle is that people refuse to understand that their thoughts and words are like a powerful radio transmission. They know that spoken words can be transmitted through space, but they do not recognize that thought, like sound, has the same degree of energy. Is it possible to persuade people that every uttered sound finds listeners, and that every thought, as a subtle manifestation, carries even farther than the word? But how many are there who care about this, when the very existence of the invisible worlds is almost universally unrecognized?

It should be pointed out that certain thoughts can be concealed, but to develop such a level of control, an understanding of the Subtle World is required. Consider how much advice might be distorted if given prematurely.

The Thinker said, "The shepherd Theokolus related that he made his way to the summit of Olympus and found nothing there. Maybe he hoped to find a holiday feast, where he would be offered intoxicating Nectar and a huge helping of Ambrosia!"

605. Urusvati knows that We approve of everything that awakens a true sense of rhythm in people. The feeling of rhythm is inherent, but the disorder of chaos deadens it. People may act rhythmically, but still be far from an understanding of the great significance of rhythm. If someone wants to take a decisive action, his instinct can correctly prompt him to first establish the necessary rhythm, and in this cadence the required harmony is found. Even a limited effort will provide beneficent results.

We demonstrated the simplest rhythms of Mahavan and Chotavan, but one can learn far more complicated rhythms. Let us recall the most ancient meters of the Sanskrit language and of the worlds of ancient Greece and Rome. In them one can find highly-developed, well-considered patterns of rhythmic sound. The ancients knew the necessity for communion with Cosmos.

During certain periods of earthly tension, one should think very much about rhythm. The people's cries of terror plunge them into the abyss of chaos. Do not think that We approve of feasting in a time of plague. But when a Hindu chants verses from the Bhagavad-Gita he acts wisely and the result is a healing harmony. Rhythm is both the cement and the wings of space.

People desire communion with Us; the first key for them will be the realization of their own inner rhythm. There can be the finest music and singing, yet nothing will resound in the heart that is deaf. In contrast, a refined heart will tremble in harmonious response to the rhythm. The seeker will then become better, more courageous and strong; he will be a worthy co-worker of the earthly and of the Supermundane, and will find joy.

Remember that Earth is suffering from an unusual state of tension. During the time of Armageddon how can one permit oneself to participate in this state of chaos? In all actions, great or small, think about this reminder. It is not well-being, but struggle, that teaches man to think. But what kind of warrior would he be if, in the first difficult hour he loses his guiding star, his thoughtfulness? How different would he then be from the unthinking ones, who cannot recognize a decisive hour, and for whom threatening events are only accidental. But he who thinks sensibly associates himself with cosmic rhythms, and in such an armor boldly accepts the battle. He is then with Us.

The Thinker said, "Muses, beautiful Muses! In your harmonious choir you give to humanity the salutary rhythm."

606. Urusvati knows that We often speak about struggle. Truly, the struggle to overcome chaos is always beautiful. There is no other way for evolution. This is a simple concept that is often misinterpreted. The sanctimonious ones resist it, for they extol some world of their own that is based upon inaction and lack of thinking. Hypocrites will argue that their own petty squabbles are also a battle. Finally, the cunning ones will make absurd accusations, so as to justify their malicious efforts.

True, for the understanding of a great battle one should learn to co-measure. People must make use of all their measuring skills in order to calculate where is the great and where the small, and should know how to find the proper balance between them. Can a single bee survive without the swarm? Is it not instructive to observe how small globules of mercury are attracted to each other, and form one whole? Likewise, scattered sand, under the influence of various rhythms, will take on different designs. Nature provides many such examples of attraction, which demonstrate the battle against chaos. One should view world events in this way, otherwise entire eras of history will pass unnoticed.

So many valuable concepts are distorted! People do not understand the great significance of love, this universal magnet. Unfortunately, people make subjective judgments, and interpret things through their ego. They think of love as imposing, and in this they clip the wings of beautiful love.

The Thinker pointed to the sculpture called Winged Victory and said, "Hold your eyes open and in purity, otherwise you will not discern where is the Light."

607. Urusvati knows how difficult it is for people to understand the idea of inner courage. It is not easy to explain to them that apparent courage may not be real. One may seem courageous, yet inwardly tremble with fear. Many examples can be cited when it was precisely the absence of inner courage that caused downfall.

Inner courage should not be confused with similar qualities. People may say we are speaking probably about calmness, and though calmness, and its neighbor, equilibrium, are related to courage, they are not quite the same. It is not easy to teach the understanding that inner courage is a constant readiness for bold thinking and action.

Great joy is felt when beautiful actions are performed freely, with no obstacles. Usually many things intrude to prevent even thinking about achievement. If heroic actions are formed first in the mind, a radiant aura is built. And when this light becomes strong enough, the dreams can be turned into action.

Not without reason it is said that each dream will at some time be turned into reality. But one should have a big store of such dreams of daring. Inner courage can dare, and this must be learned not only for the Supermundane World, but also for the earthly one. Learn to understand that whatever is useful for the Supermundane World is also useful for the earthly. Thus, in calmness, one should think about heroic achievements. Some of these thoughts will be recollections from past lives. Everyone has performed a *podvig* in the past or dreamt about it. Podvig can take place under any earthly conditions.

The Thinker said, "It is not only those who wear helmets who are warriors."

608. Urusvati knows that a great master of music must be born who will give to humanity glimpses of the symphony of the spheres. The time is coming when people will have a great need for the symphonies of space, whose harmonies will be a true panacea. The "ambassadors" of sound did come in the past, but they had little success in transmitting what they had brought with them from the subtle spheres.

In My Country a strong talent who knew the value of harmony appeared, but he could not sufficiently shield himself and departed without realizing his best possibilities. Truly, people who bring a good message must guard themselves. They are under the pressure of two forces, the earthly and the subtle, and are susceptible to special dangers. Do not think that walls must collapse upon them; there may arise petty dangers that are ruinous for them. The "messengers" should not squander themselves with carelessness in their lives. They must understand that their message is of great importance, and must carry the chalice unspilled for others. We attentively watch over them, not only on Earth, but also in the Supermundane World, where they learn the symphony of the spheres. Not much will be brought by them to Earth, but even this will assist the progress of humanity.

Urusvati heard the music of the spheres, and knows that its main power is in harmony and in rhythm. But there are no instruments on Earth that can express all the grandeur of the Calls of Space. This is one more page of Our Inner Life–We cannot live without sound, and regret that there are some people who have no need for music.

The Thinker taught, "To listen to the Beautiful and to look at the Beautiful, means to better oneself."

609. Urusvati knows how wondrously and instantaneously the consciousness of a thinking person is transformed while crossing into the Supermundane World. Some events of the life just passed gain significance, while others lose their importance. The earthly achievements believed to be most important prove to be meaningless, whereas every self-sacrificing deed in service to humanity grows in radiant glory. Those deeds bring joy, while the earthly achievements are transitory, and turn into dust.

Man reaches the highest summits through those soaring thoughts to which he may not even have paid attention. Characteristically, he ignores his valuable achievements and drowns himself in the hubbub of the bazaar. Do not regard what I say as moralizing. We are simply reminding you about the reality that is being formed on the different steps of ascent.

There are those who do not want to remember their incarnations of high earthly status, but think back to the more modest and difficult of their earthly lives. The strongest strivings in life are expressed in labor–this is the essence of the reevaluation of one's earthly existences. You may notice that sometimes the briefest encounters are recalled, for they could have been fateful moments when currents were crossed. The resultant sparks can be significant and will be recalled with gratitude. Who can say with certainty that such meetings were accidental? Perhaps they were encounters with old friends.

The Thinker said, "Here you are, calling 'Plato, Plato', but perhaps the real name is quite different."

610. Urusvati knows Our Instruction: "Be just." But what kind of justice do We mean? People invent many so-called justices. They know justice as personal, family, clan, and race. They hide behind official, school, and professional justice. One cannot enumerate all the many views of justice! But human justice is left out. People judge from many points of view, but the main one–universal justice–is never recognized.

We have already spoken about unjust judges as a shame of humanity, but We must now talk not only about judges, but about all those who are sunk in lies. Everyone, every day, pronounces judgments. People take on burdens of responsibility by shooting arrows of falsehood into space, for they judge conventionally, and often ignorantly. Also, people are often opinionated, and even spiteful, when they send their poisonous arrows of judgment.

There are many physical poisons, but many more psychic ones. Children can be poisoned from their earliest years. They are influenced by the spitefulness of adults, and their organisms can be opened to the most terrible illnesses. The efforts of humanity should not be devoted only to the development of machines and robots, but should also attend to the development of universal human justice. Otherwise, where can man go in the Supermundane World, and what kind of discourse can he have with Us? We judge humanly, but the one who converses with Us will think that he speaks justly, but he will be limited by his narrow beliefs.

One should grow accustomed to universal justice. One should test oneself–did not some partiality of judgment creep in? In daily life one should constantly examine oneself. Do not think that justice is found only in the courtroom. Everyone is a judge.

The Thinker said, "Learn true justice, for every day you pronounce judgments."

611. Urusvati knows that great attention should be paid to thoughts and feelings that arise spontaneously, that are impossible to trace to causes, and neither the past, nor the accidental can explain their origins. They can be of great significance and directed to the Common Good.

Of course, one must be in a harmonious state to be able to receive these unexpected messengers. Let everyone think how to serve the Common Good. Every farmer sows and reaps not just for himself, but also for others, unknown to him. Let him think that the grain that he produces will bring good to somebody. The thoughts themselves encourage humanity with universal understanding. All labor, especially if accompanied by good thoughts, brings help to someone.

Everyone can think about the whole of mankind. Many obstacles caused by human conventionalities will be wiped away by these benevolent currents. We harken to mental sendings. We rejoice when We hear thoughts of General Good. We are saddened when We sense that a thought sent is colored by bias. Everyone should try to eject such abhorrent impulses. Like snakes, they coil around the heart and suffocate it.

Do you notice how a sudden feeling of suffocation happens? Perhaps a suffocating thought flew in from somewhere. But We shall gather all signs that lead to the General Good, to unknown friends.

The Thinker taught, "We erect altars to the Unknown God. Should we not dedicate our labors to the Unknown Friends?"

612. Urusvati knows that one's point of view defines one's attitude to the world. It is not only external influences that cause changes in one's perceptions; many chemical processes in the human organism influence them too. Suspension of breath or its acceleration produce substances of great power, which in turn affect one's mood, or blood pressure. The brain's activity can be slowed or accelerated, and one's feelings abnormally affected. A particular circumstance can appear to be either joyous or gloomy.

Not only the way of breathing, but also the surrounding temperature, can affect the condition of one's psychic energy. Everything vibrates and is in motion, and it is necessary to consciously preserve inner balance.

People must be informed about the basic principles of psychic life. Those who do this in a clear and understandable way will perform a great deed. The time has come when people must be enlightened. This can be accomplished only in a scientific, objective way, without criticism or denial. For today's fields we shall bring a new seed, whose quality has already been tested.

Let us not dispute, because in true science true knowledge is being offered. The one who wants to be a realist must learn conscientiously. Poor is the realist who has put on dark glasses and stopped up his ears. What kind of reality will he cognize? Even verified evidence will be distorted for him.

Let the scientists prepare books for the people and speak scientifically about both the earthly and the Supermundane. The oneness of scientific principles should be demonstrated in the laboratories. If the whole of cosmos can be seen in one drop of liquid gold, then what a multitude of experiments can be made available to everyone!

This age of democracy must be distinguished by true enlightenment. This will be a great Service, and everyone can participate in it. During times of speedy progress broad measures must be applied. There is neither old nor new, there is only eternal learning. One can study ancient legends and respect them, but evolution is accelerating, and balance must be maintained. The thrust of evolution takes unanticipated leaps, from the Stone Age to the age of highest knowledge. Great is the time and great is the responsibility! Let us not fear the existence of opposing positions. Opposition is the way to progress.

The Thinker asked the disciples not to fear battle, and said, "One must learn to fly in thought."

613. Urusvati knows how diligently Our advice must be applied. A seafarer may know all his rigging, but if he cannot control it, he will perish in the first storm. Many know Our Indications, but do not apply them in their lives–little benefit can come from that. Hypocrites justify this attitude by claiming that the Supermundane World has not been shown to them. Yet they can see the entire starry firmament and already guess that there must be some kind of life everywhere. In many countries societies for psychic research are active, and try to investigate the Supermundane scientifically. Everyone, with rare exceptions, experiences the Supermundane in some way.

Science has already made many discoveries that help in the cognition of the Subtle World. Scientific conclusions do not contradict the achievements of psychic research. In the near future science will reveal to mankind the strong links to the real Supermundane World. Many myths and misconceptions will be dispelled by science's strict approach.

Even now, a new understanding of ancient legends is taking place, and many apocryphal texts are revealed to be more valid than the commonly accepted ones. We are not shaking foundations, but are simply trying to establish a proper approach. Every substantiated statement should be respected. Rigid narrow-mindedness is a condition that can be called death. We send messengers of truth, whose task is to repeat untiringly about the future steps of evolution.

The Thinker taught, "Respect those who lead others onto a right path. Only in the future will their achievements be valued, but even now we can sense where the beautiful path lies."

614. Urusvati knows how important it is that human thinking be freed. Do not take comfort in the idea that thought is in its nature free, because thinking is chained by many prejudices. Nowadays we do not burn sorcerers, but some scientific domains are regarded by many as akin to witchcraft.

Everybody knows people who consider themselves to be cultured, but whose prejudices do not permit them to accept real scientific achievements. Books can be published, new university chairs can be established, experiments can be conducted whose results have been proved, yet the "cultured" ones will cling to their worn-out prejudices. They are not ashamed to call themselves cynics or skeptics, but it would be better were they to call themselves fools. It is not so bad if a fool denies reality, except that many of them are in high governmental positions and oppose all efforts at enlightenment.

It is impossible to enumerate the many ways in which people's thinking is constricted! The psychic level of thinking today is hardly different from that of the Middle Ages! Centuries ago the fools attacked Leonardo da Vinci, and one can observe the same attitude in our time. The teacher who speaks about the discipline of thinking knows that it is still impossible to speak about some simple truths. Those in authority know how to close the mouth of the bold one who dares to speak about freedom of thought.

The Thinker used to say, "Heavy chains bind each one of us."

615. Urusvati knows how carefully one must choose the baggage that is suitable for the Supermundane World. I will read to you from a treatise called About the Great Boundary, by a Greek philosopher. "Picture a ship that is caught in a storm. The captain orders evacuation into the lifeboats. In their terror, passengers are faced with the need to leave their valuables behind. They have never before thought about which of their possessions will be indispensable to them. In their anguish they seize the least necessary things, and many perish because of their indecision about what is most needed.

"But one traveler, without hesitation, puts a small casket under his cloak and succeeds in saving himself. He has pondered long before about what is the most important, and has prepared himself for the great boundary. The Teaching about the Supermundane convinces everyone about the necessity of crossing the border with an appropriate load. It is too late to think about this while climbing into the last lifeboat."

I am quoting these lines to remind you again that the thinkers long ago taught people to understand the true essence of Existence. They knew that the beautiful eternal life has many boundaries that must be crossed with dignity. These boundaries are numerous, and one must learn from the beginning how to cross them. Yet We see that even those who study the books do not apply them to their hearts. Ask yourself–can one think of oneself as learned, yet speak slander against one's co-workers? I do not see that such self-important people have the proper baggage for the Great Boundary.

The Thinker said, "Luckily, we do not need a porter to help carry our most important load."

616. Urusvati knows that rapport or animosity are more easily established between people who have already met in previous lives. This demonstrates the constancy of energy and the durability of the rhythm once before established. But rarely do people recognize such encounters; they do not know that groups of people who were once linked can incarnate again in one place. Yet this is quite natural–some strive to return to a familiar place, and others are attracted to it by a kind of magnetism.

People in primitive cultures often recognize each other, for they know about reincarnating to Earth.

They say, "I will go to rest, in order to return again." Naturally, they wish to return to familiar ground. Among developed consciousnesses there may be a need to continue some unfinished work; that is why former co-workers or enemies often meet again. The magnet of animosity is quite strong, but few understand that the path of animosity is detrimental.

Sworn enemies are usually eager to return more quickly to Earth, in order to complete their dark intentions. Supermundane Guides experience many difficulties with such evil-minded ones. In some ways they can be persuaded, but they will not give up their desire for revenge. They are persistent, and know how to find their former adversaries. They even try to incarnate into the families of their victims, in order to more easily reach them.

Rhythm established in the past supports animosity too. Thus We can observe the rhythms of both friendship and enmity. We find ways to warn about imminent attacks by enemies without intruding upon karma. But people rarely listen to friendly advice.

The Thinker said, "The very same trumpet can proclaim defeat or victory."

617. Urusvati knows that a crude thought can forever drive away a beautiful, subtle thought. One can ask, "Is it possible? How rough the force must be to drive away a supermundane thought!" But the effect of the dense on the supermundane is obvious.

One would be astonished to see how the supermundane guest flies away from a crude touch. People do not value supermundane messages. They cannot imagine how much labor is needed for the Supermundane Friends to push a thought through dense, earthly matter. The Supermundane Friends seek the best atmospheric conditions to better transmit their messages. They wait for a time when the earthly dwellers can open their psychic ears in a calm mood. But, even if the best conditions are present, some messenger from the bazaar can appear, and the most subtle thought is driven away.

People brush away Our messages as if they were annoying flies. They complain that some kind of nonsense has come into their heads, not realizing that Supermundane Friends are trying to save them from misfortune. They will not admit that someone is trying to help them solve difficult problems in their lives. The earthly mind cannot imagine the cooperation that exists beyond the boundaries of Earth.

It is difficult for Supermundane Friends to send messages to Earth, even the most urgent ones. Evil scoffers do what they can to outrun a good thought. Unfortunately, the recipient is often inclined to listen to their cunning voices. The consciousness of the recipient is rarely developed and refined enough to distinguish the quality of the message. The concerns of everyday life obscure the Voice of Silence. Thus, it is difficult for Us and other Supermundane Friends, when people turn a deaf ear to Us and prefer the bazaar.

The Thinker instructed His disciples, "Be on guard day and night. You do not know the moment when a supermundane message will come to you. It is possible that you will drive it away!"

618. Urusvati knows that He who stands upon the Tower sees more than one who sits in a cellar. Is it necessary to repeat what is so obvious? If I say this, there is a need for it. Most people see no difference between a tower and a cellar. Against all evidence, they pay no attention to the Voice from the Tower.

During times of great tensions, people still think as they always do, but such a way of thinking is criminal indulgence. They should learn that every event requires an appropriate way of thinking.

People escaping from a burning house do not care if someone jostles them, for their concern for personal safety has greater urgency. But under normal conditions, people rarely recognize the true state of affairs, and live as if in a dark cellar. They dance in their cellar, they grow angry and quarrel, as if it were a suitable time for all this pettiness!

People have an amazing way of seeing everything through the color of their own glasses, yet take pride in their objectivity of judgment. It is time that they went beyond the limits of their "civilized" ways and developed powers of right judgment. Proper judgment could prevent some dark events. People have heard about Armageddon, but do not see it as real. So We must continue to repeat the obvious, because even the simplest truths are being rejected, and with what conceit! One must also keep on repeating about the need for trust–it is better seen from the Tower!

The Thinker used to say, "Even if I climb to the roof of My house, Athena upon the Acropolis will see incomparably more."

619. Urusvati knows how beautiful are the radiations generated by trust. On the foundation of trust is raised the mountain of fidelity, which is the adornment of the Universe. In the concept of faithfulness are joined the best aspects of life–love, beauty, devotion, courage, and wisdom. Faithfulness is a result of wisdom developed over many lives. The opposites of faithfulness, false-heartedness and betrayal, are the shame of humanity. If faithfulness has such an antagonist, then it is truly at the summit of the mountain. By the enemy, we can see who is being persecuted.

Fidelity is valued as a great treasure. Cosmic Justice

rewards fidelity generously, but the reward comes at the right time. Only a few can understand the role of time in this, for a high degree of trust is required. We are grateful for such trust. Mutual gratitude is the key to harmony. This simple affirmation will seem absurd to many, in whose hearts gratitude and faithfulness do not live. Urusvati knows the power of these qualities. Even in the midst of hard times they illumine the path of life. Wicked is the heart that does not know trust and gratitude.

The clever ones in the bazaar smile slyly and calculate how often they cheated and betrayed some trust. They filled their purse and gained for themselves a backbreaking load. It is better to be deceived than to deceive. The quality of trust will lead to many achievements. But do not wait for the right circumstances to then begrudge your trust. Daily life provides ample opportunities to manifest this excellent quality. Thus can you forge a strong link with Us.

One can instantaneously begin to radiate the beautiful purple rays of trust. What a powerful defensive net it is! We often speak of friends, but We always mean true friends. Friends can be lightminded and careless because of lack of faithfulness. When We value something greatly, We guard it. Thus, let the bedrock of trust and the mountain of faithfulness stand firm.

The Thinker said, "I will go now to the bazaar. Will someone cheat me? The cheat does not know that he gives me admission to the best shore of the River Styx."

620. Urusvati knows that the Supermundane should be accepted as a natural aspect of life. Listen! Listen! As long as the Supermundane is thought of as forbidden or supernatural, the consciousness will not be able to expand. It can be observed, though, that some people, when attempting to turn to the Supermundane, lose their balance, because their earthly limitations prevent proper communion with It.

Some may ask how one can turn to the Supermundane without causing harm to the physical body. They wonder whether, for an ordinary person, it is not destructive to mix earthly and subtle energies. Such an idea is mistaken. The mundane and supermundane worlds are interconnected in many subtle ways. To destroy these links would mean to destroy the planet. But one should not think that cognition of the Supermundane is available only to exceptional individuals. Everyone who begins to contemplate the Supermundane will become illumined by this wondrous and beautiful aspect of life.

Speak to those for whom the Supermundane has become natural. They will describe how from an early age they thought about the existence of beautiful heavens, stars, and an unknown Teacher who lived somewhere. It is clear that these children bring such thoughts to Earth from the Subtle World; the families into which they are born do not always have such ideas. With these thoughts begins the great process of the harmonizing of the two worlds.

For some of these children, after the age of seven, this expansion of consciousness ceases, and after the age of fourteen, they become tied to their physical, lower nature. But others know how to preserve their communion with the Supermundane, and for them the more subtle receptions multiply. No artificial practices are needed for such a natural communion to be established, and only this kind of communion is in harmony with evolution.

The Thinker said, looking at a beautiful star, "If it is true that our wishes are fulfilled, I look forward to being in that wonderful world."

621. Urusvati knows that some individuals, when in the Subtle World, consciously choose difficult incarnations. I speak of those whose karma permits them to have an easier existence, but whose refined consciousness tells them that one difficult earthly life is of more value than many easy ones. These selfless pilgrims will readily accept missions that the fainthearted would be eager to avoid.

You have mentioned Narada, called the Contentious One. His difficult task was to provoke arguments that would awaken dormant consciousnesses and prompt them to judge more intelligently. In the same way, many who are strong in spirit accept tasks to liberate people from their worn-out prejudices. One can imagine how difficult is the life of such purifiers! They withstand furious attacks, and only in the remote future will they receive their just recognition. Many of them remain unknown, and the results of their efforts are recorded in history as progressive changes that led to a renewal of thinking.

It must not be thought that there were only a few of these fighters. During various times there appeared many, strong in spirit, who confirmed by their lives the right path of progress. Let Our friends think about these toilers, who deserve to be valued, because they could have chosen an almost carefree existence, but instead decided to labor. Let these labors be the steps of luminous ascent.

The Thinker exhorted his disciples to choose difficult lives, saying, "Only by labor will you achieve."

622. Urusvati knows that a simple life, lofty and refined, is a proper path to the Supermundane. Simplicity brings knowledge and progress, whereas luxury leads to corruption and decay. History is full of examples of this. Untiring creators are simple in their daily life, but they influence all that surrounds them.

Every creative person, without intending to, emanates by the power of his strivings, but he must learn to balance his actions with his own needs. He must avoid zealotry and fanaticism, and must not impose on himself the simple life. This quality must develop naturally, with a full sense of harmony.

It must be well understood that taking pride in one's own simplicity is wrong. Simplicity must be one's normal state. We have spoken often about one's achievements coming about in a natural way. This approach brings true calmness, without envy, and without following absurd conventional ways. Certain nations may think that luxury is their goal, or better said, stigma. Such a life is full of corruption and cannot last. Some nations were able to survive such a poisonous atmosphere for no more than one generation, and then, not luxury, but funerary processions were the result!

The Thinker said, about false simplicity, "If one's garment is torn and dirty–is this simplicity? If one's words are coarse and abusive–is this simplicity? If a simple thought masks evil and cunning–is this simplicity?"

623. Urusvati knows how often people are unable to see the links between kindred concepts. Thus, flexibility and unwaveringness are regarded by them as contradictory. They think of flexibility as vacillation and unwaveringness as rigidity. This does not take into account the existence of flexibility in firmness, or firmness in mobility.

One must be ever ready to change, and be prepared for achievement, but must lean on a staff of unwaveringness. Only with such a combination will the pilgrim succeed. The Supermundane World should not be regarded as outside of earthly laws. There, too, a staff is needed, and a striving toward achievement can be felt. Many in the Supermundane World dream about beautiful flights and regret the load that impedes them. Actually, such a load is amassed on Earth not only by one's crimes, but also by the many confusions and vacillations that one experiences. Do not confuse vacillation with the quest for progress, whose flexibility We consider to be lofty. And the firm-rootedness of one's understanding of the foundations We consider beneficent.

The Thinker taught recognition of kindred concepts. He said, "It is we ourselves who are guilty of severing the great unity of Be-ness."

624. Urusvati knows that violent negation can coexist with enthusiastic acceptance. Let us imagine a serpent that is coiled in a circle, and let us assume that its head represents the highest degree of acceptance. Then, like the body of a snake, the acceptance diminishes gradually to the point of indifference, and then turns into rejection. At the tail of the serpent, the negation becomes furious, to such a degree that one might discern signs of recognition in it–many examples can be found, where the most avid persecutors turned into the most devoted followers.

Thus, one should especially beware of indifference as the precursor of negation. It later develops into the basest kind of negation. Yet, at the depths of the consciousness a storm is brewing, and the polarity creates a tension in which the Truth rings out. Chaos is a state of war, and manifests itself in fury, but the tensed psychic energy overcomes this darkness, and a beautiful apotheosis becomes possible.

Therefore observe the degree of negation. Let it hasten on its path to condemnation. In its weaker stages, no energy will be found for enlightenment, but when the explosion of furious denial takes place, the radiance of Light will open the gates to Truth. One can often observe such practical examples in life. By now, those on Earth appear to be irreconcilably divided, and only the coming explosion can bring about the change.

The Thinker said, "The King hounds and slanders me so much that I am beginning to think there are germs of friendship in him. But it cannot be so, for he is not sufficiently raging."

625. Urusvati knows how incorrectly chaos and the battle with it are understood. The very concept of chaos was born in remote antiquity. The classical thinkers defined chaos as primordial, unmastered matter. Later, there came into being a symbolic image of a point manifested in the circle of the Unmanifest. Such an image is correct, and yet it causes misconceptions. One could conclude, by this symbol, that the Unmanifest, or chaos, and the manifest are completely separate. Many think this way, and find comfort in the belief that they exist outside of chaos.

In reality, everyone is subject to the action of chaos, which penetrates into each human heart. One cannot say that these influences are known only to the lower organisms. All are under assault by this unseen enemy. The difference is that a low organism attracts such influences, whereas the elevated consciousness resists the uninvited intruder. We have said that cruelty, rudeness, and ignorance are nurseries of chaos. Dangerous epidemics arise around these hearths. You can observe how during times of upheaval human consciousness is changed. The gates to the spiritual stronghold open, and waves of chaos pour in unopposed, and poison the organism. Thinking is changed, logic disappears, and honesty is destroyed. Isolated achievements are engulfed by the waves of chaos. Humanity has summoned to itself a deadly ally.

It is regrettable that after millions of years people do not understand what dangers they evoke from space! But even during the days of Armageddon one can begin beneficial self-improvement. If there is not sufficient energy to banish malice, cruelty, and coarseness, one can at least restrain them. Everyone can apply his efforts to this work. Tension is great and it is time to abandon light-mindedness, that most pernicious ignorance.

The Thinker instructed, "Everyone can declare war on his own ignorance. Such a war is honorable; it is a guarantee of achievement and a service to his nation."

626. Urusvati knows that there are those who insist that We do not exist at all. They engage in such passionate denial that one would suspect that they needed to persuade themselves! No proof or logic convinces them. They will even call the people who have met Us liars, and will claim that these people were under hypnotic suggestion.

Comparisons of mental sendings to wireless telegraphy and television have no effect on the deniers. People believe what they want to believe. Nothing can change their mind. They say that they are willing to believe, if they see proof, but when the confirmation comes they say that it seemed to be so, but was not. Examples of this attitude can readily be given.

I assert that such deniers serve forces about which they have no idea. Why do they insist on what they do not know? Let them demonstrate that Our existence is not possible.

Can a conscientious investigator insist that, in his field, all has been discovered and explained? Only a dull, conventional mind dares to insist that all is known to him. Each new discovery is but one more step into the Unknown. Not long ago only the Northern Lights were known, but now the Himalayan Lights have been seen too, yet no one can point out their cause. One can speak of the intensification of the energy, and of the electric phenomena, but these are nothing but vague assumptions.

Why, somewhere behind Everest, does an unusual intensification of energy take place? And why does this phenomenon cause such varied effects? Many questions arise but as yet the essence is still unexplained. Think about this. Also, information should be gathered about different strange encounters, many of which are mentioned in literature.

The Thinker said, "Many unknown fires light the way for the travelers."

627. Urusvati knows that people should not only acknowledge the existence of the subtle energies, but should also work with them. Must one be some kind of giant to even think about such cooperation? In a well-designed machine each of its parts is necessary. One should more often imagine oneself as part of the Universe, by joining one's own energy with the universal energy.

Thought is the finest energy that one can send forth, inexhaustibly, into the vault of the Universe. Thought can rise, as a pillar of light, and be united with the great Apparatus of energy. The duty of man is to share his possessions, and the best of them is the energy of his thought. It is the energy, consciously directed, that serves as a true yoga, the link with the Higher Worlds. We have spoken many times about the significance of awareness; it alone is life-giving. Even prana must be inhaled consciously.

The Thinker said, "Each one of us, when ready for

sleep, should send a beautiful thought of greeting to the forces of nature."

628. Urusvati knows that a leader must be like a solicitous gardener. Usually, one pays more attention to safeguarding one's most beautiful plants, but the simple ones can be of equal value and usefulness and must be cared for too. The ignorant can trample upon them and think of them as weeds. So also through the whole of life one should pay particular attention to recognizing the value of those modest, unnoticed workers, out of whose ranks can come the best co-workers. One should not regret their lack of knowledge, for it is they who can bypass the middle-level intellectual knowledge and strive toward the higher spiritual knowledge.

We and Our close ones are much attracted to those who are modest and simple, untouched by cunning. Even if their thoughts at first distress Us by their primitiveness, they at least do not fall into the swamp of sophistry. Thus Our people can go directly from the small to the great, and will not take pride in their greatness. Even the great spiritual toilers did not succumb to pride. They understood that the greatest earthly labor is nothing but a threshold to the supermundane existence.

They could see the fire and the luminous flame, but this ability did not make them arrogant. Their simplicity was not self-abasement or meekness, it was the life of the heart, the life of renunciation. They did not desire special recognition, for they were true toilers. They knew when to speak and when to be silent.

The Thinker said, "Let us be silent, and extinguish even the lighting-flashes of thought. The most important, the most sacred, must rise from the depths of the heart."

629. Urusvati knows how decisively the voice rings

from the depths of our consciousness. Two kinds of psychic work take place in man. One is subject to physical, earthly conditions, and the other relates to the conditions of the Subtle World. One can readily see that this second work is higher and of more fundamental importance than the first.

Often, out of the depths of consciousness rises a voice that objects to a decision made by the earthly mind. It is especially instructive to observe these inner battles that take place in one's being. "Know thyself," spoke the philosophers, and they were right. Only the one who can acknowledge the voice from the depths of his own consciousness can consider himself to be on the path toward knowledge. It is remarkable to see how firm and fully-considered are the actions that rise from the depths of the consciousness.

One may ask, "Why are there these two, often opposing, kinds of psychic work?" and We shall answer, "They only confirm the difference between the earthly mind and the supermundane consciousness." Of course, the supermundane consciousness is more just, and sees farther and more clearly than the earthly, confused, and fearful mind.

Fortunate are those who have learned to harken to the voices of the depths of the consciousness. They will find new ways in life's struggle. They will see life with a good and just eye. They will find a true understanding of human traits. They will gather courage. Let that voice be called subconscious, or small, or great–is it not all the same? What is important is that a great psychic work is taking place.

The Thinker said, "Listen to the forewarning and encouraging voice. Your judge–your friend–is always with you."

630. Urusvati knows the different ways in which

Our replies can come. Sometimes a reply comes swiftly, even before the question itself has been fully expressed. And sometimes an answer is delayed for some days. Those cases when the answer is ahead of the question indicate that the question itself was prompted by a thought that had already been sent.

Think of the many reasons why an answer can be delayed. Some circumstances relating to the question may not yet have become fully clear, or external reasons can cause delay. But in all instances the reality of the transmissions can be observed.

Often people ask Us about circumstances or events that for them are of particular importance, but matters of greater urgency do not permit Us to immediately change the current of Our thought. In life, you often say, "Wait," and it is the same in all existence. But people are self-centered and when they want something, they do not take into consideration even cosmic conditions. One must see things in their proper perspective, and understand the scope of Our activities. We may have urgent duties, and the current of Our work cannot be interrupted. Each interrupted current is like a broken string.

The Thinker understood the need to respect another's labor. He used to say, "How can one know the flow of thought? Let us wisely wait until Our friend has completed his intense thinking."

631. Urusvati knows that people have a limited understanding of the concept of rhythm. According to general understanding, rhythm is expressed in music, song, dance, and poetry, but the fundamental rhythm, which exists throughout the Universe and permeates the whole of life, remains unrecognized. This primordial rhythm makes our earthly rhythms seem meager indeed. To counter a disorderly way of life, rhythmic actions can be helpful, but these are but a hint of the great rhythm of the Universe.

People should consider why some words and actions are persuasive, whereas others do not even touch the strings of the heart. It is the inner rhythm that convinces people and prepares them for the acceptance of what they have seen and heard. And they often will follow, without even knowing why they do it.

The movement of the great spiral is one of the expressions of the great rhythm. One reader of Our Discourses exclaimed, "Here, with each turn of the spiral, the knowledge of life is made firmer and deeper!" This is a correct observation. If we analyze the method of Our Discourses, we shall find a spiral–the best approach to the laws of life. Nothing final can be stated about any situation, for it depends not only upon what is said about it, but also upon the level of consciousness of the student. Yet the seeker's consciousness changes, and by offering him a new and higher level of understanding, the student's striving is renewed. Thus the rhythm of the Universe can be seen and utilized in the whole of life.

The Thinker knew how to awaken the realization of rhythm. "It is not in social dances and diversions, but in the beating of the heart, that we have the best example of the universal rhythm."

632. Urusvati knows the difference between the true time of events and the apparent one. The example of a physician will be particularly instructive–an experienced physician understands that a sickness does not begin when he is called, but much earlier. He will seek the true causes and will thus renew the patient's life. It is the same with the question of dates. People pay attention to the date when an event becomes evident to them, but that is not the true beginning of the event.

One can be certain that the inception of the event was earlier. It is wise to think about the real inception of an event, for only then is it possible to observe its development and resolution.

The observation of the inception of events is useful not only for the sake of truth, but as a test of one's thinking. It is necessary to learn to discard all prejudice. One's thought should be calm and free, like water in a pure well, in which one can clearly see the entire bottom. But such calm is not easily acquired. People usually prefer their preconceived notions and their own way of thinking. In the study of world events it is important to consider karmic conditions, and for this it is necessary to know the history of nations. Only with documented information can one come to just conclusions. It is necessary to learn to become a real scientist, for whom true deduction is essential, even when it does not fit one's own principles. One should learn to renounce personal opinions for the sake of truth.

The Thinker taught this too, saying, "It is not my fragile opinion, but the age-old evidence, carved in marble, that confirms our deductions."

633. Urusvati knows that a task given from the Supermundane World cannot be entirely fulfilled under earthly conditions. This should not cause distress, for the difference between subtle and earthly conditions is striking. But always remember Our Instruction, to do your utmost! Thus We remind you of the original form of the tasks assigned to you in the Subtle World.

Every dweller of the Subtle World receives a task according to his abilities. Not only are great missions given, but also some very ordinary ones, within the limits of everyday life, where one can be useful. But there are few who can remember these small missions, although they would have made the karmic burden easier.

Often people complain that there is some unknown thing that they must fulfill, yet they do not know what causes the pain in their hearts. They are trying to recall something, but in the earthly condition the subtle thought, like a frightened bird, is beyond their grasp. People cannot pursue the right path until they turn to the Supermundane World.

Pay attention to folk wisdom, which can have the deepest roots. You do right to note folkloric prophecies. It can be seen that at certain times little-known prophecies become wide-spread concerns.

It is surprising to see that the most disparate individuals begin to assert the same things, and mention the same dates. We can add that what We have just said is as true as the prophecy that lies under the rock of Ghum. One should closely observe the links between the earthly and the Supermundane.

The Thinker said, "Know how to understand the voice of the people, for the Supermundane Indications resound in it."

634. Urusvati has learned to recognize pure truth. Her experience in developing such synthesis is worthy of a whole book. Truly, it is not easy to discard all one's earthly husks and see the truth that lies at the heart of events. The insights thus gained are also useful for the Supermundane World.

It is fortunate when one is so imbued with commitment to the Good, that when crossing to the Supermundane World one can immediately continue the labor of light. It is not surprising that such harmonious continuation of work is difficult, for in it are combined both earthly and supermundane conditions. What is needed is a steadfast will that knows no obstacles. One should dare so greatly that the usual period of rest becomes unnecessary.

Man can overcome all hindrances if the goal of his journey is clear to him. When he sees the Light in the distance, he will pay no attention to the hardships of the journey. He will not count the steps to this Light, for it shines also in his heart. Thus we will find our link with the Supermundane; let it lead man to joy. Man should determine to proceed unwaveringly, without concern for the changing conditions on his journey.

The wonders of life are many, and everyone can reflect on the radiance of the heavenly bodies that reaches Earth only after millions of years. Will not such contact with Eternity give wings to man? Will he not create a new way of thinking? He can learn to love reality and find within himself the necessary level of consciousness that will enable him to sense the Supermundane. Studying the Teaching cannot provide such sensations unless the seeker accepts the Supermundane World.

The Thinker said, "Let us learn to recognize truth. It exists, although there are many veils obscuring it."

635. Urusvati knows that hatred can turn into a most destructive form of madness. Fortunately, a totally committed, consuming hatred is not often encountered. However, the power of hatred expands and attracts cunning, invisible allies. This madness can become quite dangerous, and the karma engendered by hatred is frightful. Those obsessed by hatred on Earth carry their madness into the Supermundane World. Their karma may be called hellish, for their thoughts are directed only toward the malicious satisfaction of evil.

The courage of the Guide is rendered impotent by

the malice of those who are driven by hatred, and it becomes impossible for him to turn them toward the path of perfectment. Those who do not stay on the path of progress act wrongly and quickly lose what they have previously accumulated. The one who hates cannot continue his evolution. You can imagine that the fate of the one who separates himself from evolution is terrible. People should hasten to understand that hatred is a poor counselor.

Hatred is implacable; this is what distinguishes it from other traits. Sometimes sternness is mistakenly seen as hatred. People view resolute actions by great reformers in this way, but these actions are essentially stern and far from hatred. Let us not judge the reasons for their sternness. Just imagine the abyss of ignorance and animosity that faces every reformer! It is a wonder that great leaders do not succumb to hatred, but then this is not characteristic of great leaders.

The level of one's consciousness can be judged by the presence of hatred. Only a worthless person, conceited and contemptuous of all that is unknown to him, can fall victim to the whirlpool of hatred. But his hatred does not develop instantly. He accumulates many drops of imperil, instead of drops of the healing sweat of labor. Every reformer who had to take severe measures secretly feels remorse about them, but the one who hates rejoices in his every act of cruelty.

Evolution requires that hatred be regarded as a shame of humanity, and when this requirement has been met, the many barriers raised by ignorance will be destroyed. Hatred is a special kind of ignorance. An enlightened person knows that hatred stands in the way of progress.

Do not think that a hater is always a giant of evil, for there are also petty haters. They also bear the karma of their hatred, and in this matter an earthly scale is unsuitable. Does the hater always know what he is obstructing, and what it is that he dreams to destroy? Many haters do not even know the true purpose of their hatred. They are like small stones in a riverbed, carried along by the force of the current. Even small stones can collect and form large barriers.

The Thinker said, "I pray that Destiny should preserve humanity from the madness of hatred."

636. Urusvati knows that many people pass on into the Subtle World in a wrong state of mind. Some cross over in fear and terror, others in hatred and resentment. Some cling to their earthly attachments, and others believe that when the bodily sheath dies, there is nothing else.

Many erroneous thoughts cause harm to the subtle existence. Some ideas, though useless, carry good intent. For example, some people promise to appear in the subtle body to their dear ones, and, with such an impossible promise they restrict themselves and disappoint those who wait for them. Everyone must cross the threshold free, aspiring to perfectment. It is possible that one will be required to appear in the subtle body in order to fulfill a supermundane task, but this must happen naturally, as a part of other experiences and learning.

Besides, man cannot decide to whom and when he can appear. The vibrations of the person to whom such a promise was made may remain unchanged, but they may have become more refined in another person, to whom he should appear. Such changes can be judged only from the Subtle World. It is therefore unwise to anticipate such things while in the earthly state. Everything should proceed naturally, without preconceptions. To be in full readiness requires that one not be bound by predetermined decisions. It is quite possible that someone will appear in a subtle body and thus bring benefit to people; however, it will not be a frightening ghost, but a Messenger of Light. To experience this, one must prepare oneself, and be ready to accept the Guide.

The Thinker said, "We are not in need of frightful ghosts, but may the Messenger of Light knock at our door!"

637. Urusvati knows that the human organism reacts to its surroundings to a much greater extent than is usually thought. However, people continue to believe that they live as if in a vacuum, where there are no external influences. Even the invention of radio transmission has had no effect on this belief. But now I want to remind you about an important possibility, the ability to take on someone else's pain, at a distance.

You already know that pain can be transmitted to people under hypnosis. But even without suggestion, through the power of will, pain can be taken on over great distances. Often, out of the goodness of his heart, a person desires to alleviate another's suffering and accepts not only the pain, but the illness itself. Such assumption of the illness is not produced by physical contagion, but is a psychic phenomenon involving all bodily consequences.

One can point to a number of such psychic transmissions. These attest to how sensitive the human organism is, and how rarely people pay attention to manifestations of this sensitivity. Science is of little help to most people in this area, for this knowledge is restricted to a small circle of scientists. It is imperative that the discoveries of science be made available to all people. Let us not fear broad dissemination. Many recent discoveries should belong to the people.

The Thinker said, "I do not see why the villager should know less than the urban dweller."

638. Urusvati knows that the living process of gaining knowledge will always reach out and encompass more and more, and never limit itself. By this trait, true science can be recognized. People want to see matter in everything, and they are right, but only if they acknowledge its many states and properties. The very word "matter" is a good one and is akin to the great concept of Maternal Matter. At present, in the age of the Mother of the World, one should pay special attention to all that is related to this magnificent Foundation. Besides, it should be understood that it is this concept of matter that includes all possible properties of the substance out of which all is born.

It is said that matter is crystallized spirit, but one can also say it differently, because everything, starting with the subtlest energies, is matter. It would be a great limitation for one to deny the principle of the one fundamental energy, for by doing this he will also deny matter. What then would such an ignorant person have left? It is time to return to the word "matter" its true meaning. He who considers himself a materialist must respect matter in all its forms. It is unfit to call oneself a materialist and deny the very essence of matter.

Indeed, it is wonderful to study matter and its relation to the evolutionary process. This is the only acceptable scientific approach. But even this can be distorted. A positive approach to study can never be limited. On the contrary, it must be governed by a principle of constant learning. Ponder the real meaning of many concepts and you will clearly understand how strong is Our desire to find a scientific approach to everything. For Us, such a principle does not contradict, but supports the freedom of the researcher. It only points to the beautiful matter, which is the Mother Herself.

The Thinker said, "Let us learn to revere the Mother, then we will understand the essence of Nature."

639. Urusvati knows that when visiting the Subtle World, or when passing into it, one should be accompanied by one's most joyous memories. We have spoken many times about this bridge of joy, but people rarely listen to even the best advice. Some people will say that their lives were dark and joyless. But they forget that everyone experiences moments of joy, and it is these that should be deliberately recalled from the treasury of the Chalice.

Joy is not evoked only by fanfares of victory as for a hero, or by popularity or celebrity. Pure joy is experienced in a life of labor. Everyone performs deeds of self-sacrifice, and one should learn to gather his best memories. The individual knows in his heart whether he was worthy of humanity. One should collect and cherish one's best moments. They are a precious cargo, and build a bridge of joy that glows with innumerable lights. Everyone can accept that this Indication about preserving the best memories in life is easy to follow.

One should not attach one's thoughts to dark and oppressive memories, for they, like leeches, will consume one's life-energy. Everyone experiences misfortunes, but one should not become attached to them. Why drag along a needless tail of woes? Let them be in payment for one's karma, and one's joys will be a guarantee of future success. The Guide helps best where the spark of joy glows. This page of Our Inner Life can be near to everyone.

The Thinker used to say, "One must learn to gather all sparks of joy, then the boat of Charon will not be needed."

640. Urusvati knows that many people do not understand Our repeated Indications about calmness. They err by thinking that We advise inactivity, but Our Indications about calmness are about an inner calmness. Unfortunately, this state is not easy to achieve. People may think that they are calm, when inside them a veritable volcano is raging. This state of the nervous system can bring about extreme fatigue. Is it not a contradiction that when We speak about vigilance and alertness, We also insist upon the need for inner calmness? However, these requirements are not in contradiction, but in full harmony. Vigilance succeeds when it is calm. Remember that most of the events that cause anxiety have already occurred, and are now in the past. We invite you to strive to the future. With this striving, you will be filled with subtle vibrations, and will be freed of all worry.

Only from Our Tower is it possible to see into the distance and understand how valuable is the future. One can read about the prime importance of the present moment, and whole theories exist that one should live only in the present. But the supporters of these theories must realize that the present does not exist. This reminder must be restated again and again, because people do not like the idea of living in the future.

The Thinker said, "We can remember the past and prepare for the future, but the present can neither be understood nor grasped."

641. Urusvati knows how carelessly, and even disdainfully, people regard all that concerns the Supermundane World. We will not even speak about the more subtle manifestations, but during the more gross materializations, people ask such foolish questions that one wonders why such seemingly educated people cannot speak more sensibly. They ostensibly come together for some serious purpose, but in their behavior betray signs of disbelief or mockery.

You know Our cautious attitude to so-called spiritual seances. People do not realize that besides this kind of communion, there are many more natural and unforced contacts. Thus, everyone can engage in communion with a realm so broad that it can change their entire world outlook.

We certainly do not approve of those fanatics who abandon their earthly obligations and bring nothing but confusion to all around them. They talk about higher harmonies, but at the same time forget that there must be harmony between the earthly world and the Supermundane. These fanatics consider earthly tasks to be beneath their dignity, and thus prove their ignorance. They came to Earth to fulfill some task, and should honor their obligation and love their task. With proper devotion to their earthly work, they would be able to sense the Supermundane touches. This kind of devotion is a natural link between the worlds.

One must abandon complicated analyzing, and return to the most simple. Man cannot make evolution, but must participate in it. He must harmonize himself with it. Again we come to the rhythm of labor and understand that those who just talk only encumber life. During this time of intense transformation of the world there is no place for empty talk or bigotry.

You may ask why such intense labor is needed in Infinity, and whether Infinity is co-measurable with the labor of a single individual. To the amazement of many, I must say that it is so. Each person is a living particle of humanity, which is the most powerful force on the planet. This "master of the planet" has no right to indulge in idle talk. He carries an immeasurable responsibility, and may not escape it. For him the only way is to turn as a friend to the Supermundane World.

The Thinker said, "Everyone has a great many friends, but must learn to love them. There can be no friendship without love."

642. Urusvati knows that some people do not understand the difference between the Subtle World and the Supermundane. It seems to them that both concepts are interchanged in Our Discourses, simply to avoid repetition. But it should be remembered that the Subtle World is a particular and limited realm, while the Supermundane World includes not only the various spheres, but also the world of thought–even the thought produced by those on Earth. It can even be stated that the Supermundane World is mainly the world of thought. Thought reigns, in both the supermundane and the material worlds.

It must be understood that it is not by accident that We link the essence of Our Life with the Supermundane World. People must consciously learn that the most precise understanding of the Inner Life of the Brotherhood can be achieved by studying the flow of Our thought. In everyone's life thought is the touchstone. It is said that man learns about himself by watching the current of his thought. The currents of thought are diverse; they are ceaseless and are rarely harmonious. It is not easy to watch one's own thought!

An accurate biography should reveal not just the outer actions of the individual, but also the current of his thinking. Only thus is it possible to examine the subject's essence. It is a dangerous error when experienced leaders assume that because they only thought, they are therefore not responsible for the effects of those invisible thoughts. But those thoughts become part of the foundation of their actions. It is wrong to think that thoughts have no consequences. It is difficult to know when the consequences will occur, and they may not be manifested on Earth. A great many karmic conditions can hasten or postpone dates, but the wonderful law is that each thought has its consequence. These karmic processes are related to the Supermundane World. They are based on the working of psychic energy, the primary force that fills all that exists.

The Thinker pointed out, "We are saved by our thoughts. They are our sails and our anchor."

643. Urusvati knows the necessity for a sealed memory. Many ask why it is necessary for the memory to be sealed. But they cannot imagine the horrors they would endure if humanity could continually remember past lives. A cacophonous choir would emerge, and with such a choir no progress would be possible. It is a wise law that sifts out all that is unfit for perfectment.

Inexperienced people imagine that having a knowledge of their past lives would permit them to better succeed on their path, but in reality only few would know how to properly make use of such memories. Actually, these memories are not lost, but are stored as living accumulations in the Chalice, and sometimes the Voice of the Silence reminds one of the need to draw forth and make use of an old experience. The law of concealed memory is a blessing.

Could anyone now, in this technical age, immerse himself into the mentality of times long past? This would only encumber the path. One can study the culture of antiquity, one can understand the ways in which old problems were resolved, but one cannot climb back into the skin of one's forefathers! And such an attempt would be altogether unnecessary. This is an age of astonishing discoveries, and man must adapt himself not to conditions of the past, but to the future, so as to apply his psychic energy sensibly.

The Thinker predicted, "There will come a time when people will be able to fly, and will strive toward the far-off worlds."

644. Urusvati knows that people attach little value to the development of an expanded consciousness. They are like small children who will agree to study their lessons in exchange for a piece of candy, and refuse to learn anything of importance without reward. One can observe the same thing with adults; for the promise of paradise they agree to read something, but without this promise they refuse to work for their own perfectment. The promise of a new consciousness is insufficiently persuasive. They will say, "Why do we need some new, unfamiliar consciousness? It would be better to increase our daily wage!" Thus, the Guide finds himself in the position of a benefactor building almshouses.

It is hard to believe that so few will dedicate themselves to self-perfectment without expecting reward, but simply for the sake of expanding their consciousness. Try to recall finding any true seekers of knowledge. There are many who read the Teachings of Life, but will then set conditions for reward! Some will expect payment in three years, others in seven, and some in ten. It is instructive to peruse these imaginary contracts that are expected to be satisfied by the Guide. The individual decides on the reward to suit himself, and without considering the reality, he ignores his own errors and misdeeds, and suspects the Guide of withholding payment! In his way of thinking, where are the blessings of the Supermundane World, if, at the very least, his earthly earnings are not increased? Many such earthly, secret thoughts can be recalled.

The Thinker said, "The shield may be brightly polished on the outside, but what does it cover?"

645. Urusvati is familiar with the indignation that many feel when We speak about never-ending tests. The old saying that the whole world is on trial is accepted as a metaphor with no relevance to life. Tests are seen as tiresome punishment. It would perhaps be better to use the word touchstone instead of test, for everyone knows that touchstones are a necessity during many experiments.

It would seem that people should be able to easily relate scientific knowledge to their own psychic experiences. But whenever an unexpected and unusual manifestation occurs to people, they do not believe it, not understanding that it is a sign of their own developing inner forces. Thus it is told that some Teachers purposely permitted their disciples to encounter difficult situations, so that their resourcefulness would be tested, and they would then be required to find the best solutions. Pay full attention to how people view their experiences. Only thus can one see with what degree of intelligence their acquired knowledge is applied.

Evolution is propelled by a small minority. The same relation exists between the manifested and chaos. Nonetheless, cosmic evolution advances steadily. Thus, one can see that although a minority of humanity is ready to accept the reconstruction of life, the reconstruction is taking place all the same. One can thus say that only a few are ready to follow the path of evolution, but the luminous consciousness of these few provides sufficient energy.

The Thinker said, "The few can carry the burden. It is not quantity that is essential."

646. Urusvati knows that the inseparable cannot be dissevered. This must be kept in mind when one speaks about the earthly and the Supermundane. Due to some unexplainable stubbornness people separate in their minds these two concepts, inseparable in their essence. Could any action be imagined that would have no effect on adjacent domains? All is one and indivisible. The smallest psychic action has physical consequences, and each physical action has its impact upon the psychic condition.

All this would seem simple, logical, not contradicting any truths, but the present condition of mankind does not admit it. One can trip upon even the smallest threshold. This tiny threshold, this contradiction in the human mind, exists in spite of all scientific proof. One can surmise what kind of sinister forces cultivate this idea of disunity. This belief is an obstacle to the transformation of life. People are willing to talk much about a new life, but mostly their talk is empty words.

When leaving the theater, the temple, or scientific gatherings, people at once sink into the dust of everyday life. Moments before, they were enthused, or wept, or were inspired; then followed immediate forgetfulness. One of Our co-workers performed a revealing test. He stopped to observe people leaving the theater after an inspiring performance; he did the same upon leaving a temple, and also after a lecture by a famous scientist. You would perhaps be astonished to learn that of each hundred people, only eight were still affected by their earlier impressions. The others, already at the door, quickly returned to their commonplace ways, their most impressive experiences having barely touched their stony hearts.

The same can be observed during the discourses about the Supermundane, but, as We said, evolution is advanced by a small minority. The fact remains that for most people, the Supermundane World simply does not exist. People do not wish to see those phenomena which, like a rainbow, radiate above the gulf of the everyday. Why is there this resistance, when human curiosity should lead one to an interest in the infinite realms of the Supermundane?

The Thinker begged His disciples, "Encourage people to at least glance at the starry skies. Only pigs cannot raise their heads."

647. Urusvati knows how easy it is to adopt beneficial measures in daily life. It is proper to preserve calmness before going to sleep, but unfortunately, people usually use this time for quarrels and doubts. They do not imagine the harm they cause to their health and also to their imminent visit to the Subtle World. Each one enters the sphere of that World which corresponds to his psychic state. If one falls asleep while in a state of irritation, it becomes difficult for the sleep to have beneficial effect.

Not without reason it is suggested to pregnant women to think about beauty, and to keep beautiful objects around them. This same advice should be followed by everyone, when approaching sleep. It is not difficult to spend the last minutes thinking about something lofty. Do not think that this is hypocrisy. Man must know how to control his thoughts. Even when burdened by problems, he can allow himself a moment of rest and aspire towards beautiful dreams. This is true also when conversing during meals. Experienced people know how harmful it is to partake of food during an unpleasant conversation. Every physician will confirm this. And so, in everything one can promote psychic healthfulness, which is more beneficial than many vitamins.

It is wise to ask friends not to fall into despair, because in that state they open themselves to all kinds of calamities. There are entire categories of ailments caused by sorrow and despair. It is hard to treat these ailments, because diagnosis of the stricken nerves is difficult, and physical medicines can only worsen the situation.

The Thinker said, "Aesculapius must not be angry if, prior to turning to him, we summon the Muse."

648. Urusvati knows that scientific research must soon turn to a study of the activity of the glands. Not enough is yet known about the action of the heart and of the nerve centers, and even less is known about the glands, although such knowledge is of vital importance. Only recently so little attention was given to them that physicians were too willing to simply remove them, without wondering why every organism has a developed glandular system.

At present a certain caution has developed about removing glands, but their essential purpose has not yet been sufficiently understood. The secretions of the glandular system are of great importance for communion with the Subtle World. Subtle entities utilize the glandular secretions not only for their materialization, but also for their nourishment. Thus, during their study of the activity of glands, scientists will inevitably stumble upon the discovery that the glands are links with the Subtle World.

It is not easy to observe the secretions of the glands, for, being both earthly and subtle, they are not subject to earthly measures alone. Yet, even the hardest problems must be resolved. Not only must the biologists and physiologists be summoned for this, but also the physicians. Such observations must be introduced not only among the sick, but also among those healthy people who possess great sensitivity.

Experiments must not be limited to observing only

the ill. These processes will be evident in the whole of life, and only the wisest scientist will be able to properly evaluate any unusual glandular symptoms. Therefore, We often direct attention to the study of such symptoms amidst daily life.

We ask that you not look for striking revelations, but watch closely all everyday routine, which is so full of miracles.

The Thinker insisted that the disciples observe the happenings of daily life. He said, "We are surrounded by the most striking miracles, yet do not wish to notice them."

649. Urusvati knows how wrong and harmful is the idea that the three worlds are separate. There are many bridges and ladders linking all realms. Man, in his physical state, carries within himself the subtle body, whose presence he can often sense, and also the seed of the Fiery World. Can one imagine the One, the Indivisible, with unsurmountable barriers within It?

Each refinement of feelings and broadening of consciousness opens a new possibility for communion. It is no fault of the universe that people do not wish to notice the door that is open to the next chamber. Not only at a moment of highest ecstasy, but even amidst the chores of daily life does man receive touches of the Subtle World. But instead of loving them, he fans them away as he would do to an annoying fly.

The Subtle World, in its higher strata, comes into contact with the Fiery World. And in their earthly state people, too, can sometimes receive a fiery arrow. Not without reason is each one given a fiery seed. Because of the seed's presence, the fiery arrows do not kill, but call forth an intense vibration.

These truths must be absorbed, but the majority of mankind does not acknowledge them. In many accepted teachings, the basic worlds are frequently referred to, and hints are given for the possibility of communion with them. Religions speak about this too, but people take it as a kind of abstraction, and do not admit that science also speaks about the same thing, but in its own language.

The Thinker used to say, "Man, have you already been given so much that you so easily refuse the treasures that are yours to claim?"

650. Urusvati knows that help, when sincerely given, does not violate the law of karma. There is a fanatic belief that one should not help one's neighbor because it would intrude upon his karma. This is a harmful fallacy. The fanatics do not let themselves understand that one who helps acts in accordance with karma. Man must provide all possible help, without thinking about karma.

Any offering of help radiates good, but, of course, the good deed must be sincere. In this, everyone must be his own judge. We value help when it is offered spontaneously, from the heart. There is no use in calculating whether or not to help someone. Most people would stop to help a passing stranger in distress, without thinking what a beautiful deed they are performing. And such conduct is right, for self-congratulation undermines all good results.

Timely encouragement is valuable, perhaps more valuable than many other kinds of help. The one who encourages shares part of his energy, and such distribution of one's best possession is of value. Let all those who wish to think about the Supermundane first of all experience the joy of help. Such joy is beautiful, and it belongs not only to the wealthy. Good advice can uplift and enable someone in trouble. Everyone can share valuable knowledge. In such a condition of tensed benevolence, the one who helps acquires increased strength and resourcefulness. Blessed be all help that comes from the heart!

The Thinker taught, "Learn to help; this science is blessed."

651. Urusvati knows that contemplation of the Supermundane frees one from the worst vipers, despondency and resentment. The garden of resentments is an ugly one, and the cave of depression gloomy. Still, people so often descend into these caves, and enter into the gardens to tend the thistles, that a healing remedy must be found. Contemplation of the Supermundane is precisely that needed remedy. Not for a single hour should one extinguish within oneself this flame of lofty thinking. The highest sage loses his power if he ceases to think about the future Abode. He will be defenseless, and from the bottom of his Chalice the dregs will rise.

People will ask whether prolonged thought about the Supermundane will impede their earthly activities. Indeed, this thinking should accompany one even during the hour of most intense activity. It was said long ago that the Image of the Teacher should be forever retained in the consciousness. Similarly, profound thought about the Supermundane will be not an obstacle, but a living bridge to future achievement.

It is beautiful if someone can always carry within himself a lofty thought. Let it not be the product of reasoning, but rather of wordless contemplation.

Do understand what I wish to say. Twenty years ago the understanding of these concepts may not have been clear, but now the foundation of the Teaching has been properly laid, and its basic principles have been relatively well given.

The Thinker pointed out the similarity of the work of thinking to that of sculpture.

652. Urusvati knows that, like sculptors, We shape the foundations for the broadening of consciousness. Urusvati also knows that a considerable amount of time is needed for full understanding of these foundations. One cannot learn by just grasping at fragments. The entire developing structure of Our Indications must be kept in the consciousness.

An inexperienced aspirant may think that isolated moments of attention are sufficient. An impatient student will be annoyed to hear about the necessity for a steady growth of knowledge. A selfish one will not understand why a Guide is needed. And even a rhetorician would not know the words to best express the broadening of consciousness. But you have been receiving Our Indications for twenty years, and are able to compare the levels of your consciousness as it was then, and now.

Consciousness cannot be described in words. It guides feelings, but those, too, are inexpressible. If I speak of solemnity, those who do not sense it will not understand it. Yet every important day should be accompanied by a joyous solemnity. The more difficult the day, the more solemnly it must be treated.

Our first call to you was many years ago, and the first signs were manifested to you over half a century ago—is it not so, Urusvati? Those distant signs stand as a Banner of Victory. If you rush forward too fast, the heart will not endure; the expansion of consciousness does not require destruction of the heart. A sensitive heart must be treated with care. It beats not for itself, but for the General Good. This idea must be proclaimed each Day of Remembrance.

You remember the early messages, given twenty

years ago. Every concept was investigated and revealed with an attitude of solemnity. We did not hesitate to point out that even the highest concepts can be studied. We indicated that science, too, is needed for the broadening of consciousness. We described the mental work of Our Brotherhood. The Supermundane Worlds, Our Brotherhood, and expansion of consciousness are the fundamentals of Our given Discourses. This book about the Supermundane and the Brotherhood is in fact about the broadening of consciousness. It is not possible to point to inner boundaries in the Indivisible.

All friends should know how to guard the Precious Stone. Let them place upon the work table a rock crystal in commemoration of the Solemn Day. Thus shall we preserve the memory about the most important dates.

The Thinker said, "Let us mark this Day of Remembrance with a crystal-clear stone."

653. Urusvati knows that there are many obsolete words that should be withdrawn from use. Other words have changed from their original meanings, and this results in confusion. Among these, the word occultism should be abandoned. Its history reveals that in the Middle Ages it was used infrequently, with care, by those who knew. Now it is broadcast almost without any sense of its true meaning. Science is gradually conquering all realms of knowledge, and the use of such words about secret knowledge has become a virtual challenge! Knowledge progresses, and the fires of the Inquisition are slowly retreating into the past.

Today's so-called occultists are, in most cases, laughable. They imagine their ideas to be sacred discoveries, but at the first occurrence that they cannot explain, they flee in terror. Let the truly honest researchers take the place of these prideful "occultists."

The domain of subtle energies must be studied by scientists, and now that even in the universities attention is being given to them, terms that cause confusion are no longer needed.

Equally outmoded is the term metaphysics. The manifestations of Nature, from the lowest to the highest, belong to the physical domain. It is impossible to introduce opposing views, or to separate and categorize, when there exists one, indivisible Foundation. Metaphysics appeared during the time of secret alchemy. Then, investigators had to hide from the attacks of ignorance and hypocrisy. But presently there is no need to drive science underground.

The Thinker said, "Physician, rush to help wherever health is endangered. Do not await the call. Hasten! Likewise, builders of bridges, raise them wherever they are needed!"

654. Urusvati knows that some people wonder why in Our recent Instructions they recognize things already known to them. But the new will often include variations of the old. People will rejoice to find in the new some things that seem to repeat for them ideas that long were foundations of their life. They should examine whether these foundations were real or were only empty words. If so, their illusions should be transformed into reality. Only thus should the new Instructions be understood.

Everyone has seen stars, but does everyone connect them with the idea of infinity? We often find that the starry sky as seen nowadays is very similar to the way it was seen by the ancients. All the great cosmic chemisms can have little meaning without a proper approach to the Supermundane. Likewise, the significance of thought will not be realized without a full understanding of the subtle energies. Indeed, the word thought has always existed, but its true meaning must be pondered.

The real meaning of things can be understood only by comparing their earlier significance with newly-acquired knowledge. Who can say that his former understandings were broader than his present ones? It is not easy to compare one's old and new qualities of consciousness. Man usually forgets his former level, and thinks that he used to know much that he is only now learning. It is useful to think about the new consciousness. We told you that sometimes it is instructive to visit long-forgotten places so as to recall your old understandings and compare them with the new.

The Thinker said, "Gatekeeper, hurry, open the gates! Gatekeeper, I do not know Thee, but I do know why these gates should be opened."

655. Urusvati knows that there is much confusion about the meaning of imagination. People wonder that if the imagination is so necessary for progress, how does one account for a malicious and ugly imagination? This perplexity is justified, and it is necessary to know that there are indeed many kinds of imagination.

It is not easy to help a person whose imagination is malicious, for such an imagination can be quite powerful. One can help only by directing him toward the beautiful. Only in this way can the malicious imagination be overcome, but it is very difficult and requires much time. The malicious imagination has persisted throughout time. It is firmly rooted and has survived the ages, as have so many human habits. Humanity's traditions of thinking are influenced by society, thus making it difficult for the individual to examine habitual tendencies. Such people are unable to even begin to think about the Supermundane, a realm that cannot be approached with malice.

We have watched many strong individuals who were possessed by an evil imagination. They bring much harm, and their imagination is often much stronger than that of good people. The treatment for such people is similar to that for alcoholics. It is difficult in both cases to apply mental suggestion, but it is important to provide an approach to the Beautiful, which melts away the ice of evil. The creators of things of beauty should remember the importance of their creations. I deem the Beautiful to be a powerful shield against evil.

The Thinker said, "Let everyone be provided with a reliable shield. He will receive it from the Muses."

656. Urusvati knows of the particular form of psychic activity that occurs at night. It is crudely called dreaming, but dreams include a great variety of vital manifestations. There may be projections by one's own imagination; there may be a play of memories, rising from the depth of consciousness. But there can also be influences from the Subtle World, or impressions from one's own experiences in the subtle spheres, or some distant message, sent as images. There can be many combinations of these; therefore, experiences during sleep must be scientifically studied.

Many unusual phenomena will be observed by those who study sleep. Some people insist that they never dream. This is incorrect, it is simply that they cannot remember what they have dreamt. Some people can usually remember their nightly experiences, while others not only do not remember them, but even insist, pressing the point, that they never dream.

There are night activities that are evidence of imbalance. These manifest themselves in sleepwalking, but those who experience it have no memory of it. Such people are of an unhealthy nature, and studying them is of little use to the study of healthy sleep. Their activities take place, so to speak, between the worlds, and can be of interest only for studies of physical coordination. Observations of healthy people during sleep result in more relevant conclusions.

In studying the Supermundane World, let us, first of all, not forget the process of sleep. Science should take a very attentive attitude toward the condition that is closest to the Subtle World.

The Thinker said, "We cannot speak crudely about dreams. A subtle condition requires subtle attention."

657. Urusvati knows how carefully the so-called electromagnetic phenomena must be investigated. Recently such storms assailed us, but once again no one studied them. It is essential to investigate these atmospheric manifestations, and also their effect upon the human organism.

Both the animal and vegetable kingdoms will also offer instructive evidence. Finally, all opponents of the science of subtle energies will be put to shame. It is not enough to declare that radio, telephone, and telegraph transmissions were disrupted; this is an observation of the crudest effects.

The physicians in hospitals can observe the extent to which people are subject to the effects of atmospheric storms. The symptoms are long-lasting, and provide ample opportunity for careful study. At the very least the pulse and temperature of each patient can be observed in connection with the anomalous conditions. It is not enough to note changes in the sunspots; who can assert that only those changes were the causes of cosmic storms? Maybe some other kind of energy was involved. It is not in the human power to find the Source of cosmic energy, but man can still study the influence of this energy upon his surroundings. Such a study will, in itself, be an exploration of the Supermundane.

The Thinker asked people long ago to observe all manifestations of Nature. "Not only scientists, but all people can become reliable observers."

658. Urusvati knows the danger of fragments of knowledge falling into untrustworthy hands. I warn about untrustworthy hands because ignorance is not as dangerous as treason.

It must be understood that an individual must be adequately prepared before being entrusted with knowledge. Some Guides deliberately make this preparation a lengthy process. They say, "If the consciousness is not yet ready, let the preparation be tiring, so that the immature ones will leave."

It is right to safeguard knowledge by all means. After all, when explosive materials are guarded, people apply stringent measures. They do it not because there is a secret to protect, but to avoid destruction. Similarly, knowledge in the hands of destructive people becomes a powerful explosive material.

We constantly nurture the growth of knowledge in right directions, and advise avoidance of disorderly, chaotic thinking. Nothing can be done when someone is disappointed and leaves; he is clearly not ready, and it would be impossible to coax him toward a better trend of thought. But those small grains of knowledge already gained will not be lost and may in the future be utilized by him.

When asked about knowledge that could not yet be grasped, the Thinker told the story of a youth who asked a Sage to teach him how to be the ruler of a nation. The Sage said, "Willingly, but first you must become ruler of your heart; when you have mastered that kingdom, come to me."

659. Urusvati knows that the true measure of a toiler is the extent of his labor for the Common Good. Regarding the truth of this let us recall a simple tale from ancient India.

On the outskirts of a village an unknown man settled down. The newcomer observed that the villagers were using unhealthy water from a muddy stream. He started to dig a well for them. The place for the well was a good one, and the well was quickly filled. But evil neighbors, instead of showing gratitude, whispered, "The newcomer is laboring not for us. He opened this well-spring for himself."

The newcomer said, "Then I will carry the water for myself from afar." Then the evil neighbors invented a new slander, that the water in the well had been poisoned or had an evil spell on it, that the entire village would be destroyed. After that, the newcomer left this inhospitable place for good.

The villagers avoided the well, but the cattle drank from it and were soon invigorated. After a period of time a sick little girl, suffering from thirst, drank water from the well and shortly was healed. Soon the new generation of villagers forgot the slander and discovered the healing power of the well. The newcomer who had built the well was now seen as a saint, and legends grew about him. Sadly, before the "poisoner" could become a saint, a whole new generation had to come into being. Thus one can see how the people's consciousness judges labors for the Common Good.

The Thinker knew a similar story from the life of ancient Greece, but instead of the digging of a well, it was the planting of a tree. Every nation has its unjust judges, and its valid judgments by ordinary people.

660. Urusvati knows that an ability to observe with clarity results from a life of striving, vigilance, and readiness. When We spoke about always being on watch, some thought that it had to do with some unusual circumstances. They did not grasp that the power of observation is a most normal ability, available to all. Clarity of observation is a necessity in even the simplest of tasks. Do not think that some kind of higher inspiration is a requirement for this ability.

People like to explain away their errors. They may say that their minds were scattered that day, without thinking about how unworthy such a state is. To be absent-minded means to leave oneself open to destructive influences. It is impossible to think about the Supermundane when one's thoughts are scattered. Defeat is the fate of the absent-minded leader. Courage cannot co-exist with absent-mindedness. Courage can be compared to a sword blade; never can it be compared to a handful of sand.

One should develop one's power of clear observation. No knowledge can be acquired without this ability. We cannot send a sign to an absent-minded one. Precisely, during Our discourses about the Supermundane, one's clarity of observation must be strengthened.

People may complain that due to fatigue, they have lost their ability to observe. This was answered by the Thinker, "A bird in a cage does not forget how to fly."

661. Urusvati knows that thought transmission is most easily received by a person with whom a vibrational connection has been established. Though more difficult, reception is also possible by crowds of people whose vibrations are in a chaotic state. But most difficult of all is communion with a small group that, though linked by some common goal, is in a state of disharmony.

Such groups can completely paralyze their receptivity. They imagine that they are united for a common action, but in reality, they usually can be unmasked as hypocrites. Their hypocrisy may be conscious or unconscious. It is especially difficult for Us when some united group action is needed, but instead, they pierce one another's hearts with invisible arrows of disunity.

How can success be hoped for when each member rejoices at the defeat of another? There is no way to show them that in such behavior they invite their own defeat. Examples of this can be cited from the history of all nations and of all ages. And even now, in spite of having the books of the Teaching, the same lack of harmony can be seen among Ours. Such disorderly conditions provoke consequences that the participants cannot even suspect.

With one wave of his hand man can produce a conflagration. He could, afterwards, regret his carelessness, but what can such regretting accomplish? It is time to put aside the outworn thinking that whispers, "There is no confession if one does not first sin."

The Thinker told the citizens who maligned Pericles after his death, "Ugly stunted ones, you must have seen Pericles in the dark if you imagine him to be as ugly as you yourselves are."

662. Urusvati knows that biology, a science of life, and ethics are inseparable. Some time ago this was sensed, then later forgotten, but now it is again being remembered. We speak much about straight-knowledge; in this concept are contained both biology and ethics. Biology cannot be a dry science; it must contain within itself an understanding of psychic life. It is precisely this that must be studied, for only then will it be possible to speak about the fullness of life.

Certain branches of science have their boundaries; others are unlimited, and therein lies their captivating power. The most primitive materialist cannot deny the scientific importance of biology, and this acknowledgment links him with those tasks that expand knowledge. It is impossible to categorize biology; each of its pages is firmly fastened to the next. This realm without boundaries has a special attraction for the unprejudiced scientist. How many other sciences also serve this science of life!

One of Our friends called himself a biologist, but said that at the same time he was a psychologist. This is a correct description, but is rarely heard. Unfortunately, biologists often turn away from life and shut themselves up in laboratories. But can true biology exist without a broad study of life? We wish to tell all friends that they should not fear to think of themselves as biologists. It is better to describe one's work with widely-accepted terms.

Some may think that those who reflect upon the Supermundane would be more suitably called astronomers, but this name is ill-chosen. Even now many astronomers deny the possibility of life on other planets. Their way is not Our way; biology, however, is easily linked with ethics, and the result is a natural cooperation. This is why We, from Our first discourses, advised the development of the power of observation. Independent observation leads to true scientific learning.

Many think that the term straight-knowledge somehow demeans the dignity of knowledge. This is another error. But some of the better scientists recognize the role of intuition, and in this We concur. We arm Our friends, so to speak, for a distant journey. They may meet all kinds of criticisms and should at all times be ready to reply. On the one side the superstitious ones will drag them to the stake, and on the other, those serving science will demand to see their diploma.

What is needed is steadfastness based on real knowledge, and the maintaining of an awareness of the existence of a Hierarchy of Cooperation. The student of life is not alone.

The Thinker understood the existence of life on all planets. He said, "It would be madness to think that only our Earth is inhabited."

663. Urusvati knows the futility of reasoning with a prejudiced opponent. There are limits to the benefit of laboring to spread the Truth. It is useless to insist where a heart of stone refuses to accept.

It is not always easy to discern lack of receptivity. Straight-knowledge alone can whisper, "Leave, for no understanding is possible here." The right understanding must be cultivated, and it is better to tell too little than too much. Some people will insist on the right to disseminate further the knowledge that was given to them. They are correct in asserting this right, but the responsibility is theirs to know to whom the knowledge may be transmitted. The teacher must not prematurely overload the consciousness of the student.

All must be molded goal-fittingly. To this end, acquaint children from an early age with the grandeur of the Universe. Both microscopes and telescopes should be given to young children. It would be even better to take them to an observatory. Such an experience will be impressed in their minds forever, and will encourage a higher way of thinking. It need not be feared that children will not understand what they have been shown. They will be reminded of what they had learned long before, and will take joy from it. Children will not be shocked by such experiences of cosmic dimensions. On the contrary, it is the petty things, like family quarrels, that will unsettle their world view.

Appreciation of teachers must be increased, so that they are understood to be among the primary shapers of a nation. It distresses Us to see teachers demeaned. In all countries, teachers should be the educators of the people. Their devotion to this task is so great that the nation must provide them with a life that encourages achievement. Can a teacher, when denigrated and impoverished, speak about the Supermundane, or point out the beauty of the heavens, to broaden the thinking of his small students?

Acquaintance with a telescope should begin even earlier than school age. Small children must be given the opportunity to make their own majestic observations. But of course, when we see the poor conditions in many villages, advice about providing telescopes can be seen as utopian. Nevertheless, one should make a start toward the Common Good.

The Thinker said, "Soon the human eye will not suffice to see all the riches that are predestined for mankind."

664. Urusvati knows the many forms of heroism. It is said that circumstances make the hero; it would be better to say that circumstances awaken the hero. Many people do not understand this phenomenon, but others know what is destined for them and carry out their mission from an early age. Some sense that they must fulfill something, but their consciousness does not provide a clear indication. For such born heroes circumstances will be the key. They will force the sounding of the deep inner strings and bring about the required *podvig*.

Today, people do not usually speak about heroes and their achievements. When history narrates heroic deeds, they shrug their shoulders, saying, "It is not for us to perform heroic achievements!" Thus they affirm their own ignorance!

Every era has a place for heroism, beginning with the humble conditions of family life up to cosmic manifestations. One must be able to elevate oneself above the demands of daily life and attend to the needs of the Common Good. Many great opportunities for achievement will then be found; people should not think of *podvig* as inappropriate.

It is instructive to observe in what nation the word heroism is more often used. Let us ask small children to name their heroes. They will not hesitate to reply, and should be encouraged to maintain this awareness throughout their lives.

There was a game in India in which everyone had to name his greatest hero. A small child spoke of Krishna. He was rebuked, and was told that Krishna was a God. But the child insisted that Krishna was primarily a hero, for he labored for the good of his country. The child also pointed out that Krishna knew the language of the animals. He was corrected, "He played his flute and thus charmed the wild animals." But the child insisted, "That means that Krishna knew the language of the animals."

The Thinker kept in mind the myth about Orpheus and always reminded his disciples that Orpheus was a human being.

665. Urusvati knows that when We speak about Krishna, Orpheus, Zoroaster, and other Teachers of mankind, We have important reasons for this. All of them gave instruction, differing in language and custom, but the essence of their teaching was the same.

As yet, the work of comparing these Teachings has not been accomplished. One can point to studies in comparative religion, but We now have in mind an analysis of the common foundations given by the Teachers. A scholar who sifts through the characteristics of all nations and ages will find at their foundations teachings that are as if given by one source. One could mention those few individualities who in succession fulfilled their mission of teaching humanity, thus helping mankind's progress.

At different periods, Teachers, at times without knowing the teachings of others, pronounced ideas that were similar to the others, not only in language but also in feeling. Even someone ignorant of this might think that one individual alone gave these teachings. But those who knew more will draw their own conclusions.

The work that will reveal the universality of these teachings will be of great benefit. Such work will be very difficult, for, in order to be believed, it will be necessary to utilize the recognized sources. The most valuable of the apocryphal writings cannot be cited, for they are not trusted by people. But even the accepted historical data permit useful comparisons. Truth must be proven by recognized methods of reasoning. In spite of the tragic loss of materials beyond counting, many valuable records can still be found. For example, the writings of the disciples of Apollonius of Tyana and Pythagoras can be studied. Perhaps only some words from these will be found dependable, but even these fragments will sufficiently convey the essence of the Teaching. It will become evident that the Teachers, though belonging to different religions, affirmed the same principles. In studying Origen, ancient ideas will be found that he himself could not have previously heard. During deep study, every individual will come to similar understandings.

The Thinker used to say, "When I listen to the narrations of the pilgrims, it sometimes seems to me that it is one person who speaks. I see different garb, hear different tongues, but my heart recognizes the one source."

666. Urusvati knows the preordained plan. Following the plan is like guiding a fragile boat through boulder-strewn rapids. The boat must proceed in its indicated direction, and deliver its load to the proper destination; but the riverbed changes constantly, with dangerous rocks continuously shifting. While guiding the boat the helmsman must at each moment find the safest course.

Those living near the shore rejoice, thinking that the boat is proceeding happily to its destination. They say, "The helmsman knows the way." They do not see the dangers averted by each move of the rudder. The helmsman cannot escape into a quiet backwater, for then there would be no way to proceed. Much must be sacrificed so as not to lose the right direction. The river spray blends with the helmsman's sweat, but for the onlookers this struggle is no more than a merry race.

All of this applies to understanding preordained plans. Few understand the needed intensity of focused vibration. Everyone sees the future according to his own habitual way of thinking, and in the same way sets his goals, without foreseeing the dangers, and unaware that any exist. He insists on circumstances being as he imagines them, and does not realize the dangers he can cause. The onlookers unwittingly confuse the helmsman with their intrusions. Yet, the more dangerous the situation, the more carefully the onlookers should behave. Truly, very few can fully understand preordained plans wisely, and without self-interest.

There is a multitude of rays irradiated by each organism. There is nothing new in this, but when thinking about the rays, new conclusions will be reached. The paths of mental sending are complicated due to the intrusion of many emanations from without. Therefore, the vibrations of the communications must be strong.

Urusvati noticed correctly how often We return, seemingly with great haste, to matters already discussed. But there are really no repetitions, simply expansions. It can be seen how, within the briefest of intervals, a new plan is indicated. This should not cause surprise; despite the seeming variety of preordained plans, they are in fact inwardly linked. Actually, at present, in the flow of world events, the inner connections underlying external differences can be discerned. It must be understood that the boat is speeding through dangerous rapids, but its goal is unshakable. Many rocky obstacles must be avoided. This is not a distortion of the ordained way, but sensible goalfitness.

We say this not amidst inaction, but during tense striving. It is one more page of Our Inner Life.

The Thinker said, "It is easy for me to picture myself as a helmsman amidst a raging current. Right now, the sun is shining, the stillness is complete, but My heart senses the approaching turmoil."

667. Urusvati knows that the Great Teachers of humanity were subjected to cruel persecution. This is so well known to people that they do not like to be reminded of it. Yet they are ever ready to similarly persecute every bearer of the Good. Moreover, people do not like to hear that the persecuted accept their tortures with joy, and that they understand their treatment as recognition of their *podvig*.

One can also point to the experiences of one of the Great Leaders, whom We call the Incomparable Singer. This name suits Him, for He was the first to indicate the power of sound. True, His teaching was later distorted by the people. It must be pointed out that He understood the meaning of Unity. He explained each discord as a result of ignorance. But His dedication to the concept of Unity did not prevent Him from donning armor whenever His people were endangered.

Many will not understand why the renowned Singer can become a warrior. People thus reveal their own limitations. But each human being is a perfect microcosm, carrying lightnings within himself that, when the currents are over-tensed, can be discharged into space to relieve the tension. There is no need to restrain oneself when life demands active achievement. Thus one can trace how Leaders were able to contain within themselves the most diverse qualities. People, regrettably, paid no attention to the Leaders' motives, and thus their deeds were misinterpreted, and they were often criticized.

The Thinker used to say, "I am not a warrior, but when the trumpet calls, I will find within Myself the strength to help the world."

668. Urusvati knows that mental creations are indestructible. They are subject to many influences, but they can all be manifested in a physical state. We remind you of this because some people are confused about it, knowing that in Our Repositories there are many still-unrealized ideas. There is no contradiction in this. If a plan is not fulfilled today, that does not mean that it cannot be accomplished tomorrow, perhaps in even a better way.

People see contradictions where there are none. One could show them many examples of thought beginning to manifest itself physically, but their self-imposed mental limitations prevent them from accepting them. Here again We touch upon the need for trust. Trust would make evident the cement that binds a mental structure with its physical embodiment.

Ethical principles should be seen as practical solutions for life. Wisdom is not something in a fairy tale. It is based, first of all, on trust, which guards against wavering. In the same way, goalfitness results from the application of higher principles; only in this way can seeming contradictions be reconciled. Not without reason did Buddha measure the disciples by their ability to contain.

The Thinker taught, "A path is for walking in two directions. One should also be able to return home."

669. Urusvati knows that thoughts can create, but can also destroy. And thought itself is indestructible. There is nothing contradictory in this. Destruction is not annihilation. Matter, which is created by thought, cannot be annihilated. The builder cannot eliminate his materials. He can break down the structure, he can transform the condition of his materials, but he cannot annihilate them. Knowing this puts a special responsibility upon the thinking person.

Among the unmanifested subtle constructions there are many ugly ones, which should be improved. But what degree of energy is needed so that out of imperfect materials something beautiful can be made! We are often saddened when We see the needless expenditure of precious energy! Many an energetic and even rational mind can occasionally create ugliness. You already know that in earthly life, too, the mind can be a poor counselor.

It is amazing to see how distant from understanding beauty some thinkers are. In their own domains they demonstrate the logic of their thinking, but in the domain of the Beautiful their eyes are blind. This kind of failing is often seen, and it is, as a rule, accompanied by a distinguishing trait–self-conceit. Usually they are beyond rescue in this earthly life, and in the Subtle World they commit much harm. It is not possible to even mention the Supermundane in their earthly life, and in the Subtle World they do not perceive the beauty of Cosmos.

The Thinker said, "Man, you drag behind you a long tail of ugly thoughts. Do you really intend that in the Supermundane World you will also be surrounded by the same mean little companions?"

670. Urusvati knows to what extent people, because of their nature, are at the same time attracted to and fearful of whatever appears unusual to them. Keeping in mind this human trait, it is therefore necessary to speak cautiously about unusual phenomena. Even then, it is advisable to say that the information was obtained from others–witnesses–and not to point to oneself as the authority. Otherwise, people will grow fearful, though they may attempt to conceal their fear.

As an example, We can cite the Incomparable, Perfect Singer. He possessed many phenomenal abilities, but knew not to speak about them, so that He would not be seen as participating in the manifestations that took place near Him. His music made an impression on those around him, but did not reveal that He, Himself, was the cause of the more profound transformations that were felt.

His Teachings were given as if coming from antiquity. He possessed enough wisdom to avoid letting people even notice His powers. But when some who envied Him suspected that He possessed phenomenal faculties, they began persecutions that then led to murder. Thus it can be seen that people do not forgive others for their special abilities, yet wish to possess them themselves. A great sensitivity is needed, in order to know when the word "Supermundane" may be pronounced.

The Thinker said, "Beware lest the Highest be turned into the lowest."

671. Urusvati knows that cosmography, as a most interesting and important subject, should be taught in all schools. This study comprises all aspects of knowledge about the universe. Those who wish to transform the consciousness of their nation must provide the people with knowledge of the fundamental structure of the universe, and present it in a scientific and attractive way.

This should not entail difficult examinations that often alienate the students' interest in the subject, but should be in the form of discussions that do not make demands. If the consciousness of the student preserves fragments of distant memories, his enthusiasm for this knowledge will be more easily kindled. Truly, cosmography must be taught in an interesting way. New scientific discoveries must also be presented. Textbooks should be produced in a way that permits them to be easily re-edited with new information.

Many subjects will be synthesized in the teaching of cosmography. Astronomy, astrochemistry, astrology, and folk knowledge–all will find their place in the scientific structure. Probably the older generations will regard such teaching as unrealizable, but We have in mind the young ones. Thus will the Supermundane enter into the sensitive consciousness.

The Thinker said that all the separate sciences will at some time come together as faithful co-workers.

672. Urusvati knows how persistent are Our mental sendings. An uninformed person would wonder why We sometimes repeat almost literally what We have said before, but an experienced recipient understands that repetition is a deepening and has as its purpose the intensification of energy in space. There are many reasons for the ways in which Our communications are sent. People, in their self-centeredness, think that all is done only for them, for their separate selves, forgetting the common good.

Our communications vary greatly in their rhythm and the quality of their sound. They often move fleetingly, and are difficult to grasp, but they can also be distinctly articulated, sent with an insistence that provokes a strong response. Also, Our communications can be sent either speedily, or quite slowly. Our complicated work requires many methods.

Thus, as one repeats a mantra, it may be necessary for the rhythm to dominate, with the words of the mantra almost obliterated; or a sonorous pronunciation may be needed, in which every word is clear.

The Thinker used to say, "Do not think that everything is done only for you. There are many ways and reasons for a higher thought to be sent."

673. Urusvati knows that in every significant event, there are strong cosmic influences, but four levels of human thinking are involved. The first level is that of those who, with full understanding, participate physically in the resolving of conflicting forces. For them each event can be seen as the result of a battle. On the second level are those who participate in the Subtle World. They also have a clear understanding, and are involved no less than the incarnate ones. The third level consists of those who are involved, but without understanding. The fourth level consists of the leaders, whether visible or invisible.

The first two and the fourth levels have been discussed by Us many times, but the third level must be spoken about, for it includes more and more people who, consciously or unconsciously, participate in the most complex events. It can be understood that their thoughts form a powerful force, which can be dangerous because of their chaotic nature.

Irresponsible, with a low level of consciousness, subject to any influence, ready for any betrayal, filled with malice, such people fill space with the debris of their disorderly thinking. Their enthusiasms are unpredictable and can change daily; thus, they become sources of psychic epidemics.

Moreover, they endanger the mental sending of conscious co-workers of Good. They poison the atmosphere, and much energy is required to neutralize their dark sendings. They do not understand the scope of the harm inflicted by them, and do not wish to know what barriers they set up on the path of evolution.

Some may wonder what is new in all this, for malicious ignorance has been recognized as destructive for a long time. But precisely at present, during this time of Armageddon, the legions of destroyers multiply. They render useless the labors of the co-workers of Good, and special warnings should be proclaimed against their madness. Their disruptions of harmony must not be tolerated. The great majority, unknowing, can easily succumb to falsehood.

The Thinker constantly pointed out that ignorance is a most powerful force and therefore dangerous.

674. Urusvati knows that lack of co-measurement is a psychic blindness. People sometimes choose to ignore a devastating fire just to be able to finish their porridge, yet the same people will jump in alarm at the sight of a fly coming through their window. The sense of discrimination must be developed at all costs, otherwise man will fall prey to a particular kind of barbarism.

Is it not strange that people do not care to develop their abilities or to think about the psychic side of life? They make it more difficult for Us to direct human thinking toward the Supermundane. It becomes impossible to provide to so-called civilized people an understanding of the supermundane realms. They believe that they have already attained a high level of scientific knowledge, but they have no idea about harmonizing spiritual understanding with science.

Do not think that We see many co-workers who can introduce supermundane ideas into their lives. You have received letters in which Our Indications are called not concrete, inapplicable to life. A real tragedy is revealed by these unthinking judgments. People who complain about the impracticable abstractness of Our Teaching do not ponder where the boundary lies between concrete reality and theoretical abstraction.

It is precisely now that reality is so urgently needed, because the world is passing through a dangerous stage of reconstruction. At such a time it is inadmissible to indulge in abstractions, when every hour demands a real, concrete decision. But the psychic blind cannot discriminate between urgent, practical reality, and harmful abstraction. They fill their lives with useless abstractions and do not see how harmful they become. Urusvati remembers how an overdressed crowd rushed to an entertainment when the building in which it was to be presented was already falling in.

The Thinker taught, "Cognize reality, and thus liberate yourself from the chains of slavish thinking."

675. Urusvati knows that some people will insist that physical participation in a battle is more effective and more difficult than battle on a psychic level. Such a misconception occurs because of a lack of understanding of the psychic life. It is impossible to compare physical and psychic tensions, for psychic tensions are so much more significant in all ways.

Subtle energies are stronger than any physical ones, but this cannot be accepted by people, because of their wrong attitude to life. It must be frequently repeated that physical suffering is nothing compared with the suffering of the subtle body. Similarly, physical dangers cannot be compared to psychic dangers. The greatest physical upheavals are as naught if compared with the psychic changes in the world.

At present, when humanity is tensed in the battle for the reconstruction of the world, attention must be given to the psychic side of life. Yet there are many obstacles on the path of this natural evolution. People will resist with all their might the idea that useful knowledge should penetrate their limited consciousnesses. There will be many rebellions against efforts to broaden the consciousness, and many despicable measures will be taken to stop the spreading of the needed knowledge.

It is instructive to observe the state of mind of the adversaries. They will invent all kinds of arguments to ridicule psychic energy. Every one of you can cite examples from your own experience when you witnessed denial of psychic energy.

The Thinker taught, "Do not fear ignoramuses, and hasten on the path to knowledge."

676. Urusvati knows that every revelation of new knowledge is received and disseminated only by a small minority of people. The majority responds to new revelations with animosity. Opposition, and even fierce hatred follow in the wake of all beneficial discoveries.

Some may think that this can be attributed to envy, but in reality the cause lies much deeper. It is the opposition by chaos to all constructiveness. One can even measure the value of any new knowledge by the degree of hatred that it provokes. Not only malicious mockery, but also ruinous hatred will attack all that serves the renewal of life. Observe how close to treason the cultivation of such hatred is. They are ready to engage in any subtle attack that will damage what has inflicted no harm on them.

Haters can be divided into two kinds. The first, by attacking a truth, draws attention to it. Such people are incarnated sometimes for a specific purpose: to become unwitting promoters of an entire movement. It must be understood that their karma is not worsened by serving such an intended mission.

The second kind of hater, however, is very harmful, for he attempts to plant falsehoods on the paths of mankind's progress. You often have met such spoilers. They cannot be excused for being possessed, otherwise every weak-willed person would find similar justification for himself. We must beware of those who fall into the grip of possession.

Remember that these haters react with particular rage to the revelations of the Supermundane World. They prefer to remain surrounded by outworn ways, but under a mask of relevance and reason. Many fine paths have been littered with obstacles by these hypocrites. Science must find a broader way to lead to unlimited learning.

The Thinker fought such haters. He warned the disciples that they should not leave their philosophical treatises unguarded. "Do not forget that even among family and friends there may be haters."

677. Urusvati knows that even small indispositions of a leader can have a decisive influence upon important events. Historians may call this coincidence, but actually, many causes can be perceived; these causes may be human or cosmic, or the inexorable action of the Wheel of Law.

It should not be thought that a large event must be caused by large influences. The fate of nations can depend on seemingly small circumstances. It would be instructive to study this, to observe the correlations of things, not according to their physical traits, but according to the correspondences of their most subtle energies. It is especially important to perceive how the great events of Armageddon are connected with imponderable karmic conditions.

Karma always overtakes the perpetrators of injustice. The ways of this perfect law are inexorable, but they are circuitous. People generally cannot perceive the subtle correlations, and because the supermundane conditions are so different from the earthly ones, even an act of supreme justice may be seen as unacceptable to them. Yet the earthly and supermundane correlations involved in the most complex occurrences must be studied. This requires the cultivation of an ability to think deeply. And no one can teach what can be perceived only by straight-knowledge.

The Thinker taught His disciples to discern the essence of all events. He observed that, usually, the superficial appearance of events does not reflect their inner meaning.

678. Urusvati knows that predictions and their fulfilment as events depend on many factors. A weak person should make no attempt to predict. Such a one can judge solely from his own limited understanding, and thus will only impede the flow of important events. Everyone, due to his own limitations, can to some degree be an impediment. A weak thinker can often become in some respect a fanatic and will see everything through his own prejudices. Therefore it would be better for people not to make predictions, and, even more, it is dangerous to make predictions and attach contrived dates to them.

Understand that a prediction, before its earthly fulfillment, has its psychological influence in space, and in some invisible way has an effect on events. It is instructive to study how Our predictions are fulfilled.

The Thinker used to say, "Do not think that only what you can see has reality; many things are born in space before they become visible to you."

679. Urusvati knows that the Supermundane can be studied in many ways, but the approach must always be without prejudice or limitation. Every field of science can open a way to the Supermundane. Astronomy will be transformed into a study of life in other worlds. Physics will give room to astrophysics. Chemistry will include astrochemistry. The Supermundane will enhance philosophy and psychology. Physiology will find the links between the human organism and Cosmos. History will take care of finding valuable knowledge in the ancient writings.

One can easily see that radio and television transmission will serve to reveal new discoveries about the Supermundane. In this way even the so-called positivist sciences will serve the broadening of consciousness.

There is no need to await great epochal changes, when each unlimited mind can at any time enhance its understanding. Even the ridiculed sciences, such as astrology and alchemy, will be raised from the ashes, together with other ways of studying the subtle energies. Humanity, without rejecting former achievements, can regenerate life. What is necessary for this is to substitute the word "possible" wherever one sees "impossible." Only through this self-revelation will people be able to approach the study of the most fundamental realms. Even geology can remind us of layering that occurred because of supermundane processes.

The Thinker pointed to the earth, saying, "And you, Earth, remind us about the grandeur of the Supermundane."

680. Urusvati knows that the degree of readiness determines the level of success. And what is the readiness that We refer to? One may know conventional rules and be ready to obey them, but such readiness achieves nothing. True readiness is found in the harmony of knowledge and straight-knowledge. Then one is strengthened by Our sendings, which are received consciously and with care.

People are often committed to a labor that is imposed on them as a duty, but nothing good can come from such coercion. No task, no matter how elevated, has meaning if it is coerced. It is time for humanity to understand wherein lies true readiness, without which there can be no heroes. A high state of mind results when man accepts naturally the beauty of intense readiness.

The Thinker used to say, "He who will not lift the food to his mouth will not have his hunger satisfied."

681. Urusvati knows that silence can be a sign of the intensity of inner power. It has long been said that stillness can be more powerful than the storm or whirlwind. But how many understand this universal fact? Silence is usually understood as just a reluctance to speak.

People generally see everything through the filters of their own ego. They would like to learn things, but only petty things, and do not understand the silence in others. They do not understand that there can be such states of great tension, especially in the realm of the Supermundane. When people do recognize the Supermundane, they can only bow in reverent silence; but foolishness will tempt some to turn the great into selfish pettiness. It is difficult to discuss the Supermundane with those who always try to turn any conversation toward matters of personal concern. People should compare the Supermundane with their personal concerns and understand that the great includes the small, and thus is of help to it.

The Thinker required that His disciples be imbued with an understanding of the significance of silence.

682. Urusvati knows why We often discuss calmness. All that is said about Nirvana also applies to calmness. For those whose consciousness is weak, calmness is perceived as not thinking, indifference, and absence of will; but for those of strong consciousness, calmness is a sign of the highest tension, indicating a broad consciousness, wisdom, and courage. Calmness is a manifestation of a great inner potential. One must consciously develop it and understand that, in this state, discharges of psychic energy are unavoidable.

Urusvati rightly understands that a discharge of psychic energy is needed during times of significant world events. The subtler the organism, the greater the discharge. This is the cause of an unexplainable fatigue that can be observed in increasing numbers of people, a fatigue of epidemic proportions that is as yet not understood by science. Only later will people be able to understand the purpose for which their energy was discharged, and what magnet attracted it.

In observing these manifestations, one can clearly see the coming together of the Supermundane with the earthly. Know how to preserve true calmness.

The Thinker said, "I do not know where my strength flies to. May it fly to the most worthy."

683. Urusvati knows that anyone who loses equilibrium and calmness becomes unreceptive to health-giving vibrations and subject to destructive ones. Such a one suffers great torment, and becomes a source of infection to others. Such agents of disease should themselves receive medical help, but, of course, physicians must first recognize the cause of their condition. The doctors must not poison the organism with narcotics, which would simply dull the consciousness without removing the cause. On the contrary, when the narcotics lose their strength, agitation and imbalance will increase, and doubly assail the unprotected organism.

Only treatment by use of psychic energy can provide the best means for cure. This energy can be directed from a distance, but only if the patient does not resist. Many manias develop out of states of imbalance. This can be more clearly seen from the Subtle World. It is astonishing to observe how insignificant are the things that cause people to lose their equilibrium.

Time itself shows people that the phantoms that frighten them have no reality, as they realize that they have survived their frights and anxieties quite well. But the harm in it all is just that during such petty turbulence they could not think about the Supermundane.

The Thinker told a neighbor who became ill, "Friend, was it worth inviting illness just because of concern about a shipload of merchandise?"

684. Urusvati knows that each one of Us at some time in the past had to adapt His psychic energy to function properly in the dense conditions on Earth. It is impossible to make such difficult adjustments quickly. It must be remembered too that such processes must be performed by earthly means.

Do not think that some kind of magic or sorcery can be resorted to for the initial adjustments. First of all, We had to develop the quality of observation, in order to learn to note the point of contact with cosmic forces. What We had to learn is the same as We teach all of you to do, but in reverse.

People should not complain that manifestations of the Supermundane are rare. They are numerous, but one must learn to sense them; however, one should not exaggerate what one feels. Many newcomers are ever ready to see each fleeting perception as something momentous. It must not be expected that the process of refinement of consciousness can be hurried; the microcosm needs systematic and steady development, else it will never become a reflection of the Macrocosm.

Yet, the main achievement is that each refinement is inalienable, for nothing can destroy the qualities of psychic energy. Therefore it is important to develop these qualities. Everyone, at any time, can apply himself to the benevolent task of cultivating all aspects of psychic energy. This is a work that leads to the attainment of knowledge of the Supermundane.

Begin your observations from the simplest, the smallest. In any environment cosmic signs can be sensed. Just as meteorological and seismographic observations can be made, so also can one make cosmic observations, which is what we will call supermundane observations.

Everyone can begin a diary recording premonitions, sensations in connection with events, and all unusual occurrences. In time, many mistakes will be seen in the diaries. They are unavoidable, for the interaction of currents is perceived with great difficulty. Do not be distressed by this, for We too have always accumulated Our observations under difficult conditions.

However, note that cosmic observations can be made by all, without discrimination. The way to unlimited knowledge is open for all. Any realization of one's mistakes will bring new understanding. How wonderful it is, gradually, from one's own experience, to develop an understanding of the psychic conditions that bring about the best results.

A sense of premonition is a first step toward straight-knowledge; but the tendency to exaggerate must not coarsen the subtlety of straight-knowledge. Remember that everyone must make firm his commitment to refine his straight-knowledge. Desire and strive!

The Thinker said, "Out of my small window I can see the grandeur of the starry vault."

685. Urusvati knows that a new era of science began a century ago. Every great advance until now has carried with it the legacy of earlier knowledge, but knowledge was always divided into categories. This is a harmful limitation. At present humanity is approaching the next step, when we are again reminded of ancient truths; but now there is a need for synthesis.

What is it then that brings about a renovation? It cannot be assumed that a school education is sufficient to cause it. And we cannot rely just on knowing that predicted dates are imminent, and that cosmic currents will act on mankind in some new way. There are other factors that must be sought that will help to raise the thinking of humanity to a new level. Among these are new applications of electrical energy, and new developments in the chemical industries. Very material and physical forces can influence thinking, and also the functioning of the glands.

Man does not notice how even the most narrow, utilitarian ways can lead to the refinement of consciousness. Of course, we should not think that such utilitarian approaches can bring about a new era, but if jinns can build temples, then ordinary chemical advances can turn mankind toward a higher quest. Thus, even this time of Armageddon can sow seeds of progressive change.

The Thinker foresaw long ago that mankind would wail much, and out of these wails will emerge cries of victory.

686. Urusvati knows that Our cosmic observations will always provoke skeptical responses. Scoffers will say, "What importance can insignificant human attempts have in the face of Infinity? It is like a butterfly trying to fly to the Moon." Such comparisons are inappropriate, for the skeptics overlook the power of the psychic energy of man.

Not all diamonds were found by great scientists. Let us recall what magnificent discoveries were made by simple, untrained people. Let us not look too hard for causes–nothing happens without cause–but remember that even children have often been excellent observers and discoverers. And when cosmic dates are approaching, human thinking develops more quickly and independently.

One must beware of people who call themselves initiates. Not one of the great philosophers allowed himself such conceit. Not one of Our co-workers takes pride in his knowledge. Every one of Us possesses a certain degree of experience, but We realize that the measure of Our knowledge is relative. Only with this approach can one gather strength for advancement. Spatial research cannot ever be discouraging, for each moment may provide the joy of discovery. Let us not be hasty, weighing the significance of our discoveries, for both the discoverer and the interpreter meet upon Supermundane ways.

The Thinker understood the beauty of such supermundane meetings. They are not accidental and the reasons for them are beautiful.

687. Urusvati knows that Avidya–ignorance–can easily be turned into knowledge, if there is any inclination at all toward learning. The sowers of knowledge can be called light-bearers. This definition is by no means symbolic; it reflects reality. In truth, when one reveals a desire to pass on one's knowledge, one's radiation grows and shines with beauty. Such radiation is like the aura of one who performs *podvig*. During each transmission of knowledge a certain *podvig* takes place. And if that knowledge is absorbed with equal enthusiasm, an enveloping flame of superb light is ignited. Thus one can see that Our use of the word "light-bearer" is based upon reality.

To Our regret, when We say about ignorance that it is darkness, this too is a reality, though a sad one. When people permit themselves to drown in ignorance and negation, all radiation is extinguished. They open themselves to the most dangerous illnesses, for their protective nets are weakened. Such extinguishers of Light are incurable, and only a new experience in the Subtle World can reveal to them a further way. Sooner or later these people will understand that their behavior cannot lead to any good.

During your conversations, there should be agreement about the precise meaning of terms utilized. A difference in understanding leads to unresolved conflicts. Many philosophical systems collapse, precisely because of imprecise understanding. Thus many do not understand the difference between innocent and intentional ignorance. They think of them as synonymous, and dangerous misjudgments can then take place.

Remember that when discussing the Supermundane one may fall victim to harmful misunderstandings. One person may speak in terms of religious dogma, and another in those of astronomy; both will miss the true, vast concept that is the Supermundane.

The Thinker, after several disputes, remarked, "It is sad when people speak about opposite things using the very same words."

688. Urusvati knows that each human organism reacts to cosmic perturbations in its own way. A more refined organism resounds more strongly. One should not try to suppress such reactions–that would not be natural–but one should adjust one's behavior during these periods of tension.

At present, humanity is undergoing unusual tests. It must be noted that the vast majority is not ready to understand the true meaning of events. Some, like ostriches, hide their heads in the sand, others poison themselves with hatred, thus creating new karmic burdens; still others keep repeating outworn formulas. Humanity reacts in many strange and inappropriate ways, instead of trying to understand the true meaning of events. Those reliable ways that could help humanity are again ignored.

Many will think Our discourses about the Supermundane irrelevant, even though only a correct understanding of the Supermundane can resolve their problems. During a storm one should at least know the whereabouts of the longed-for harbor.

A common, powerful striving will enable development of the needed sense of assurance. But a general striving is not enough; everyone must also be an individual, conscious unit. You know that an army is strong when each warrior acts on his own conscious, heroic impulse.

We have spoken much about unity, and all that We said remains valid. But think about what is required to build a beneficial unity. A coerced unity produces nothing. Therefore, We frequently advise that the harmful elements fall away. An infected limb must be amputated. There can be a physical, as well as a psychic, gangrene. Many illnesses can be noted where preventive measures were not taken.

The predestined moment of danger has come. One can see how wrong are the predictions of self-absorbed people.

The Thinker said, "We think that something important takes place when a thousand citizens are making noise in a public square, but what will happen when thousands of thousands grow agitated?"

689. Urusvati knows how often the most basic truths must be repeated so that they will penetrate the human consciousness. Clairvoyance and clairaudience are not acquired by earthly ways, yet people demand some kind of system that can be derived from their usual daily routine. One instruction can be given: observe clearly and closely, observe vigilantly each sign of subtle sensations.

Do not expect and await these manifestations, but remain open to receive them. Expectation is a human attitude, but it is an obstacle to the approach of higher manifestations. It is well-known that the strongest manifestations are received unexpectedly, and are only disturbed when the voice of the mind rings out. The subtle nature must not be forced, but its every expression should be welcomed.

Let us not calculate precisely what kind of manifestation is most important. Sometimes the seemingly small revelations are more significant than the most soul-shaking ones. Learn how to sense the manifestations. Which one will sound deep in the heart? Truth is in the heart, knowledge is in the heart, revelation is in the heart. It is said that the Yoga of Love is the shortest path. Truly, it can be called the Yoga of the Heart.

All cognitions of the Supermundane are formed in the heart. Thought has its origin in the heart, and is then conveyed to the brain. Let everyone who wishes to turn to the Supermundane summon the power of his heart, for it alone will resound to Infinity.

The Thinker taught, "Every teacher must be a pupil of the heart, without it all our aspirations will end in destruction. Woe to those with hearts of stone."

690. Urusvati knows how differently Our Abode is imagined by people. Some think of it as a kind of monastery, while others call it a den of sorcery; some insist upon its having royal splendor, while others think of it as a place of austere asceticism; and some deny Our existence altogether, while others think that Our Ashrams exist everywhere.

Many such examples can be given, but one opinion, not without significance, should be mentioned. It says that We do not live in the physical body, that there is one place in the Himalayas, filled with the emanations of many minerals, where a constant whirl of supermundane energies exists, which permits special connections with the Supermundane World. And so, abandon the idea that We have a physical body, and affirm the image of Our link with the supermundane whirl, which assists in producing special chemical combinations. At least in this way people will be reminded about their link with the Supermundane.

Do not insist upon a full explanation, when only partially-useful understanding has been offered. The many partial paths of knowledge can then be combined. We do not reject any knowledge, however fragmentary, as long as it does not deny the most important things.

Do not laugh if, out of ignorance, impossible characteristics are ascribed to Us, such as royal splendor and luxury. Simple people for whom luxury is the pinnacle of achievement, usually think thus. In their own way they wish to adorn Us, but they can think of nothing finer than royal splendor. They place precious stones upon Our Image and think that they act rightly, believing that supermundane forces must serve the power of their luxurious embellishments.

The Thinker used to say, "Friend, if you want to see a clear reflection in a basin of water, wait until its surface becomes calm. Calmness is the garment of wisdom."

691. Urusvati knows that even when one is thinking clearly and in a focused way, unrelated thoughts can unexpectedly intrude. Intense thinking does not permit such thoughts to rise from the depths of the consciousness; this means that they are spatial sendings. Do not think that such intrusions occur because of imperfection of thinking. Messages received can be urgent and grand, or can be quite ordinary. Even the ordinary ones are evidence of the harmony of vibrations between sender and receiver.

The experienced observer knows that similarities of vibration can exist on any level, whether that of great thoughts or of simple, everyday thoughts. Therefore, when spatial thoughts intrude, one must be alert to them. It is possible that help is being requested, or that useful advice is being sent; in this way new supermundane cooperation can be established. Great illuminations begin from one small spark.

Cooperation with the Highest is woven not from coercion, but from joy. What would Our labor be without voluntary cooperation? A lone worker cannot succeed in all the worlds. It is beautiful when a friend, unasked, hastens to help with and continue the urgent work. Urusvati remembers how Sister Yu. provided medical help. No one asked or demanded it, but true cooperation is hundred-eyed and hundred-armed.

Those who can think about the Supermundane can understand the meaning of cooperation with the Highest. We are ever ready to speak, and have spoken for decades, about cooperation, but the first lack of understanding by people is enough to destroy the fragile beauty of cooperation. There is little point in reading words if confusion about their meaning plunges one into doubt. Recognizing the value of supermundane knowledge will inevitably lead one toward conscious cooperation with the Highest.

We are ready to repeat, for thus We saturate space, but let those who abandon Us ponder whether their actions are goal-fitting.

The Thinker, when abandoned by a disciple, asked His remaining followers if they wanted to join the departing one. "Let the husks be separated from the grain."

692. Urusvati knows that some people imagine Us to be omnipotent, but those who think more deeply understand that degrees of power are relative. No one can claim absolute power, because there are so many limiting conditions that must be considered. Influence must be carefully prepared, and all those involved, on all sides, must assent willingly.

Cosmic currents can present a significant obstacle; therefore, one must choose carefully those that are harmonious. Not without reason are they called the harp of space. In ancient times a poet said, "You can put me out of tune but you cannot play me." Thus, people can disrupt any harmony, but they do not want to think about the labor needed to tune a great harp.

Also, people do not understand when I speak about Our relative power. Human nature regards it as a sign of weakness and powerlessness. In everything, the Golden Mean must be observed; this is the only true way.

The Thinker said, "Even the most powerful is limited in Infinity."

693. Urusvati knows that Our judgments are not accepted by many. Even when Our Indications bring predicted results, people pay no attention. Only few will remember how exact Our Indications were. It is not easy to promote the Teaching of Good if it is not applied in life. Who could understand the full meaning of the Supermundane if even the simplest advice is rejected? It would seem easy to apply timely, useful advice, but something prevents people from remembering it. This something may be ill will, but usually the cause is much less significant, and may simply be laxity. But people dislike having such traits attributed to them. They insist that they are on constant watch. Therefore, do not expect of people what they, in their present state of consciousness, cannot even grasp.

Especially harmful are those who read much, but assimilate nothing. It is often better to deal with those who lack knowledge, but have a benevolent nature. Students should not be offended if We point out failings caused by their laxity. The Supermundane requires focused striving. Laxity can never lead one to soaring flights.

We point out that during these days of Armageddon one must draw from within oneself the highest degree of vigilance. You have read in the earlier books many urgent Indications, but how many of you have given due attention to them?

The Thinker used to say, "Do not sweep out the pearls with the dust."

694. Urusvati knows how attentively the poor should be treated. Most of the population is poor, but it is they whose labor serves to renew earthly forces. Therefore it is unworthy to look upon the poor as inferior. History shows us that what people think of as wealth is transitory and short-lived.

Also, remember that there are many who voluntarily accept the mission to live among the poor and share their destiny. Outwardly such messengers do not differ from the crowd. One must know them well to sense their inner riches. They are very receptive to matters of the Supermundane World. They are transmitters of essential knowledge to those who are most deprived. The pompous rich would not enter a poor dwelling, but even if they did, they would not find a common language.

We constantly direct Our friends to the poor, for the source of the future is there. Those nations that understand the principles of Common Good and strive to the future, will gain power. In these discourses about the Supermundane let us be affirmed in our commitment to the principles of humaneness to all; this is a step forward on the path to knowledge.

The Thinker said, "The future belongs to the poor; the rich own only the past."

695. Urusvati knows that exposure to subtle energies is similar to exposure to radioactive energies. If one is careful when dealing with radium, harmful effects can be avoided. Similarly, subtle energies can be either healing or destructive. Though they saturate the atmosphere, most people do not know how to make use of them for improvement of health. We feel an obligation to point this out.

It is because of ignorance that some suggest having nothing to do with these dangerous energies. But this is impossible, because humanity is surrounded by chemical and other powerful influences. There is no other way but to learn to accept supermundane sendings. Everyone is already aware of the value of pure air and takes appropriate measures to utilize it in his daily life. One should think about what subtle conditions of the human organism correspond to the subtle energies.

We have spoken sufficiently about imperil, and everyone should understand the destructive power he carries within himself. The heart cannot assimilate subtle energies if it is assaulted by destructive arrows. Similarly, one cannot assimilate the supermundane gifts when the germ of illness is already rooted within. That is why so much is said about timely preventive measures. Everyone can receive beneficial supermundane energies by maintaining a benevolent attitude.

The Thinker said, "No physician can contrive a better panacea than benevolence."

696. Urusvati knows that We, too, strive to maintain a state of harmony when in contact with especially powerful subtle energies. In addition to maintaining an inner striving, We arrange Ourselves in a circle. This circle is highly harmonized, and in it each of Us keeps to a particular place. Everyone has in front of

Him, on a small table, an apparatus that intensifies the current. When atmospheric conditions are obstructive, this apparatus can also be used to amplify Our voices.

We also make sure that Our co-workers do not add their own messages while We are striving to make contact with powerful subtle energies. Conditions must be observed precisely, for any disturbance can be destructive. This should not be seen as a sign of Our weakness, but as a sign of the great power of the current. Therefore We repeat about the importance of harmony, which must be built steadily, over time. However, the destruction of harmony can happen in a moment.

Many will wonder about this, if they themselves have violated harmony but have felt no consequences. This is akin to the attitude of a criminal, who thinks that the consequence of his deeds will pass him by; but he forgets that every cause has its effect, and that the law governing this process is beyond earthly understanding.

Similarly, inner disruptions of harmony are not easily perceived. We can affirm that communion among Ourselves does not cause disruptions, for We have strengthened it through Our self-sacrificing labor.

Likewise, Our harmonious meetings should not be thought of as some kind of magical ritual. We gather simply to initiate undelayable actions for the Common Good.

The Thinker said, "Even an offence is forgiven if it is performed for the Common Good."

697. Urusvati knows how harmful it is to limit great concepts by one's own understanding of them. For example, people speak about humaneness and think that it is limited to mercy and compassion, but humaneness is a manifestation of all that is good in the microcosm.

Man cannot live without at least some idea about the Supermundane World. In this, one may recall the parable about a man who denied the existence of that World: A certain pompous fool argued that his life was connected only to the Earth. A Rishi asked him, "Do you really insist that you need only the Earth, and nothing of the Supermundane?" The fool persisted, and the Rishi requested that he conduct a test, "Lie down with your face in the dirt and see how long you can survive with the Earth alone!" The fool answered indignantly, "Do you wish me to suffocate?" But the Rishi smiled, "Apparently you cannot live even a short time without the Supermundane." Thus in a few words, the presence of the Supermundane World was affirmed.

Connected with this, the Wisdom of the East tells us also about the essential need for sleep. Even the most powerful ruler cannot survive without sleep, which is a path to the Supermundane.

True humaneness discerns those moments when events of significance are taking place. People, as a rule, do not recognize an important, decisive hour. They connect events to arbitrarily chosen causes, and overlook true causes. It is therefore impossible to speak to them about dates, because they do not perceive the inception of events.

Even thinking people can allow harmful limitation of concepts. They say, "My psychic energy" when they know that the primary energy cannot be owned. It vibrates and constantly changes throughout the cosmos. When expended, it is replenished not from within, but from without.

The seed of the spirit is clothed in radiant psychic energy. This garb may be shabby or beautiful, but it belongs to no one. Man has been given a great gift, because the microcosm is a condenser of psychic energy. This ability, sent for the cognition of the Supermundane, cannot be thought of as a possession.

People do not correctly understand the great concept of justice. They often regard justice as some decision handed down by a court, but it is really achieved by man himself being summoned to authentic knowledge, by directing his heart toward the Truth. The Supermundane World can broaden the consciousness. Just as a dowsing rod can point to underground water and metals, so can the scepter of the spirit point out the Truth.

Many qualities must be realized, but such realization cannot be achieved by resorting to arbitrary, personal opinions. It can be achieved only by grasping the real nature, the Supermundane essence, of things. People rarely understand this simple expression, the essence. To realize it a certain amount of synthesis is needed, but first of all it is necessary to cognize the significance of the Supermundane World in all things.

The Thinker taught His disciples to perceive the Supermundane influence in all manifestations of life. The Supermundane is not simply a realm; it is also a level of consciousness.

698. Urusvati knows that Our Teaching is inexhaustible, just as is My care for you. But no care can be fruitful without cooperation. Cooperation grows wondrously when there is undivided striving. The coming together of energies generates the needed fruitful spark. These sparks are indicators of advancement; success in labor depends upon them. Once again let us affirm the importance of labor.

It is particularly sad for Us when people speak about wasted labor, because no labor disappears, and all labor produces its harvest. But do not decide on the expected time of such a harvest beforehand, for a harvest can be gathered only long after the seeds have been laid in the ground.

The labor of learning must be honored, because all knowledge adds to the expansion of consciousness. It is an error to think that only spiritual or philosophical labor can contribute to the growth of consciousness. Remember that the labor of learning is a kind of motion, in which the consciousness expands.

Cosmos continuously unfolds, and the consciousness of the microcosm unfolds also. Truly, it can be said, "On any path toward the Supermundane I will meet Thee." It is impossible to foretell which of the approaching ones will outstrip the others in his quest. For everyone a word of encouragement will be found.

The hypocrites and the cunning ones multiply, because they have no idea of the Supermundane. They do not understand that in lying they primarily deceive themselves. People cannot subsist on abstractions. Explanations of virtue should be based on scientific foundations, defined in terms of the human organism itself. The time is coming when even the loftiest concepts will be proven by science.

There is no need to fear that humane ideas will suffer when contacted by the realms of science; on the contrary, one can only foresee a broader expansion of consciousness. We can only welcome those scientists who will study the moral foundations of humanity from the point of view of physiology and other sciences, and thus explain the functioning of the microcosm. Then, at last, man will be able to reflect upon the true workings of the nations.

Let us not forget that even in ancient times voices were calling for the organizing of society according to principles of community. Unfortunately, every attempt to renew the consciousness in this way was undermined by the opposition of ignorance.

Even so, nations are drawing closer to a manifest, essential reconstruction of the world. This reconstruction is based on the same ancient principles, though new terms may be used for them. Thus the renewal of the world is hastening. It could have taken place bloodlessly, but the human consciousness had not yet assimilated the principles of humaneness.

The Thinker said, "People are social beings, and must ponder the building of a humane state." We can now recall how the Thinker dreamt about a state founded upon higher principles.

699. Urusvati knows how necessary it is to give people knowledge about the attainments of science, art, and culture. Governments must send out, even to the smallest villages, publications in which will be described the people's heroes and leaders, their popular medical traditions, and their folk wisdom and lore. A monthly "Friend of the People," such as this, would bring joy to all generations.

The joy of labor has been pointed out by Us many times, but it must be strengthened by a healthy competition. It is precisely the "Friend of the People" that will inform the people about the best products of their resourcefulness. People who are isolated in remote areas, who had to teach and train themselves, still can establish links with other members of the same crafts or trades. Every craftsman will understand that he can become a master and continually perfect himself in his craft. You know how often self-taught people have introduced useful improvements to life.

Steadfastly and joyfully numberless ways of cooperation can be formed. But steadfastness should be based upon wise equilibrium. It will manifest itself when the earthly labor will soar through a realization of the Supermundane. Thus We suggest that all earthly efforts be combined with gaining knowledge of the Supermundane. At present, people see these domains as opposing each other, but they must join in friendly cooperation.

The concept of cooperation is often distorted. People imagine that being under the same roof with others, or participating with them in the same work, is enough to make them co-workers, but the main requirement, the harmony of their psychic energy, is overlooked by them. Besides, healthy cooperation provides the possibility for progress and perfectment for every participant.

You may encounter opposition to the "Friend of the People." Some will say that such an inclusive publication is not scientific. Others will point out that ordinary people will not understand scientific terminology. Much like this will be said, but these objections are outworn. Synthesis is always beneficial. The most difficult scientific concepts can be explained in understandable ways. It may even be good to reward those scientists who know how to use understandable language!

The Thinker said, "Citizens, be collectors of knowledge, not possessors." No one understood this Advice, and regarded it as a contradiction.

700. Urusvati knows that every appeal for the renewal of life must address the needs of women and the young. Some people think that both of these aspects of life are secure, and are developing successfully, but in reality the position of woman and the education of the young are not at all in a satisfactory condition. Only a small number of women can assume equal rights in the conditions of life, and in most schools the foundations of a sound life are not taught. Evolution cannot proceed successfully when two pillars of support have not yet been made secure. It should not be thought that evolution proceeds under any conditions; it can be obstructed, and much precious energy will be wasted.

The world convulses from the horrors of Armageddon, yet life grows ever uglier. People may believe that they work for some higher ideals, though their deeds reveal the opposite. One can find in life the very same agonies that burdened mankind thousands of years ago. These wounds cannot be justified by blaming the intolerable conditions of life, when people make no effort to improve these conditions, even to some small degree. Small groups can point to their useful achievements, but now We are discussing not the exceptions, but the masses of humanity, who are the real movers of evolution.

The Thinker said, "O, ye wise men, your efforts will be fruitless if woman does not stretch out her hand to you, and if you do not raise a generation of heroes!"

701. Urusvati knows how lightminded many people are about their own state of readiness. One would think that there exists a great number of heroes ready for self-sacrificing *podvig*.

Readiness can be flaming, or can be lukewarm. The lukewarm people cheat not only those around them, but also themselves. They do not even notice their own lies, and thus worsen their condition. Truly, it is better for those who acknowledge their unreadiness; at least they can improve themselves. But the cunning one and the boaster close off the path of advancement. Thus We must constantly remind you about the state of readiness. It alone gives one courage for overcoming all obstacles.

Many speak of their readiness to work with Us, but at the first sign of difficulty they retreat in cowardice. One of the main causes for this is a lack of understanding of the meaning of life. They do not ponder upon the Supermundane Infinity, and are chained to the earthly mirage. Just as a horse kept always in a corral loses the ability to race, so also does the prisoner of Earth lose the ability for rapid advancement.

Thus, when I speak of readiness, I am reminding you about advancement. One should be ever ready for *podvig*. One must think much about *podvig*, before putting it into action. It must first be performed mentally, and thought about with such conviction that its implementation in life is unavoidable. Only thus is that living cooperation, about which so many words have been spoken, created.

The Thinker said, "Do you not think that lukewarm readiness is like one drop of nectar diluted by an entire sea?"

702. Urusvati knows how much humanity is plagued by the phantoms of contradiction. Humanity itself created and nurtured these phantoms. Even the most fundamental concept, that of primary energy, is surrounded by irreconcilable opinions. We have said that energy is inexhaustible, yet at the same time recommend all possible care in utilizing it. And people see contradiction in that, even though every thoughtful individual knows that everything of value must be safeguarded. We have also spoken about the stability of the primal energy, but people then point to its changeability. But actually, its true nature is not its changeability, but its multiformity. Also, people try to apply earthly dates and qualities to it, forgetting that the Subtle World does not live in accordance with earthly calendars.

It was not without reason that in ancient times students were required to learn to reconcile contradictions. A pupil, stumbling against contradictions, was often held back for a long time at that threshold. He not only could not reflect upon the Supermundane, but even lost his earthly path. He could find a solution only if he understood the significance of goalfitness, but by not understanding goalfitness he was lost.

The Thinker said, "If all that was read reminded us about goalfitness, we could have conquered the dragon of contradictions."

703. Urusvati knows that an attitude of solemnity is needed for thinking about the Supermundane. This attitude is ignited when one conceives an idea about the Supermundane. The slanderers will say, "Again a contradiction!" But they do not understand that with the fiery quality of striving, many things are revealed almost simultaneously, faster even than the speed of light. Truly, in fieriness is found a key to the treasure-box of all possibilities.

Likewise, people do not want to understand that something can take place in the Subtle World before its earthly manifestation. Urusvati knows that occurrences in the Subtle and the earthly worlds are not necessarily simultaneous. This delay may be natural, for the purpose of shaping a distant earthly event, but it also can be caused by circumstances that intrude upon and deflect the order of events. A stormy sea can serve as the best example of the complexity of rhythm on the different worlds.

Most people are not able to make the idea of the Subtle World a part of their lives, and thus they obstruct evolution. It is difficult to reveal to the earthly consciousness that the Subtle World is the true source of events in the earthly world. Whole decades can pass between an event in the Subtle World and its counterpart in the physical world, even though by being formed in the Subtle World it became inevitable.

One could wonder why some events are beacons that determine many subsequent events. One must remember that events follow a very complex course that cannot be accounted for by a simple explanation. Who would dare to decide which of the stream of events is the most significant, and what are the causes and what the effects? One must train oneself to think about the Supermundane.

The Thinker said, "The eye did not perceive, the ear did not hear, but the heart knew that something had taken place."

704. Urusvati knows that inspiration, exaltation, and also enthusiasm, as it is called, must be consciously sustained. But patience, containment, and tolerance are also created consciously. It is a mistake to surmise that the rewards of self-development come from without; a fiery hearth lives in the depths of the consciousness. Man must perceive it, must safeguard it lovingly, and must summon its forces. Only then can outward help be given.

Even a simple mechanic understands the basic laws of the application of energy. So much the more should a thinker adopt the application of his own abilities. Therefore, when We speak about the Supermundane, We speak according to the fundamentals of human nature. Thus, in your discourses about the perfectment of life, use the most ordinary examples. Most people are good listeners when spoken to in simple words. A simple word is a great gift.

The Thinker said, "Find the most simple about the Great; love enters only through a plain gate."

705. Urusvati knows how careful one should be about the expenditure of psychic energy. Even experienced workers have been guilty of expending it improperly and excessively. One should not wonder that, though inexhaustible, psychic energy requires a very careful attitude. It is also important that the inexhaustible spatial energy be in harmony with human energy. Otherwise, human energy could be fully spent, having lost its link with the Highest Conduit. For this, co-measurement and goalfitness should be remembered. People usually try to call these concepts abstract, forgetting that there can be nothing abstract in the Universe.

People should remember that they live in constant danger, and that their participation in the Supermundane World is not an abstraction. These simple reminders are needed not only upon the beginning steps, but always.

The Thinker advised his followers never to consider themselves immune to danger, for anyone who depends only upon the protection of the teacher has already ceased to be a true co-worker.

"Beauty lives in conscious cooperation."

706. Urusvati understands rightly that knowledge is the entryway to excellence in labor. The quality of one's labor is defined by one's knowledge. Without knowledge, a high quality is not possible. All labor requires at least some knowledge. This knowledge does not come only outwardly, but can also be awakened inwardly.

There is much knowledge in man; some of it is awakened easily, but much requires deep concentration to be brought out into the consciousness. A vigilant concentration can only be developed by using the manifestations of earthly life. Therefore, withdrawal from the earthly life can be only a temporary one.

Spirit is a quality of matter; therefore We repeat: Do not withdraw from the earthly life, for in it too are found spiritual joys, and joy is needed for supermundane feelings. It is especially necessary to care for those who labor, in order that the proper rhythm of labor may generate in them the joy of the heart. The humblest worker can be a great vessel of joy, if he perceives the supermundane vibrations.

Do not complain if you have to speak of things simply and repeatedly; multitudes of hearts await a simple word. They wish to warm themselves at a welcoming fire, and thus can raise themselves to the Supermundane.

The Thinker taught, "Observe the course of the luminaries. Everything earthly strives to the Supermundane."

707. Urusvati rightly resists prejudices and restrictions imposed on knowledge. People particularly love to talk about the freedom of science, and at the same time try to prevent scientific cooperation. One can only remind them about the significance of synthesis, because so many people do not want to realize the important meaning of this concept.

It is necessary to teach in school that all scientific domains are linked to one another. One should warn against prejudices, for even the scientists suffer from this repugnant illness.

It should not be forgotten that prejudice can become the most dangerous barrier in the attainment of the Supermundane. The time will come, indeed, has already come, when cognition of the Supermundane will be a very real science. Armageddon directs the people toward this.

People are perceptive enough to notice the many striking manifestations that fill everyday life. The observable combinations of psychic and physical conditions do not occur by accident. There has never before been such confusion in life. Verily, man could be a king of nature, for he can induce shocks in it and his thought is like a fiery arrow. Therefore, study the consequences of human thinking. Remember that a prayer for destruction is alien to true knowledge.

The Thinker said, "The symbol of knowledge is Infinity."

708. Urusvati knows the value of *podvig* as an action of the free will. A teaching must be an instruction for the one embarking on the spiritual path, without coercion. It must be remembered that even the slightest forcing will impede evolution.

It may be asked what relationship exists between the idea of *podvig* and the Supermundane. But the individual cannot progress without such a relationship. One must develop an understanding of the Supermundane as a helpful reality. It is not enough to accept the Supermundane, but not admit it into one's everyday life. Care should be taken that the young generations think about the Supermundane from their early years.

Let these thoughts begin with study of the paths of the luminaries, or upon the basis of philosophy. There are many ways to the Supermundane Heights. But it is essential that through all one's labor and difficulties should always shine the Beacon of the Highest World.

It is not to be expected that people, gripped by Armageddon, could easily realize the urgent need for thoughts about the Supermundane, yet everyone, within his limitations, can sow useful knowledge. Let it be multiform. Let each nation color knowledge with its own hue. And finally, let them recall containment and patience. Let there be no rejection, but always a gentle reminder about the destiny common to all humanity. Only by knowing this can we guarantee the humaneness of progress.

The Thinker taught, "I have chosen my way voluntarily, and nothing will divert me from learning about the Supermundane."

709. Urusvati knows the beneficence of regularity of rhythm. The beat of the heart is constant. Any irregular beat of the heart is an unnatural, unhealthy condition.

Likewise, a break in one's striving to the Supermundane is also an unnatural condition. Some will say, "But the majority of people do not think at all about the Supermundane." And you may reply that the psychic condition of most people is not natural.

One should learn to distinguish between a living and a dead calmness. Often one's striving turns into a dead habit; that kind of regularity brings no benefit. Every sensible structure is in need of goalfitness. Only in a state of living receptivity is it possible to affirm oneself on the path and to go forward. Again it is necessary to remember all the seeming contradictions that must be reconciled.

We have often said that realization of the Supermundane can be increased under any conditions. Not only calm contemplation, but also powerful inner conflicts can provide the necessary impetus for advancement. Outer conditions have their role also, and people must always maintain a state of constancy.

This idea must be accepted as simply as possible. Blissful joy is in the acceptance of the Supermundane energy. It is available to everyone who desires to turn to it. In this will also grow co-measurement, which allows one to distinguish what is the most urgent and needed.

The Thinker advised, "Accept the command of the heart, but first of all think about where the heart is and by what it lives."

710. Urusvati knows how to recognize the various strata of thinking. It is usually believed that the exterior layer of thought is the most perfect one, for it is more easily expressed in words, but that idea is incorrect. Far more significant is the inner layer, which is expressed through feeling. This layer has a much stronger hold on man; from it rise the actions that affect one's karma. The sensitive, elevated consciousness knows how to heed the inner thinking. It needs no words and knows that ascent is forged in the hearth of silence.

Concentration is a companion to true achievement. Patiently and tenderly is this constant companion summoned. External, chance currents can disrupt the growth of inner thinking. You observed that the collective thinking of crowds is quite primitive, not because the crowd consists of fools, but because the external, random, inter-crossing currents and irregular rhythms destroy the highest expressions.

The crowd will never express any idea about the Supermundane. Their best feelings will be buried under heaps of words. Rarely, quite rarely, mass thinking can be effective, but in the history of humanity there are almost no indications of important collective decisions made by the masses. The crowd cries out yes or no, but it does not express the higher concepts. Therefore, do not be disturbed if the crowd does not listen to talk about the Supermundane. Solitary thoughts can merge into special currents, and their powerful effects will even dissolve rocks.

The Thinker used to say, "Teach me to hear the Voice of Silence."

711. Urusvati knows the power of faith, but knows also that straight-knowledge is even stronger. In faith there are assumptions, but with straight-knowledge there is only active affirmation, without deviations. It is not enough to accept, even in full trust. It is necessary to actively affirm, as a command; only thus can the way to the Supermundane be found. Let us not think that every thought about the Supermundane will be fruitful. Many mayflies flash by, without leaving any trace in the existing Universe. Just wandering aimlessly in thought, without developing a firm consciousness of where and how to look for indications about the Supermundane life, is fruitless. We have spoken much about the reality of the Supermundane World, but man loves to separate the Supermundane World from the earthly, and therein lies great harm, for first of all there must be accepted the one energy that abides in everything.

One should explain in schools that man lives in three worlds. It is easy for children to understand the idea of human mobility. And how much will the beauty of the world be multiplied when man will be admitted to the hearth of progress! Much has been spoken already about the filling of space. Every physicist and chemist can, however primitively, confirm these laws. Let one speak about matter, beginning with any level of the worlds, and (It is acceptable if he only speaks about matter; it is irrelevant from what level of the worlds to begin one's exploration, for) Infinity will broaden the outlook.

The Thinker did not deny anything that could give birth to an expansion of thinking.

712. Urusvati knows the natural applications of psychic energy. Cosmic activity is rhythmic, as are all psycho-cosmic manifestations. It is impossible to be a dwarf today and a giant tomorrow. Much ongoing intensification of one's forces must be undertaken before a natural evolution can take place. Many times have people attained considerable heights and then, instead of continued perfectment, have fallen into everyday routine. It is necessary to understand the value of gradual perfectment, which alone provides true achievement.

Even experienced investigators do not always maintain a proper continuity of experiments. They fear that their short lives will not permit them to complete what they began. Yet, if they understood the continuity of life and consciousness, their attitude to their tasks would change.

Earthly language is of no use in describing eternity. For this, a supermundane language is needed. Only with straight-knowledge can one silently express the concept of eternity. Man must proceed on his endless path without thinking about the brevity of earthly existences. Man can bring his lives closer together, and can transmute them into a garland of spiritual victories. The most valued by Us is when one's psychic energy is applied naturally, daily, untiringly, here on Earth. In this way does Our sister Urusvati proceed.

The Thinker advised, "Gather all forces before entering the higher path. There can be no retreat after one begins to strive toward the Supermundane."

713. Urusvati knows that only a few are able to discern the experiences of former existences. People often complain that they do not have knowledge of

their former lives. Yet, when they do obtain some of that knowledge, they either become distressed or fall into conceit.

People are rarely so developed in their consciousness that they can properly evaluate the lessons learned from previous lives. They cannot often recall useful achievements or recognize past errors and the consequences generated by them. People frequently complain about the law of karma because they think about it in earthly ways; but the law of karma is a cosmic one.

A single earthly life is less than a mustard seed in Infinity, but we must address ourselves to the Supermundane, for we participate in it. It is not a conceit to consider oneself a citizen of the Universe, and only in this state of mind can one realize the scope of responsibility of participating in the Great Construction. Not many can picture themselves as co-workers, united with the Great Construction. People obstruct their flight of thought with conventionalities, and, instead of liberating their thinking, they condemn themselves to a dark dungeon.

Regrettably, millions of years of earthly existence have been insufficient for humanity to liberate its thinking. The art of thinking is ignored and nowhere is it taught in schools. But how can one realize the Supermundane if there are everywhere barriers and prohibitions? The way to learning must be liberated, so that the New World can be built.

Do not think about the New World as something unattainable, but see yourself as its participant. It is no idle dream—the striving toward regenerated life, when the best creativity of the nations will merge in indomitable progress.

The Thinker said, "O Teacher, guide me to understand and to apply the experience of my former existences."

714. Urusvati knows that intolerance is the sister of ignorance. A broad tolerance begets open-mindedness, from which issues daring. The strongest striving requires straight-knowledge, and also a balanced open-mindedness. It is impossible to embrace the Supermundane World without both these foundations. Straight-knowledge can whisper to the heart, but the brain must also accept the possibility that the Supermundane World exists.

It has been said many times that man is the co-worker of creation. It is precisely so. Every thought impresses a mental image. This creativeness is indestructible, and it is time for people to realize their responsibility for this creative work.

Many lightminded and harmful mental obstructions pollute space. People do not usually believe that their feeble thoughts could leave any trace in space, but they must be reminded that even a fleeting feeling can inscribe an indelible hieroglyph there.

Only a full understanding of the meaning of thinking can lead to luminous daring. Do not think that this word has anything in common with audacity; in audacity there is rudeness, but higher daring is always benevolent. It opens ways to beautiful, mental creativeness.

Each beautiful thought must be safeguarded. Let it expand in space. It is a real gift to the structure of the Universe. But people must begin to think about the Supermundane World as natural and sense its touches in everyday life.

We speak about daily routine as a constant link to the Supermundane, which has its place in everyday life. Losing understanding of this can be the source of much grief.

The Thinker used to say, "Realization of the Supermundane comes not only from without, it is also born within ourselves. Let this sign of daring glow in the heart."

715. Urusvati knows that a chemical compound is affected by the addition of even a minimal amount of any substance. In this way, a poison can be transformed into a healing remedy—and the opposite is also true. This very simple fact should be mentioned as an example to those who do not consider that, in the same way, the participation or removal of just one person can affect great events.

Ignorant people will say, "How can one individual influence the course of events?" They do not realize that We have in mind not so much someone's physical presence as his psychic influence. Many such examples could be cited in which one person brought a positive influence to a problem. Likewise, instances could be pointed out in which nations expelled their most valuable people, and thus made their path more difficult.

It is not a fantasy that the aura of a person can have enormous influence. It can transform the most poisonous substance into a panacea, but the ignorant ones do not accept this scientific consideration. They prefer to drink the bitter chalice, rather than admit an intelligent approach. There is much unhappiness in the world because of such ignorance! The Supermundane World cannot be revealed to those who prefer their own downfall to liberating the thinking of humanity. Many rulers have choked off the finest flights of thought. Evolution should not be tortured thus! The Supermundane world knocks at the door of the consciousness; great must be the ignorance of those who oppose a natural eagerness for knowledge.

The Thinker said, "The persecutors of freedom of thought prepare a frightful path for themselves."

716. Urusvati knows that even in remote antiquity the significance of human emanations was understood. Sickness was often treated by the laying on of hands or by surrounding patients with healthy organisms. Over time, people did not develop these healing abilities within themselves, and even forgot about them.

Thus, when mesmerism reminded people about these influences, they regarded it as something quite new and unusual. I speak about this in order to point out how often mankind forgets its own achievements. It only seems that science advances steadily; in reality, advances in learning move in waves. But people should not take this as an excuse for inaction. They may one day be able to rediscover many long-forgotten achievements.

It would be useful to write a book about the rediscovery of forgotten ways. This book would deal not only with the supernatural, but would also explore natural history, in which many pages were once known, but later forgotten. One must educate people about the forgotten achievements. It will be difficult to accomplish this, for ideas were expressed differently, and in different tongues. One has to know many languages and the mentality of many nations to be able to trace the chain of achievements in knowledge whose links were broken for centuries.

In such research attention should be given to the supermundane data that is generously strewn in the treasuries of folk wisdom. It is wrong to reject former achievements. It is unwise to say, "Let us begin from today," when the treasures were collected yesterday.

The Supermundane World was many times described in legends, and in such beautiful imagery! Thus one can move forward without throwing mud at the past.

The Thinker said, "Beware of the paths of ignorance, they are muddy."

717. Urusvati knows what true cooperation is. I have already said that everyone, under all circumstances, unavoidably participates in the Supermundane World. But this unconscious cooperation is in a sense an animal one; what We expect is human, conscious cooperation.

Such cooperation is born naturally, when one first recognizes the Supermundane World. This realization takes place gradually, when one begins to think about something existing beyond the physical. Thus does the fire of cognition begin to blaze.

The Thinker said, "Teacher, let me become Thy helper."

718. Urusvati knows how inseparable are the sciences and ethics. In ancient times religions were strong links, directing man toward the Higher World, but later crime, superstition, and hypocrisy coiled themselves around the religions. Many people began to search for another sensible approach to the Supermundane World. Learning and science offered new possibilities for an approach to the Higher World, but the thinkers understood that science without a moral foundation is lifeless. Thus we must always remember that science cannot advance without the realization of living ethics.

From the earliest school years, it is necessary to lay the foundations of the sciences and indicate how they should be studied. Prior to immersion into scientific formulas, it is necessary to lay firm, practical foundations. Only thus can be found a living way to living successes.

We do not deny anything useful. The foundation was offered to humanity many times, but was not accepted with certainty. Therefore let us welcome knowledge, but we must accompany it with an understanding of ethics. Understand clearly that a scientist without ethics is not working for evolution. Powerful thinkers must also be ethical people.

The Thinker said, "Teacher, show me the path of the beauty of the spirit."

719. Urusvati knows that man cannot properly measure the value of his actions while in an earthly state. Often, those deeds that seem to be the best are polluted by self-interest, and the truly self-sacrificing ones are forgotten in the dust of everyday life.

I affirm that the motivating causes for one's actions lie in the depths of the consciousness. Even enlightened spirits cannot discern the reasons for their actions. Of course, in the subtle body this discernment is easier, but even that is relative.

It must not be thought that an inability to evaluate properly is a calamity. It is unnecessary to involve oneself in all this reasoning when one's main purpose is to do good. Every act of good brings benefit. The more good we do the more we increase the beneficial accumulations. The reasoning mind must not be allowed into the domain where the heart should reign. The reasoning mind can always validate self-interest, but the heart will recognize untruth.

Psychic energy is directed mainly by the heart. The science that does not understand the foundations of psychic energy cannot succeed. The new world, of which the better part of mankind is dreaming, can be formed only upon a correct understanding of psychic energy. Man can live with it in friendship, or in enmity—but this would be a terrible deviation.

You may hear cunning suggestions that will say, "Is it not better to leave all these considerations about psychic energy to the scientists? When science will express its opinion about this energy the ordinary citizen will begin to talk about it." However, the cunning destroyers know well enough that psychic energy is the possession of all.

All of humanity must learn to recognize the various manifestations of psychic energy; it would be wrong to restrict these studies to a small group of scientists. Besides, there may be found among scientists self-interested people with preconceived ideas. The development of humanity is now at a level that summons all to cooperation, because the basis of Be-ness is sensible cooperation and cognition of psychic energy, without which mankind will be thrown into chaos. External accomplishments will not save man from self-destruction.

It is impossible to imagine how Armageddon can be concluded in the right way without an understanding of the foundations of Be-ness! I speak thus so that people will know to what extent the Supermundane provides the solutions for earthly problems. Do not think that the Supermundane can remain at rest when earthly confusion corrupts everything. Yet, Urusvati knows how greatly proper education can ward off the danger of savagery. After all their discoveries, people still turn to savagery! Do not regard this as an exaggeration. The convulsions of Armageddon threaten incalculable calamities. Thus the Thinker said, "The time is coming when people will have to think about the Infinite in everything."

720. Urusvati knows that one of the most valued

human qualities is keenness of observation. Everyone who can see should develop this keenness. But actually, the opposite occurs. People obscure their minds with superstition and prejudices. This becomes a kind of super-maya. Therefore, the power of keen observation must be cultivated.

It is not without reason that We insist upon the need for good upbringing and education, that We speak repeatedly about certain qualities that are forgotten in humanity's confusion. As always, ignorance reigns and the voices of enlightenment are solitary and subject to persecutions, which, though different from those of the Dark Ages, are equally inhumane.

Let us not boast of culture, which now is taking on ugly forms. What kind of culture can succeed when the very art of thinking is not cultivated in the young! Even the reading of books will not help if their contents are not pondered. Therefore it is so necessary to sharpen attentiveness so that world events will be seen in their true significance.

People attempt to justify their behavior by saying that the universe is engulfed by chaos against which human thought is powerless. But such a notion cannot be applied to thought. Thought is powerful in everything. The aspiring consciousness is already successful in space, and even the germ of a thought has power. Keen observation will help to perceive how thought moves not only the muscles, but even the most complex processes of life. Amidst everyday life the most wonderful manifestations can be observed.

The Thinker said, "I wish to observe the manifestations of the Infinite."

721. Urusvati knows and has tested her abilities to see and hear the Invisible and Inaudible Worlds. It is significant that her considerable achievements were acquired in a natural way. Even in ancient times, people knew artificial methods for opening the way to the Invisible, but no unnatural approach is of any value.

It can be seen that all in the Universe is goalfitting, and can be attained by natural means; therefore the attainment of Urusvati is treasured. True, such levels of attainment cannot be reached quickly. Many vibrations must be assimilated, and this can be done only through many years of labor—indeed, it is better to say not years, but centuries. These attainments must be safe-guarded, for they have as their goal not personal benefit, but the progress of the people.

Attainments gained naturally must be protected against the opposition of today's scientists, who often impede rather than help. Mediocre scientists have their own prejudices and think that they are expelling superstition, when in reality they are creating new, harmful obstacles. In everything, search for natural ways.

The Thinker said, "Teacher, reveal to me the way—the most simple and straight."

722. Urusvati knows the importance of rhythm when in continuous communion with the Higher World. The rhythm of the highest energy is attained only through many years of labor, and cannot be achieved as a result of sudden illumination. One must begin with words, and later with wordless aspirations. Finally these flow together into a rhythm that resounds constantly in the heart, both when awake and when asleep. There is one basic quality that increases the vibration. Let us call this quality ecstatic Love, for in it are the highest devotion, inextinguishable trust, and untiring power. This step of ascent is a high one, but there is no ultimate stage in anything.

When any step of ascent is achieved in earthly

life, without departing from one's daily routine, it can be called the highest test. True, it is difficult to hold one's torch high amidst crude vibrations, malice, and ignorance, but then the greater is the achievement. By maintaining a constant striving toward the Higher Worlds without turning away from daily life, that containment will be found which people call synthesis. But how rarely does one find in life the toilers who have dedicated themselves to the service of the Higher World!

People sometimes talk about the Common Good, yet this goal will only be possible through the embracing of the Higher World. Only then will the process of perfectment become a wise one, and unite all quests of humanity. The varied paths of all pilgrims will then be accepted and understood. They all walk the one path, and only their words differ.

The Thinker said to the disciples, "Embrace all, understand, and love."

723. Urusvati knows how difficult it is for people to understand divisibility of the spirit. They think that this concept contradicts science, but they overlook that the newest discoveries do confirm this utilization of psychic energy.

Radio and television transmission demonstrate how energy can be transmitted simultaneously in many directions. Of course, for this, proper transmitting and receiving apparatuses are needed. The human organism is a perfect apparatus for the transmission of energies. It should be understood that not only the natural abilities of man, but also his free will are involved in every psychic transmission.

Often, a thought is sent correctly, but for some reason is rejected by the recipient. Also, a recipient may be sensitive enough and ready to receive it, but the message itself may have been improperly sent. Often, people hear something, but are unable to attune themselves to the vibrations, and thus receive only senseless chatter.

It must not be thought that transmission of thought and images is possible only at high altitudes. Transmission of psychic energy can take place anywhere. Of course, highly populated cities hinder the clarity of transmission. Nevertheless, one should train oneself so that psychic energy will work regardless of physical conditions.

Urusvati can attest that at first every external sound caused her pain, but later, when her vibrations were strengthened, the transmission could proceed under any conditions. Such vigilance and keenness are quite difficult to develop and demand considerable time, but the psychic world merits special attention.

The Thinker said, "Let us not return to the time when thunder was regarded as Divine Wrath."

724. Urusvati knows how often, due to misinterpretations, people do harm to the fundamental concepts. They speak about superhuman efforts, even though in the earthly life all is human. Even when one speaks about efforts that are noble or exalted, they nevertheless are always human. By their misinterpretations and distortions, people demean themselves.

The time is coming when all treasures in man's possession should be recognized. A true science, devoted to the study of the primary energy, must be accepted. People know about the salt that permeates the oceans, but they prefer not to acknowledge the energy of space. We call it psychic energy, but other names can be applied to it. Perhaps you have heard about grace? It exists, and its essence is nothing else than psychic energy.

Terms for psychic energy can be found in the various languages of the East, but their meaning was much distorted. We call on scientists to acknowledge the fundamental principle of energy—the foundation for all teachings.

We do not deny, We do not destroy—We construct in accordance with the mental condition of mankind. Each century brings its own conditions, which cannot be ignored. Often the Great seems to become obscured, and waves of destroyers engulf it. These signs must be observed closely, for they too contain within themselves the steps for the future. Evolution must be loved in all its stages. Eternal change is the basis of life.

The Thinker used to say, "Traveler, hasten to the goal, do not get caught overnight in an icy stream."

725. Urusvati knows how much people can distort even the simplest concepts. They understand calmness as deathlike inaction, but calmness is really a state of intense psychic activity, like a still and luminous body of water fed at the bottom by healing springs bringing sustenance for the benefit of humanity. Thus calmness should be understood as work, absorbing and enlightening.

The Teacher first of all tests His disciples' ability to maintain calmness during times of special tension. It is surprising to see how few pass this test. This is because people do not acknowledge the Primal Energy and the Higher Worlds. They believe that coarse physical conditions are all that exist, and many best possibilities are destroyed by such ignorance. You have often seen that even educated people do not wish to accept scientific developments. Their science drags along its old wagon-load like a lazy horse with blinders.

We will not tire of speaking about paths free of prejudice. One may ask—what is new in this? But let them consider how new are the paths that lie before humanity. Let all become participants of the new stage of evolution. Precisely, not just those especially chosen, but all those who call themselves human; let them approach the common work that reveals the Higher World.

Let us not utter pompous words. Let the honest work of learning be one's daily labor. All must participate in this labor. Let us not forget that everyone is a bearer of psychic energy and can observe at least some of its manifestations. Thus humanity will come closer to a new happiness and will understand what is the Common Good.

The Thinker indicated that he who can preserve calmness has already looked into the healing well.

726. Urusvati knows that emotions provide the propelling power for psychic energy. Love is the most powerful, but hatred has almost equal power.

Does this mean that one can live in hatred? Of course, it is possible, but it brings only loss. Not only does hatred bring an accumulation of imperil and through sicknesses shorten life, but mainly, its effect in the Subtle World is disastrous. You already know that in the Subtle World all feelings are intensified, and also their consequences. Now imagine how difficult it is for the hater to tear himself away from his destructive passion. Not only does he surround himself with evil, but his entire being is permeated with the poison of evil. He suffers because he himself has invited his torture. Thus, let us say, it is profitable to live in goodness and love. And this state becomes more intense in the Subtle World and a source of great happiness.

Much is available to the one who has embraced Good. He can sense the vibrations of the Higher Worlds, he can hear the music of the spheres, he ascends the steps of the harmony of beauty. Those philosophers are right who affirmed that beauty is goodness, and goodness beautiful.

True, many will regard these formulas as abstract and not applicable to earthly life. But the deniers will have to experience the conditions of the Subtle World many times, so that Truth will affirm itself in their consciousness. One can pity those people who, having learned reading and writing, imagine that they have already mastered the Teaching of Life.

Let us not condemn lack of knowledge, but let us sternly condemn deliberate ignorance. It must be understood where the boundary between insufficient knowledge and determined ignorance lies. One is curable, but the other is often irreparable. The one who denies knowledge is always self-conceited and pompous. Thus, by one's everyday behavior can one's essence be recognized.

The Thinker said, "We may forgive lack of knowledge, but intentional ignorance is unfit for cooperation."

727. Urusvati knows that there is but one Source for the advancement of knowledge. Many people prefer that everything should have a scientific foundation. Let us offer them the opportunity to conduct scientific research in a new way. Science has already branched out into a multitude of fields, some of which seem so contradictory that it would be impossible to find common ground. But if the scientists observe the psychic condition of the different researchers during their moments of greatest mental tension, they will find striking similarities in the tension of the researchers' creative centers. A philosopher and a physicist, a geographer and a psychologist, will all be alike in their moments of discovery.

Start the observation from that point on and you

will come to the conclusion that the science of gaining knowledge is one Tree, and its branches can grow only from that one root. Thus one can make instructive observations, and this path will lead one to cognition of the Supermundane World.

Let us not wonder that many thoughts are born simultaneously in different parts of the world; these scientists do not know each other, they proceed by different ways, and are influenced by the restrictions of their particular national cultures; yet, there is one thing that inspires them to work for the good of humanity. How many beautiful observations can be made when the consciousness is expanded without negation, which is a sign of ignorance! Thus let us learn to embrace all and let us look upwards, with free eyes.

The Thinker asserted that the ancients knew much that was later forgotten.

728. Urusvati knows that psychology must be transformed into an objective science, as tangible as physiology. It is necessary to start teaching it in the lowest primary grades and then continue in all the higher educational institutions.

All branches of education must include a study of the foundations of psychology. This science should perhaps be named slightly differently, but let the accepted name remain. We try to avoid making changes in terminology when a useful goal can be reached with conventional terms.

Psychology must study the hidden forces of man. It will not only hearken to the ancient philosophies, but also will walk its own free, scientific path. Even the study of comparative religion will be thought of as a psychological study, because all spiritual studies have at their basis the acquiring of knowledge about the Supermundane World.

Let us not, out of pride, ignore the ancient achievements, for under different names are hidden the same experiences and deductions. Free scientific methods should be applied, for life in all its manifestations opens the way to cognition of the Unseen World. Many different energies merge into and flow out from the one primary energy. The study of the branching out of the one power, in individual ways, into every living being, is of great value. The abundant diversity of individualities should be treasured and explored, because it is precisely this study that will help the scientists to reconcile the seeming contradictions.

The Thinker said, "One can construct a sonorous choir with many different voices. People have the will, but few know how to apply it wisely."

729. Urusvati knows that the will is psychic energy, transmuted and sharpened. In antiquity the arrow was a symbol of the will. At present much is spoken about the development of the will and many artificial methods are proposed for strengthening it, but it can only be developed by active work.

When you meet people who lack will power, you can be certain that they suffer from laziness and are in a state of obscured consciousness, unwilling to attempt any independent activity. There are many such people and they will not readily understand that such creative labor sharpens their arrow of attainment. It can be stated that lack of will is accompanied by fear, depression, ingratitude, and other terrors of ignorance.

When we strive to the Supermundane World, we must gather all our will in order to courageously conquer all the lower strata, which nail people to a state of ignorance. Let us not pity those who deprive themselves of the possibility of advancement. Out of compassion We will point out to such people how much they lose—but you can be certain that many of them will not be able to heed Our advice.

Only a life of labor will teach them to value quality in their work, and on this path of struggle they will garb themselves in the armor of will. Amidst everyday life one can find excellent exercises for development of the will, and these natural ways will be blessed.

The Thinker admonished the disciples not to allow despondency.

730. Urusvati knows that attentiveness is one of the first conditions for successfully conducting experiments with psychic energy. People often speak about their striving, keenness, or vigilance, but they ignore the simplest trait, attentiveness. For them, the phrase "to live in danger" is understood in an absurd way. It is true that an expanded consciousness brings with it natural attentiveness, but there are not many such consciousnesses.

It is fortunate that attentiveness can be developed, but it must be cultivated early, in the family and in school. The attention of schoolchildren must be directed not only to major events, but also to the smallest details of everyday life. The Subtle World manifests itself first of all in one's daily life. The most valued traits of the spirit can be perceived amidst everyday routine. Let us not regard as heroes only those who strive for the welfare of humanity, but let us pay due attention also to those who perform daily, ordinary labor. Attentive observation of these people will reveal many manifestations of natural psychic energy.

When We speak about the Subtle World, We must also include the subtlest energies. These energies should be observed in real life. One should not think that miraculous powers can be found only elsewhere; they are ready to manifest in every individual, but they can be discerned only through attentiveness. And We offer this attentiveness in everyday life to all who want to think about the Supermundane World. Do not assume that such an exercise is an easy one; it requires steadfastness—a quality that few people possess. They are too often eager to fly in their fantasies to the far-off worlds, speeding through space without effect. And We advise, amidst the routine of daily life, to learn beautiful attentiveness. Let it grow from the earliest years.

The Thinker said, "Look under your own feet, or you will stumble."

731. Urusvati knows that people should not only acknowledge the reality of the psychic world, but also feel its influence in earthly life. Many speak about the existence of "something," but do not admit the presence of a powerful psychic energy in their everyday life. But the time has come when man should pay attention to his moods, enthusiasms, anxieties, and certain pains.

We do not foresee man's progress without the development of conscious association with the psychic world. But it must be remembered that We have warned frequently against psychism and mediumship. Let people understand that these unhealthy, artificial deviations will not bring a salutary broadening of consciousness. We speak again and again about how much man must uplift his thinking, so that he can then advance on the path to the Supermundane World.

Let us not prescribe conventional rituals. It is first of all necessary to safeguard each person's individuality. The individual will, pure and noble, will lead in its way to the goal of united consciousness. It will help to cleanse the eyes and ears for the ultimate acceptance of universality. Only with this individual inclusiveness will man walk the path of true knowledge. Let us ask scientists to remain sensitive and not deny any individual observations that can lead to further research. There is so much that can be implemented only through mutual respect.

Nations should learn to think about the Common Good, for self-interest will prove to be a major obstacle to progress. The terrible trials that affect humanity simply hasten the approach of new world constructions.

The Thinker said, "Teacher, impart to me the words that I must use to summon others to the most urgent tasks."

732. Urusvati knows that illumination that comes through joy and love is stronger than any insight that comes through suffering. Yet, people insist that it is suffering that purifies humanity.

Why is it that man is not capable of utilizing the higher path to illumination? The answer is simple—suffering is sown by man himself in the earthly world, and it partially penetrates into the Subtle World. But pure joy and love live in the Fiery World, and are seldom experienced by man. During the coming evolution people will realize where their treasure lies, and will turn to this panacea of light.

Among the new scientific achievements will be the discovery of the power of the emotions of love and joy. Humanity must steadily grow closer to these impelling forces of light, and understand that any thought of joy has healing power. Even amidst sorrows one can find signs of love and compassion. Let these signposts help the weary traveler. Scientists must learn how much the rhythm of joy opens the gates to an influx of psychic energy. Science should demonstrate how the power of joy heals.

The ignorant will say that such advice is not practical, because humanity is drowning in suffering. Only such people would choose to sink into darkness rather than turn to the quest for Light. Only such people would say that man can never learn to utilize the energy of thought.

One must strive ardently toward the renewal of life. Everyone can think of heroism, of joy, and of exalted love. Everyone can gain the power of the healing remedy and spread these emanations in every direction.

The Thinker said, "Sorrow is transitory, joy is everlasting. Love the Light and love the Beautiful." Thus did the Thinker direct His disciples to the simplest solution.

733. Urusvati knows that an arrow aimed true flies unwaveringly to its goal. Compare the arrow to a human thought. A trembling hand will not aim the arrow truly, and, similarly, wavering thought will not reach its goal.

Avoid scattered thinking. Often people do not notice that many thoughts rage simultaneously within them. As they swarm about like flies, it is impossible to discern which thought has the most significance. This circumstance must be studied. Future apparatuses will demonstrate the harm of such confused thinking. It would be better not to think at all than to permit such confusion within oneself, for it is a kind of madness.

You may ask, What measures can help? Do not seek outside yourself for forcible means, but rather observe your thinking, so that you can naturally purify it. When man becomes aware of confusion in his thinking, he should evaluate his thoughts, to determine which are the most needed.

It is not easy to follow little insects in the depths of the consciousness. They can disfigure any beautiful thought. But if man will assume the task of learning the dangers of scattered thinking, he may begin little by little to banish extraneous thoughts.

Clarity of thought is very necessary for thinking about the Supermundane World. One does not prepare laboratory ingredients with dirty hands; likewise it is impermissible to approach the high chemisms of the Supermundane World with a soiled mind. People should think more purely about the higher worlds.

The Thinker advised His disciples to think about the Supermundane as if participating in it personally.

734. Urusvati knows how lightning-fast, resounding spirals of thought envelope the planet. The resulting sheathe can be either beneficial or harmful. Through free will man can cause healing or destruction. Man cannot say that he suffers without cause. It is man himself who at some point in the past introduced poison into the cosmic fabric.

Cosmic soundings are already being studied and it is understood that every thought, every word expressed by man is engraved on indestructible tablets. The time is coming when human thought must be studied. It is quicker than light, and forms a tenacious cover over the Earth. But how often are thoughts benevolent?

People already know how to grasp the superficial expression of thought, but are not yet fully capable of understanding its meaning. In the future, there will be sensitive apparatuses that can record the precise meaning of a thought. People whose thoughts are devoted to the Common Good will rejoice at this research, but all those who live in hatred, malice, lies, and envy, will oppose it by all means. The scientist with enough resolve to conduct the research leading to this discovery will hardly be called a friend by contemporary humanity.

Simple is the admonishment that one should not

live in hatred, but the proclamations of today's leaders often encourage it. They do not know the power of thought and of karma. He who thinks that evil can be exterminated by evil is gravely mistaken. Even the horror of war cannot be stopped by hatred. It is noble thoughts that will save mankind. Heroism is shaped not by hatred, but by fiery good will.

The Thinker said, "A fiery warrior knows no obstacles."

735. Urusvati knows that heroism is an expression of self-sacrifice and fiery enthusiasm. When performing a heroic deed, one's vibrations are raised, awareness of physical sensations disappears, and the entire being is filled with a fiery insight.

Only the unknowing would ask—why speak about heroism when discussing the Supermundane? They do not understand that striving toward the Supermundane is itself an act of heroism. They do not know that each thought about the Supermundane raises the vibrations and fills the consciousness with fiery striving.

If the thought is weak, its effect will be negligible, but a clear-cut, strong thought has powerful effects. It must be said repeatedly that thought about the Supermundane produces healing vibrations. Also one should remind often about the importance of exalted thinking. Soon physicians will recommend, in cases of psychic imbalance, thought about the Supermundane. The first attempts will be primitive, and the people will not fully recognize the importance of such communion, but even the smallest drop of this panacea will produce beneficial results. Indeed, thinking about the Supermundane is in itself a panacea.

It is not an exaggeration to say that people carry within themselves a talisman, but this would first require that they experience the exaltation connected with thought about the Supermundane. A man walking without his staff may stumble, but a strong staff can be given from Above. It must be accepted for the brave ascent to continue.

The Thinker asked His disciples to love the climbing of mountains. It helps turn one's gaze upward.

736. Urusvati knows that one approaches the Supermundane World not so much through reason as through love. Great is the magnetic power of the feeling of love, but, regrettably, science does not know the true significance of this magnet. A loving man responds to the cosmic law of attraction, and thus receives special qualities which are characteristic of this law.

It is possible to sharpen one's insight and be imbued with valor, to become ready for *podvig*. Even one's health is improved when the mind and heart are turned toward exalted thinking.

It is incorrect to assume that people who are subject to so-called hysteria can more easily commune with the Supermundane World. They do tend to mediumship, but We desire another approach, wholesome and goalfitting. The perfect path will be love for the Supermundane World.

It is impossible without love to gain knowledge of the Supermundane. It is impossible to approach only through reading. An intensified will is needed, but this will can be developed only through love.

Also, We advise you not to separate yourself from earthly life, for this life is given to us as our field of battle. One can test oneself only in life, and all such tests will be beautiful if they are under a dome of love for the Supermundane World.

Children should become accustomed to a recognition of the Supermundane World from their early years. Thoughts about higher manifestations should be engendered in the mind of the child. The most ordinary person can have this sacred treasure, and cherish these hours of exaltation.

The Thinker advised His disciples to learn to love their reveries about the Higher World, when their consciousness is renewed.

737. Urusvati knows that at times of upheaval, both enlightenment and negation manifest themselves. Every example of exalted knowledge meets with negation, not only because of savage ignorance, but also due to superstitions based upon bigotry. Science is attacked from both sides. People speak about the freedom of science, but in fact this freedom is limited to physical learning. All that has to do with the Supermundane World is suppressed, no less than during the Middle Ages.

Let us not forget that only strong minds can think freely. Ordinary thinking is constrained by the emanations of negation. This circumstance must be taken into consideration during any discussions about the state of science. At present the need for liberating science must be proclaimed with all one's forces.

The best thinkers have suffered enough; they have been afflicted enough by the whistling and curses of the ignorant. There has been enough mockery of all that is not understood by the savages. Let the New Era be distinguished by a veritable liberation of science!

Do not think that this is a truism. On the contrary, it is a cry in the desert. People do not realize that times of world upheaval are filled with special vibrations.

People talk about taking vitamins, forgetting that their moral state is far more important than the taking of medicines, which actually can turn into poison when their moral conditions are unhealthy. It is grievous for Us to see how the solitary thinkers are turned upon by savage ignorance. They have shut themselves away in order to preserve their freedom of thought. But they could be of great help to humanity, precisely now, when the world is convulsed. May they find the strength to outlive the present time, when Kali Yuga is already near its end!

The Thinker advised His disciples to affirm the freedom of knowledge, and the freedom of thought, for the sake of the salvation of the World.

738. Urusvati knows the importance of equilibrium. We have already pointed out that man should strive with all his power toward the Supermundane World. By doing this, he will develop a conscious awareness that he participates continuously in the Supermundane World. At the same time he must treasure his earthly life, must learn to rejoice at high quality in his labor, and must continue with the earthly life, as he finds new ways of perfectment in it.

One might ask how it is possible to reconcile these seemingly contradictory ways. Truly, it can be done, for man can perfect his consciousness. Many examples from different ages can be cited in all of which a remarkable fact will be noted—most of those who embraced these "opposites" were not of the clergy. No one would guess that these toilers carried within themselves a commitment to the Supermundane World. They worked conscientiously. They loved labor in its highest quality, and they guarded their own acute realization of the Supermundane World as a sacred treasure.

It should be understood that such workers are especially useful for the perfectment of the world. They do not conceal the existence of the Supermundane World, but they can sense where revealing it is appropriate. They strengthen their magnetism and thus naturally attract the hearts of disciples.

However, it is not only the above-mentioned "opposites" that can surprise those who are inexperienced. Many seeming contradictions can be mentioned that would appear strange to them. For example, man should not succumb to passion, yet he should not be without feeling. Everywhere the Golden Mean must be realized, just as was said so long ago.

The Thinker said, "Man has two arms, one serves his labor, the other serves his heart. If one hand is shorter than the other, people call it ugliness; so is it also in heavenly and earthly affairs."

739. Urusvati knows that even important words are meaningless if they are not accompanied by a sending of psychic energy; such dead words only clutter space. People must understand the necessary power that is given by psychic energy. For this reason, much was said throughout the centuries about the need for faith.

Confidence makes speech convincing, but one should understand the meaning of confidence. To this, therefore, we shall add one more concept, that of command. Of course, command should not be understood as coarse aggressiveness, which only antagonizes the listeners. We have in mind inner command, which gives immutability to one's words. Regrettably, evil intentions too often are accompanied by a strong will, and thus cause great harm; this means that one should learn to master the power of benevolent command.

It is not often that people can intensify their will for the sake of good. No one told them in childhood what a powerful weapon they could possess, and how many supermundane helpers would be attracted by their benevolent command. Only exceptional consciousnesses understand the significance of command. They do not allow their will to turn toward evil. Such examples could be cited from many centuries. We call them Beacons of humanity. They acted consciously in harmony with the Supermundane World and thus multiplied their psychic energy.

The Thinker said, "Learn to be imbued with a good command; it will multiply your forces."

740. Urusvati knows that every phenomenon in the atmosphere has its effect on man. It would seem that knowing this would lead to new scientific achievements, but, unfortunately, since contemporary science places such great importance on classifying each phenomenon, scientists forget that the influence of phenomena on the individual differs from one person to the next. Thus the influences they may not have personally experienced are excluded from their observations.

Scientists must leave behind conventional limitations, and then they will enter upon new, boundless ways. For the sake of this it must be realized that each individual is a microcosm in the full sense of this word. Also, it is not difficult to understand that each microcosm is individual and unique.

The chemism of each microcosm is a special one, just as every small particle of Macrocosm is individual. This does not contradict the essence of universal laws. They embrace all possible conditions and find in the unrepeatable individuality of all Be-ness a furnace of new combinations of energies. Energies, universal and individual, cannot be renewed without individual interactions. Thus it can be understood that the Unity pointed out so long ago is a system based on a multitude of individualities.

Wise rulers have always understood that the individuality of a person must be carefully protected. An experienced schoolteacher can sense how the individuality of the pupils should be safeguarded. Only the ignorant can suppose that everyone can be cut to the same pattern. Such ignorance acts against the cosmic laws, and people exhibiting it can never be considered scientists, for every true researcher must possess a broad and open mind. We must often repeat these basic ideas, because most people, hypnotized by dead terminology, do not wish to open their eyes to the most simple manifestations of nature. It would seem that the individuality of all that exists would strike joy in people, for it is precisely this that gives everyone a special place in the universe and opens the way to new achievements. This infinite wealth will lead the science of the future toward new discoveries that today would seem like impossible fairy tales.

People often say that for cooperation between individuals, similarity of character is needed, but they should speak not of similarity, but of harmony. Only the harmony of energies can be useful. Harmony is not repetition, it produces a chord. May this chord be strong and sonorous. It is hard to imagine a symphony built of monotonous octaves. People should love polyphony; the richer it is the more human hearts it will touch and call to action. Thus we will be open to the rich multiformity of perceptions. Nature must not be dealt with as if impoverished.

The Thinker said, "Nature is inexhaustible."

741. Urusvati knows how essential it is to know how to live in a state of joyous readiness. About readiness We have spoken many times, but remember that the readiness should be joyous, otherwise it becomes transformed into something dismal, doomed. In such a state one's readiness to cross into the subtle realm is harmed. It must not be thought that We are speaking about this effect as just emotional; on the contrary, We have in mind its scientific aspect.

It should be reasoned that first of all the highest vibrations must be maintained. Joy provides such vibrations, just as does exalted striving. But people often misunderstand the feeling of exaltation, and for them the feeling of joy is more accessible. Let them think about good encounters in their lives; let them choose the most joyous images; let people in their quiet moment evoke their fond memories.

But one must prepare at length and patiently for each new revelation of cosmic order. We always advise that one concentrate and find the power to protect the secrecy of these high attainments. These pearls are gathered with difficulty, but can easily be scattered. He who prattles too easily will break the lock of the sacred repository. Constant equilibrium is the adornment of the wise. They will gather their seeds amidst everyday labor. This labor will sow joy in their consciousness and provide consolation against offences and injustices. Any achievement must grow out of a state of joyous readiness.

The Thinker always called for the realization of joy as the highest form of healing.

742. Urusvati knows the value of pure imagination, for its neighbors are enthusiasm, exaltation, and other helpers of the ascent. Purity of imagination must be especially stressed, otherwise even criminals will think that their imagination has value.

It would be wrong to assume that quality of imagination is formed by itself and does not need cultivating. This is a big error! All such faculties must be developed. Imagination must be nourished by the best examples of self-sacrificing heroes. All the highest aspects of humanity must be taught, and also the many achievements that can be found in nature itself. That is why the natural sciences must be taught. Let children understand that great ways are open to them, and in improving themselves they will ask about the Supermundane World.

People often destroy their own possibilities by limiting their thinking. For instance, they think that their thoughts and words disappear into space—an error! For all is transmuted, and nothing disappears. For the development of imagination it is necessary to recognize this omnipresence.

Man has discovered ways to transmit sound to a distance, but is mistaken in thinking that sound's reach, however distant, is limited. It is not possible to intentionally limit the reach of sound. Man imagines that he has already attained the boundary of cosmic law, but even a flight into the stratosphere is nothing but a child's attempt. Imagination alone can save man from reaching premature conclusions. It is impossible to think about the Supermundane world without a developed imagination. It must be understood that science should be free, without limitation.

The Thinker said, "People dream about having wings, but the swiftest wings are already contained within themselves."

743. Urusvati knows that the greatest plants grow from small seeds. In the tiniest seed is contained their vivid colors, strong aromas, and plentiful substances, healing or poisonous. And indeed the vital capacity of the seed is of long duration! People receive indifferently these wonderful gifts of nature, not aware that the very same vital force acts in all domains of life.

People do not ponder that each seed of psychic energy possesses the very same capacity for marvelous transformation. Of course, not all people are so light-minded; there are many passionate observers, but they are divided into many degrees of ability. They often do not differentiate between the early stages of manifestation and those of realized attainment. They may accept a momentary spark as the ultimate achievement, forgetting that from a spark to a fiery "Lotus" the way is long.

The development of true equilibrium, called the Golden Path, permits one to distinguish the various steps of achievement. People should rejoice at each fiery spark, but remember always how lengthy the path of achievement is. Amidst a normal path of perfectment man will think with common sense about the Supermundane World. We are most solicitous about sensible self-perfectment; it will come through reflection—continuous and intelligent.

The Thinker summoned all to the Supermundane World, inviting them to see the wonderful manifestations of Nature.

744. Urusvati knows that man must beware of indifference; it is the ruin of high vibration, it is the killer of ascent; it is the path to apathy. They will say, "But indifference should free one from desire." This is an error, for no one speaks against the desire for heroic self-sacrifice. Such desires should be understood as darings, as milestones of ascent. Rejoice when you see daring attempts. They prove that the one who dares never falls prey to indifference.

One may notice the beginnings of daring amidst daily life; such glimpses are valuable. They can be even more treasured than the daring that is born of violent commotions and calamities.

They will say, "Necessity breeds heroes," yet it is still loftier when heroism is engendered freely, when the broadened consciousness perceives the beauty of *podvig*. Let the *podvig* be prepared from the early years. Let children sense that they are able to create beauty independently. Amidst everyday life, one can see a child's thoughts take wing. No one taught them, no one offered them examples, yet their consciousness told them that something unusual, and useful for someone, could and should be done.

The Thinker said, "Replace indifference with magnanimity."

745. Urusvati knows that psychology, as a science, must be put on a tangible, measurable basis, just as biology is, and thus develop knowledge about the Supermundane World. It was a great error that psychology was presented as something purely theoretical. Truly, it is a continuation of physiology. Thus must be learned all aspects of Nature.

But why did scientists offer psychology in this way? The reason is simple—they did not know the Supermundane World. To them the Supermundane World was a fairy tale for uneducated peasants. The big question is—who are the more ignorant, the scientists or the peasants?

How can one discuss psychology without knowing the properties of psychic energy? The complete reality of the Supermundane World must be accepted. One should learn to patiently collect the scattered fragments of this knowledge and treat them without prejudice. We advise you not to encumber science with new terminology, but to continue its evolution. Categorizing leads to undesirable complication. We always advise you to strive for synthesis.

The Thinker pointed out the ancients, who in some of their observations outstripped the discoveries of later centuries.

746. Urusvati knows that a good physician, prior to recommending a treatment, will examine in detail both the physical and mental states of his patient. The physician understands that the mental condition can be a friend or an enemy.

Every physician should be a psychiatrist in the best meaning of this word. Thus he would know that prescribing the same medicine to patients in different mental states will produce completely different results. This example is relevant to everything in life, especially when the Supermundane World is involved.

Even the least mental indisposition can turn a faithful co-worker into a harmful one. The mental state of your interlocutor must be understood with care, so as not to worsen his condition. It is better to remain silent than to begin a harmful dispute.

People with an understanding of psychology can be recognized—they are oblivious to offense, and thus avoid arguments that might lead to unnecessary discord. Sometimes one must wait for a day, or perhaps just an hour, when the mood of the co-worker will change and a receptive state will arise. It is valuable to sense such vibrations and use the opportunity to convey information about the Supermundane World.

The Thinker said, "Learn to unite, not to divide."

747. Urusvati knows that an integrated memory is the product of vast accumulations. First the person accumulates a great quantity of information, which later is consolidated when the consciousness has expanded and new knowledge is gained by perceiving events in their entirety. And then the shell of the unnecessary cracks and falls away, and the crystal of understanding of the perfection of humanity emerges.

This process of transformation of memory may sometimes feel like a loss of memory, but this is incorrect, for much information is transmuted into a new understanding. A person who is not firm in his consciousness must be shown how much more rapidly synthesis can lead to a wise all-embracingness. The greatest discoveries demonstrate the synthesizing abilities of the mind of the explorer. These experiences are justly called inspiration; that is, the accumulated mass of information falls away, and the arrow flies to its target. Such synthesis is particularly evident when contemplating the Supermundane. Therefore let us always be ready to fly in thought to the most essential, which is the purpose of earthly existence. Let us learn to understand that superior to all earthly sciences is the pursuit of knowledge of the Supermundane.

The Thinker said, "Shed all that impedes learning of the Supermundane."

748. Urusvati knows that the creation of good is the duty of man. This benevolent activity takes many forms, and one should carefully choose the ways of influencing others according to their consciousness. The consciousness of your interlocutor may be self-absorbed, but you can, according to your ability, make him aware of useful information.

Let us not forget that the greatest want in humanity is not the result of material poverty, but of spiritual ignorance. The belief is widespread that nothing exists after physical death. Unfortunately, this harmful misperception is growing. Religions are of little help, for they just repeat their obscure formulas. Science also offers little help. It is in no hurry to perform the scientific research that will prove the existence of the Supermundane World.

Nor does science point out that one who believes in non-existence will find himself in a most pitiful condition in the Subtle World after his earthly demise. He will be in a worse situation than any follower of the most primitive religion. Having trained his consciousness in negation, he will find himself in a continuing mirage, incomprehensible and frightening.

One's thinking can be very stubborn, in affirmation as well as in negation. One can imagine how greatly shamed will be the denier when he embarks on his new life in the Supermundane World. Thus, every explanation of the essence of the Supermundane World will be of great benefit if given earlier.

Help the unknowing ones when you can.

The Thinker demanded that His disciples always affirm the Supermundane World.

749. Urusvati knows how physical manifestations can be compared with psychic ones. For instance, fliers fear air pockets and inexperienced pilots greatly fear these and blame them for accidents. Mental "pockets" exist too, and people think that their abilities become dulled or disappear because of them, but experience proves that such lapses are caused by psychic, cosmic energies.

I will offer a still simpler comparison. Look at your reflection in calm water, then ripple the surface of the water. The image will first disappear, then reappear in a distorted form, and only after some time will it become clear again. Mental agitation acts similarly—for a long time the human appearance becomes lost and distorted into an ugly mask. Could one possibly turn to the Supermundane World with such an ugly expression? Even it would appear ugly too! Much time is needed for the spiritual surface to provide a true reflection again. Thus, with simple examples, remind yourself of the conditions that can assist in a better understanding of the Supermundane World.

It is impossible in the earthly life to always have

the best conditions, but without such conditions one should not attempt to make contact with the subtle realms. The agitations that occur must pass, and with calm restored one can more easily turn to lofty concepts. Without calm sacrilege may result, and you know how harmful that is. Thus, by observing oneself, one can remember how ugly are the distorted reflections.

The Thinker advised, "Stir the surface of water, and study what happens to your reflection."

750. Urusvati knows how precious is a solemn, joyous mood. Some people call this mood the Torch of the Supermundane World; others the Gateway to the Subtle World. One should enter joyously this beloved motherland. Everyone can make the passage easier. The magnetic vibrations of the Supermundane draw one closer, and it is therefore desirable to heighten one's own vibrations. The easiest way is to fill oneself with solemn joy.

One should not think that such a state is easily achieved. It is not one of boisterous merriment! Many people do not see the difference between supermundane joy and earthly merriment, yet the difference is enormous. One should train oneself to learn to discern solemn joy. In Our Abode, We first of all establish a mood of solemnity. One can live in such a happy state, in which all earthly sorrows acquire a special meaning. Of course, We do not speak about artificial solemnity. Some people feign an air of solemnity, but in reality simply deceive themselves.

People should develop a desire to think about the Supermundane World in a state of solemn joy. Let the most beautiful images accompany such thoughts. Let the highest harmonies help to elevate one's vibrations.

The Thinker ordained, "Beautiful Images and Harmonies will be the Beacons of the Supermundane."

751. Urusvati knows that fearlessness is stronger than any conjurations. But you also know that just as any minor fault decreases the value of a precious stone, fearlessness loses its power when it is not absolute and complete. People should find no consolation in thinking that it is possible to be more or less fearless. Without full immunity from fear, how could they dare to peer into the Infinite? Man should learn fearlessness, otherwise the Supermundane World will terrify him.

It is not easy to learn fearlessness if no daring was accumulated in former lives. Every past obstacle was a lesson in how to overcome it. Past victories point the way to new successes.

Let man understand that no one can deprive him of life. It is mistaken to think that life exists only in one's earthly existence. Courage is strengthened by the realization that life is indestructible. Certainty about this is the way to fearlessness, and the certainty must be complete to be effective. Any magician knows that his formulas must be uttered with full confidence, otherwise the most powerful words lose their value. Thus, man must strive to attain full fearlessness if he wishes to perceive the Supermundane World. Fearlessness heightens one's vibrations.

The Thinker said, "At times it seems to me that I am fearless, but will I be able to face dreadful danger? I will command myself to stand firm against it!"

752. Urusvati knows that patience is the parent of tolerance. Intolerance is the offspring of ignorance. Nothing obstructs achievement as much as does intolerance. One must become attuned to an attitude of tolerance from one's earliest years. And compassion is akin to it. Tolerance is the best way. Those who argue should not be dismissed if their words contain just one particle of truth. This particle could serve as a bridge for unity. But patience is needed to discover such particles of truth.

When in the Subtle World one can observe that it is precisely tolerance that leads to the attaining of higher vibrations. Consciousness will indicate where the likeminded ones are. They may be different in their looks and ways of expression, but their vibrations will be similar. Only real tolerance will make it possible to come close to them.

Let the Teaching of the Supermundane World indicate all the qualities needed for this achievement. A common moral basis is needed, and also an understanding of the mutual benefit, when thinking about the Supermundane existence.

The Thinker instructed His disciples first of all to demonstrate a beautiful tolerance.

753. Urusvati knows why the primary energy had different names at different times. This is quite natural, for the name of the energy must correspond to the level of consciousness. Also, the effect of the energy on any of the nerve centers would make it seem that the energy was something particular, rather than universal.

The primary energy is the foundation upon which the phenomenon of thinking rests. When one is mentally tensed, one attracts the spatial energy, and thus can more readily develop. People sometimes cannot understand why they are unable to use the energy that appears to assist everyone else. This is because they do not develop their thinking and fail to strengthen their magnet, thus depriving themselves of help from above.

Scientists already speak about some kind of spatial force, but they cannot explain how greatly the laboratory of man is in need of spatial currents. Man cannot approach the Supermundane World if he is a stranger to the realization of spatial energy. Note that We are now calling the primary energy spatial, so that scientists will not think there is something religious in it. We do not want to antagonize; let everyone advance by his own way, but if he is thinking, he will arrive at a recognition of the power of the primary energy.

Let man, through studying his own reactions, double his attention to surrounding phenomena. He will then understand that these are all natural and ordinary manifestations of the one powerful energy.

The Thinker pointed to the magnet of the heart. He knew which center is the best receiver of the primary energy.

754. Urusvati knows the painful reactions caused by certain sounds during the process of thought transmission. At such times it sometimes can be observed that a very loud noise is more easily tolerated than a highly charged but quieter sound. It would seem that such phenomena should be studied, but where is the physician who would be able to perceive the transmutation that is taking place in one's organism? The physician must be open to an understanding of such processes, but many physicians, by their presence alone, interrupt all manifestations of psychic energy.

It must be conceded that there are many such deadly negaters, especially among so-called scientists. Instead of refining their feelings, they irreparably kill them. Because of this they must not be present during the processes of thought transmission, and are unable to investigate the condition of the organism receiving remote currents. But it is possible to find refined, positive observers who will not only not impede, but will even strengthen the process.

Human thought should aspire to psychic observations. During such quests people inevitably come closer, and they can cooperate usefully. Let them travel in thought through the Supermundane World. If their first attempts are primitive, they should not be discouraged. Help will come if the striving is sincere.

The Thinker said, "When will the physicians appear who have full knowledge of the entire human being?"

755. Urusvati knows that he who progresses spiritually knows how to discern what is the most important and the most undelayable. Do not think that the reasoning mind can help in this. The mind can lead one astray into an abyss of faulty interpretation. Only psychic energy, when in communion with the Higher World, can direct one's discernment to the way of truth.

The most important, though absolute, is still individual for everyone. It must be understood to what an extent the individuality is molded out of many conditions, over many centuries, amidst the most varied causes. Even so, the one who advances spiritually can discern the sparks of the absolute.

It is not easy to recognize, amid earthly existence, the most important to which one should strive in the face of the obstacles. We have already pointed out that obstacles, like the flow of the waters, help one to sense the main salutary current. Only spiritual tension can provide an understanding of how much the Guiding Power can be sensed everywhere and always. Only thought about the Supermundane World can help one to perceive the particle of the Absolute that is accessible to humanity.

The Thinker believed that everyone can choose to understand how the Highest is manifested in all earthly turmoil.

756. Urusvati knows that man must develop a deep understanding that he is in eternal motion and in a state of continuous transformation. This can be scientifically proven, yet people do not take it into consideration. Transformation, especially, is difficult for people to understand. They can recognize a change caused by age or the state of their health, but will not acknowledge that they change steadily, every moment.

Of course, especially sensitive apparatuses can record the changes in man's vibrations and in his entire nervous system, but such apparatuses are not yet in use, and the science of the study of nerves and glands is still young. Thus, the most important requirements for the realization of the Supermundane World are not given proper attention.

Likewise the study of thought is still neglected, and the very atmosphere surrounding man is not sufficiently studied. The composition of air was discovered, but the vibrational nature of the atmosphere, and the powerful chemical process that affects all that exists is not yet understood. Can one speak about transformation, when it is easier for people to think of themselves as unchanging?

On the path of transformation remember the Instruction of the Thinker, "Learn to find the patience to listen to others speak of their pain. Find the benevolence to give wings to the joy of others. You do not know the source of their sufferings. You do not know the cause of their joy, but learn to offer warmth and encouragement to others."

757. Urusvati knows that in the near future the study of the Supermundane World will be intensified. Science will help, but also the people's consciousness will be more attentive to the manifestations of everyday life. People must be assured that attention to psychic manifestations is not superstition. It has been sufficiently indicated that superstition and prejudice result from ignorance. Now it must be said that lack of attention to subtle manifestations is also an act of ignorance.

One should strengthen the striving toward observation of the surrounding subtle phenomena. The eye and the ear must be made more acute so that the link with the Subtle World can be recognized in everyday life. It must be made clear that the Subtle World is close to every being. One should remember that these observations will be of benefit to science. But there should be no derision if inexperienced observers arrive at the wrong conclusions. Each observation can contain a spark of truth, and scientists can recognize it.

Let a benevolent attitude prevail in the work of psychic research; otherwise people will shut themselves away in silence, and much that is valuable will be lost. Manifestations of the Subtle World are like the finest cobweb; it can be torn, but the presence of something, very subtle, will be felt for a long time. Remember that the Subtle World is revealed in very subtle ways. Science, therefore, must adapt itself to the subtlest manifestations.

The words of the Thinker should be remembered, "The most subtle can be perceived only with great attention."

758. Urusvati knows why We often mention the value of labor. Labor begets rhythm. Through labor one experiences supermundane vibrations; that is why quality of labor is so important. In this way every good worker refines his vibrations and can begin the ascent.

One should not think of certain fields of labor as special, for in each labor high tensions can be attained. Labor must be rhythmic and therefore daily. There is no need to await some special inspiration to begin labor. The prayer of labor can begin at any time, and through it man attains a new perfectment.

Let us not reject manual labor, for in the application of one's hands is found true mastery. Who can dare to draw a boundary between craftsmanship and creative artistry? Truly, the conscious worker is also a creator in his domain. Luckily, each domain can be perfected; in this, man, without even thinking about it, makes contact with the highest vibrations and the Supermundane World. Each moment of such communion can bring a useful discovery, and can be strengthened by benevolent cooperation.

Perfectment of labor is the next task. Not in the distant future, but in the coming years will labor be victorious; along with it will approach the beneficent vibrations of the New Era. Let us not forget that on the eve of the Era of Light one should learn to revere labor.

The Thinker said, "One may respect labor, but one should also understand its lofty purpose."

759. Urusvati knows the value of silent communion with the Supermundane World. Each verbal, mental address has within it a plea, a wish, or some kind of human feeling, but the essence of the Supermundane World is beyond words. Communion with the great essence must also be beyond words.

Let human thought be silenced for a moment, let the eyesight be dimmed, let the ear be dulled, and the sigh will transfer man into the higher Supermundane Worlds. He does not plead, does not demand, does not praise, but is experiencing the great Be-ness. Everyone can find a moment for such exaltation. Everyone can feel rejuvenation from this kind of contact with the Higher Worlds.

No special incantations are needed; the spirit striving to its Motherland, attracted by the Great Magnet, is enough. Give freedom to the spirit; do not bind it with human limitations. It will soar by itself and return triumphant; thus man becomes attuned to the Supermundane World. Such communion occurs more often than one might imagine. People do not understand how the rejuvenation comes, and ascribe it to some kind of earthly process, but the value of a silent attunement to the Supermundane World is great! People should not forget about these gates.

The Thinker advised His disciples, "Learn not to demean the greatness with thoughts of earthly bustle."

760. Urusvati knows the salutary results of cooperation. Many people understand that cooperation increases productivity and heightens its quality, but at present I want to point out one valuable aspect of cooperation. Let us take as an example a choir or an army, or a team of workmen; it is probable that in such groups there can be found many people clouded by misfortune, but their common unity will lessen their personal unhappiness. Thus common striving helps turn people from their individual suffering. One should not think that common work brings about a dulling of personal feelings; on the contrary, with a high quality of labor, it can heighten one's striving. Thus working in unity is of help to all.

It should also be understood that the approach to the Supermundane World can be facilitated when following this principle of group effort. The many varieties of individual understanding can join to form a harmonious choir. A common desire can strengthen the striving.

Wherever possible, small groups should be formed, striving toward cognition of the Supermundane. Such groups could be of great help to one another. They will find mutual support when facing the derision of the crowds, and will help each one to develop attention toward the manifestations of the Supermundane World. Such groups should be small, so that the varied vibrations of individual participants do not impede the harmony. No one can forcefully command striving towards the essence of Be-ness, but the harmony of vibrations makes possible a powerful ascent.

The Thinker summoned His disciples to common labor, saying, "Let the beauty of labor heal our wounds."

761. Urusvati knows that science has established that there is a poison in the human organism that is produced by anger and irritation. Likewise, science recognizes the poison caused by fear and doubt. Doubt is a cousin of fear, and decomposes the organism.

It should be remembered that the one who doubts harms not only himself but also the benevolent forces. The very emanations of such a person prevent assimilation of the energies sent to him. Such a one cannot make contact with the Subtle World, and cannot sense the reality of subtle influences. He remains in a state of constant negation and destroys his own creativity.

Doubt is deadening, and must be distinguished from realistic, sensitive discernment. Man must think sensibly about all that occurs, utilizing the straight-knowledge that is given to him. It safeguards him against errors. It can be developed and will protect him from the viper of doubt.

Man, when filled with the poison of doubt, cannot respond to the subtle energies; an infected being cannot soar to the higher supermundane realms. Physical health alone cannot save man; health of the spirit is needed.

The Thinker said, "He who doubts is like a fleeing timid warrior."

762. Urusvati knows that science will soon identify the harmful chemism caused by despondency and envy. It can be observed that these attacks produce partial paralysis of certain nerve centers. Indeed, the color of one's emanations can show clearly to what a degree the energy of the organism is sapped. Can anyone in this condition perceive supermundane signs?

It is necessary to study human moods. A list of the positive and negative qualities of those who swim through the storm of life could be compiled. In doing this, it can be seen that between the extremes, there can be found undetermined ones that are like half-hearted, failed chemical experiments, in which reactions cannot take place and subtle energies cannot be applied.

Do not tire of repeating to beginners that the conditions of the Subtle World are completely different from those of the earthly world. Such simple considerations are quite foreign to today's humanity, which prefers to deny rather than to think of emotions and their consequences.

It would be useful for man to think more often in scientific ways. Do not think that scientific terminology can desiccate the heart that is striving to the Subtle World. The Supermundane Laboratory is close to everything in the Universe.

The Thinker said, "The one who has fallen into despair, or is possessed by envy, is like a corpse."

763. Urusvati knows that joy is a rare bird. If it perches at your window, be ready to admit it. Even the smallest, most ordinary joys transform the emanations of man. It can be imagined how much more luminous

man's essence becomes when there is joy about the Higher World.

There can be discovered beneficent chemisms produced by joy. Illnesses can be cured by joy. It is time for science to investigate the value of joy. Joy without cause is often spoken about, but this is a misperception. Nothing can happen without reason. The ability to sense a remote cause is evidence of a great refinement of one's consciousness.

There can be no limit to the flights of thought, thus the wings of joy can be directed from the Supermundane World. One should pay attention to the joy that arises in the heart. However, it should be explained to certain people that We have in mind pure joy, joy about the good, the joy of creativity, otherwise all who live in spite will laugh, and imagine that their own emanations will become filled with light.

Spite produces strong poisons and plunges people into darkness. Do not think that I speak about abstract foundations, I simply speak about the laws of the human organism.

The Thinker told the seekers of joy, "Joy is happiness."

764. Urusvati knows how carefully every positive manifestation must be protected. Thus, speaking of joy, We say, "Man, do not cloud the joy of your neighbor. It may appear to you to be strange or insignificant, nevertheless, it contributes to the health of space, and it is not for you to judge the reasons for anyone's joy. Do not belittle something useful with derision and insult.

"Remember that you have been designated a guardian of space. You can restore health to it or can defile it. You cannot aspire to the Supermundane World if you are a source of deadly poisons. With your every breath you send either restoration of health or destruction into space."

Why does man think so rarely about the great responsibility of his existence? When coming again to Earth, everyone aspires to perfection; why then in earthly life do people so seldom dream about *podvig*?

The ancient legends are to them just impossible fairy tales. Man's thinking is depressed, like the decay of death, though every beautiful thought creates a new nerve in space.

People rarely dream about their future existence; therefore it is of great importance to speak often about the reality of the Supermundane World. Let all teachers find in every object a way of mentioning the greatness of Infinity. Children should raise their imaginations more often to realms of good.

The Thinker begged, "Avoid quarrels and bad memories, for they are harm-bearing."

765. Urusvati knows how many aspects there are to the science of astrobiology. A number of institutes will be dedicated to the fields of study that are most vital to humanity. Those institutions must work equally on both physical and psychic tasks.

Along with astrobiology, the psychobiology of man must be studied. Only in such cooperation can the correlation between microcosm and Macrocosm be understood. But it is regrettable that psychobiology is so often studied in distorted ways. The Society for Psychic Research is mainly occupied with extra-ordinary phenomena, when it should be studying the phenomena of ordinary life.

People must accept the reality of the Supermundane World not as something supernatural, but as the foundation of earthly life. Only with an understanding of the reality of the Supermundane World can evolution proceed; one should strive all the more to this knowledge, since the state of contemporary life must be purified of the poisons produced by humanity itself.

The poisoning and corruption occur in full view of humanity. People introduce poisons into life and assist in the corruption of their children. It was said long ago that the mixing of blood is harmful, yet does it not now take place on a broad scale? True, it does help to save lives, but its internal effect brings irreparable harm. Mixed blood rarely is in harmony with the individual's own blood.

People love to talk about the collapse of nations. But this is a process that takes place over many years. Thus, the psychobiology of nations must be safeguarded.

The Thinker said, "It is a joy to realize that we are in constant cooperation with the Supermundane World."

766. Urusvati knows how many outworn concepts must be replaced by more appropriate ones. It must not be thought that such concepts become outworn over many centuries. Some of them are younger than a century, and have already lost their purpose. For instance, the word "spiritualism" is not an old one, yet it already lost its usefulness by being limited and vulgarized. True spiritual knowledge encompasses all aspects of the Supermundane. It is wrong to restrict it to limited spiritualistic seances, when broad psychic research provides ample opportunity for new knowledge.

Likewise, absurd scientific subdivisions should be avoided; they just divide the one body of science. Nowadays people speak about parapsychology, but what is the point of such a category when it is all contained in the vast domain of psychology? It is only when physics is insufficiently understood that metaphysics exists.

Many examples can be cited when the body of science was divided without real need. Much is spoken about synthesis, about the one great energy, but such talk is usually empty words.

People prefer to fence themselves off in narrow specialties, and thus avoid cooperation in broader concerns. As a result, they create complicated, lengthy terminology that serves no real purpose. Of course, every science has its branches, but they all must be branches of the one Tree.

At present humanity is passing through a critical period. The time has now come for true synthesis. Without conscious cooperation, people will be unable to mend the torn essence of man. It is impossible to find co-workers without mutual trust, but that can come only from straight-knowledge.

The Thinker taught His disciples to think about the source of straight-knowledge.

767. Urusvati knows that a physician who does not study man in a healthy state cannot competently help man when he is ill. Individual characteristics of the organism must be observed in order to be able to combat illness. As an example, psychic phenomena must be understood as individual; thus the importance of this concept of individuality must be understood in the microcosm and also in the Macrocosm. Though people do not understand that the Macrocosm can also be individual, every experienced observer already knows that generalizations are made only with great caution. Life does not count the varieties of its blessings.

People may ask which yoga is the shortest path to knowledge. You know the Agni Yoga—the fiery synthesis—but many have not yet familiarized themselves with this fiery knowledge. They would like to be directed to one of the earlier known yogas. I shall select the Karma Yoga: creativeness, conscious labor, striving towards higher quality, will lead to the Highest by the shortest path. However, Karma Yoga requires time, whereas Agni Yoga can be called the lightning-like way. Think how beautiful is the path of lightning, but do not forget how difficult the lightning-like tension is.

The Thinker said, "Let the most difficult be the most beautiful."

768. Urusvati knows how people attempt to justify their lack of desire to think about the Supermundane. First of all they will speak about insufficient time, about daily cares, about work beyond their strength. "We have no time," they will say. But does a lightning bolt of thought need much time?

Even the most imperfect turn to the Supermundane brings good. When one's eyes are fatigued, one closes them momentarily and receives relief; similarly, a lightning-like thought about the Supermundane improves the health of the organism.

It has already been said that realization of the Supermundane World requires acknowledgment of its existence. There can be no doubt in such a realization. I attest that a doubting thought cannot bring man close to the Supermundane World. One can see how those who study and read a great deal can remain furthest from an understanding of the Supermundane life, while others, through straight-knowledge, penetrate to the heights and receive beneficent help.

Truly, heart and feeling will remind one about the shortest path. This action is unfortunately not often understood, though without it attainment of and cooperation with the Supermundane World are impossible. We do not speak only about belief in the Supermundane World, but precisely about cooperation with it. Even everyday concerns must not deprive one of the opportunity to lift oneself up in thought. Words are not needed when the heart flies high. No one should attempt to justify his laziness and ignorance.

The Thinker said, "We will tell those burdened with sorrow that a flight to the Supermundane brings relief."

769. Urusvati knows the feeling with which one should approach the Supermundane World. Fear is a poor guide. The mind will not bring one to the Heights. It is essential to love the Supermundane World.

The skeptics should not wonder that instead of complex scientific formulas, We speak of the universal, human feeling of love as the best conductor. The best success is attained in any field if the investigator loves his subject. Only love can create the highest attraction. You know enough about the significance of attraction. This magnet is laid in the heart of man, and he is drawn toward the great magnet of the Supermundane World.

It must be understood that We have in mind not the isolated, easily-extinguished flashes of love; these mirages have no significance. It is steadfast love that is needed, devotion that burns unextinguished, through all of life's trials; such love leads to the Motherland of the heart, where, as in one's beloved Motherland, all is familiar, dear, beautiful. Such love will not be destroyed by earthly cares; on the contrary it will strengthen the spirit, enabling one to overcome the gravest of difficulties.

Attraction will bring active help from the Supermundane World; such communion will become true cooperation. Thus should it be in everything, but people too rarely realize the cosmic law of attraction and its foundation, Love. Even the most imperfect love contains a particle of good within itself. Thus, after all mental accumulations, man arrives at the very natural feeling by which all kingdoms of Nature live.

The Thinker taught, "Love is the most fiery feeling. Maintain the flame of your love for the Supermundane World."

770. Urusvati knows that some people cannot overcome the terror they feel during manifestations of the Supermundane World. In no way can one explain such a feeling except by the presence of inharmonious vibrations. True, during high manifestations, trembling is inevitable, but it is not a sign of fear.

In the future, it will be possible to a certain degree to harmonize the vibrations by the use of electricity, but at present such a device does not exist. At present, it is possible to help by the power of suggestion, but such psychic intrusion can be harmful. Suggestion must be applied very carefully when dealing with supermundane powers. It could be possible to cause a deadly dividing of psychic energy.

We have already spoken of the need to love the Supermundane World in order to draw close to it. One cannot be terrified by something one loves deeply. Therefore, people who are terrified by manifestations of the Supermundane World do not love it. They can acknowledge the Supermundane World, can accept its reality with their mind, but the mind is of no help when standing to face the Supermundane World. Only love will alter their vibrations so that they can approach and greet each manifestation of the Supermundane World.

There is no need to return to the superstition of past ages, when people venerated the Sky because of their fear of thunderstorms. Let us not imitate ignorant savages, but rather perceive the Supermundane World scientifically. Let people's desire to approach the Supermundane World be prompted by love. Their free will empowers people to accept the signs of the Supermundane World voluntarily and conscientiously.

The Thinker advised to avoid frustration and despondency, for they are obstacles to the cognition of the Supermundane World.

771. Urusvati knows how often people utter correct words without understanding their true meaning. For example, they may say, "This man is mentally unbalanced." They would then call a physician, who would begin killing the patient with narcotics. The physician may speak about sick nerves, but will not understand that the affliction of the nerves is a result of a disorder of the consciousness, that might also be spoken of as a derangement of psychic energy.

An unbalanced person is like a badly tuned stringed instrument. In such a state he is not fit for creative labor, just as the out-of-tune instrument is not fit for music. Strings must be put into harmony, and that must be done by someone with a knowledge of music.

Likewise, one's free will can strengthen the consciousness and bring the nervous system into harmony. Let us not forget that a deranged person cannot approach the Supermundane World, and will even inflict harm on all those surrounding him because his emanations are poisonous.

Remember that people often become upset because of trifles that are not worth thinking about. Moreover, they encumber their consciousness with petty details, and during times of difficulty become so depressed that their nerves are deadened and they are incapable of finding a sensible way out. There are many calamities in these times, and people must think about strengthening their consciousness. During times of world upheaval people are drawn closer to the Supermundane World, but they must first restore balance to their consciousness. Free will is given to them for this. They should command themselves not to lose their own equilibrium during the epidemics of derangement that threaten mankind.

The Thinker said, "Keep the strings of your heart in harmony."

772. Urusvati knows that this is a time of painful progress for nations. Each nation evolves in its own way: one by war, another by calamity, by labor, by knowledge, or by *podvig*. Each nation bears its own karma. This karma can be light, but many nations carry a heavy and difficult karma.

You must tell people that in this evolution of peoples there can be no return to the past. Everyone who realizes the immutability of evolution, has already made his own destiny easier. Everyone who understands the law of labor in the service of humanity helps his own ascent. Everyone who learns to love to serve the evolution of peoples also serves his own evolution. Thus, a great responsibility turns into a light burden.

It will be asked, "Why is this time called the Era of the Mother of the World?" Truly, it must be so named. Woman will bring great help, not only by bringing enlightenment, but also by affirming equilibrium. At times of confusion, the magnet of equilibrium is disturbed, and free will is needed to reunite the broken whole. Maitreya, the Compassionate One, needs co-workers. He who sacrifices himself for the Great Era will reap an abundant harvest.

The Thinker said, "Learn how to labor for all humanity."

773. Urusvati knows how solicitously one should relate to each advance of science. It is time to put aside the ignorant misconception about the division of sciences into applied and theoretical: all sciences are vital.

A scientist, in the breadth of his research, cannot foresee what scientific realms he will have to deal with. He realizes that the many categories of scientific discipline are all connected by one unifying principle. Therefore, it is necessary to begin the teaching of all scientific studies with a philosophical analysis. Thus it will be possible to lay a foundation for the unity of knowledge.

It is impossible to point to any domain of science as less significant. In contemporary research every science can open new horizons. Recall how astronomy, after a time of dry computations, turned into a science of the Universe. The same occurs with many sciences that find their true mission.

Likewise the needs of the people should not be forgotten. They require scientific explanation in an accessible form, though always strictly authenticated. A full range of books on all subjects must be made available, but they should not be published at random. Governments must undertake a program of broad publication of small books covering all the fields of science, all branches of knowledge. These books must be written in a way that allows inclusion of the newest scientific discoveries and achievements. Also, the books should be well-written, so that beautiful language will serve as an attraction. Let us not forget, either, that psychology and biology must lead the way. The Supermundane World must be presented beautifully.

The Thinker said, "The victor will be the one who finds the simplest word about the Highest."

774. Urusvati knows how diverse are the paths to the Supermundane World. This multiformity must be kept in mind when helping the young in their quest for the Higher World. Most important, they must be protected from developing a narrow world view.

Beginning with the earliest school years, it is necessary to lay down in an accessible way a proper foundation for broad thinking. The young should also be taught to be dynamic in their explorations, for nothing can compare to personal encounters with different ways of thinking.

One must understand that for most of those who enter the Supermundane World, it will appear to be beyond compare. People find there a life based on immutable laws that are quite different from those of ordinary, earthly life; only flexibility of mind can help the newcomer to adapt quickly to new conditions.

Schools should familiarize students with the various levels of existence. Let the schools teach them to seek a broad way, based upon the wisdom teaching of the Thinkers. Reason and creativeness will reveal the possibilities available to everyone. One should be concerned that each child become aware of his own internal possibilities. Separate from karmic considerations, the ulcer of despair can often be seen in humanity. Man falls into the darkness of a prison built by himself. Everyone should help such prisoners, pointing out to them the near and joyous way.

The Thinker advised that, first of all, one must cast out the misconceptions about hopelessness and consider it the enemy of man.

775. Urusvati knows that in ancient communities service to mankind was considered to be a lofty and difficult test. The tested one did not have to change his activity, but its essence was to be dedicated not to himself, not to his city, not to his country, but to the entire humanity. Thus, the scope of his activity broadened and resulted in good for all.

It was not easy in ancient times to imagine the magnitude of humanity, and the possibilities for expansion of mental transmissions. We say this because at the present time humanity finds itself in a similar state of mind about the Supermundane World. We advise you not to withdraw from earthly activity, but to preserve thoughts about the Supermundane World, which will cease being seen as abstract and will enter life. It should be remembered that all one's earthly labor can be dedicated to the Supermundane World. The greatness of the Highest World will inspire the highest quality in every human endeavor.

High quality can only raise the consciousness of mankind and bring it closer to the Supermundane World. The consciousness will affirm the meaning of the Higher World, but also, the inner, indescribable feeling will help, with a single sigh, the approach to the Highest. The improvement of quality in every activity will become an invisible bridge toward beautiful achievement.

The reasoning mind should not cloud the creative feeling, which will be of real service to mankind and to the Supermundane World. Especially now, with mankind in a state of confusion, hope should be given that everyone is destined to come closer to the Higher Worlds. Any labor is a trustworthy path. Only in commitment to high quality can one succeed on the path of ascent.

The Thinker used to say to His disciples, "Let each one of you affirm yourselves in quality of labor. Each one will labor in service to the Supermundane World."

776. Urusvati knows that one should bring into daily life a realization of the Supermundane World by every means possible. People complain about obstacles to this, but usually these complaints are without foundation.

Thus, people speak about cruel shocks in their lives,

but do not mention the chief obstacles to their successful development. They forget that a shock is like an explosion that can reveal deep-hidden riches. But earthly life is overwhelmed with petty quarrels that obscure, like the smoke from a leaky oven door. It is impossible to ascend when each day is filled with such poisons. Therefore, people should not complain about the explosions and cruel shocks, and should ponder how to free themselves from the small vipers.

People often fall into despair, thinking that their labor is not needed, but they forget that the energy generated by labor has cosmic value. Man cannot know where his energy will be manifested, or how and when it will bring good. Perhaps the man himself will sense this good and intentionally offer it for the benefit of his neighbors. If the labor is good in its essence, then not despair, but joy, will be the reward of the one who labors. Many examples can be cited when people have robbed themselves of joy; because the value of the sense of joy is not often realized.

The Thinker said, "Do not fear explosions, but beware of petty quarrels, for they swarm with ignorance."

777. Urusvati knows about the widespread increase in criminality. It occurs in many forms, but its harmful essence is always the same. It can be noted that some primitive societies are more moral than those that consider themselves to be enlightened by civilization.

An instructive book could be written about the corruption of humanity, for which no help is availing. It is particularly ugly when a known criminal preaches about morality and continues to perform traditional ceremonies. It was said long ago that the best ritual, in the hands of a criminal, turns into sacrilege.

Science is of little help if it is not unbiased. Even

though it is precisely science that could be expected to help to purify the consciousness. Morality and biology have unrecognized connections. It is inconceivable that humanity, even amidst today's armageddonal calamities and terrors, does not learn to look beyond the ashes of their own hearths! Man does not properly apply the wonderful inventions that fill this present life. It would seem that radio, for example, should prompt him to think about thought transmission, but in fact this invention is mainly used for deception.

Where lies the solution? Again, one should turn to the Supermundane World. It must be accepted in full reality; only thus can an immoral man be warned. But how much must be accomplished in this direction! Science must assist; science should be free; science should penetrate the depths of the human consciousness. Civilized humanity must ponder upon why primitive societies often are the most moral!

The Thinker warned people to look higher than the roof of their own dwellings.

778. Urusvati knows that the free will is of value only when it is truly free. Pitiable is the madman who imagines himself to be free, when in reality he is burdened with all kinds of fetters. Can the will be called free when it is blind and deaf, and crawls in the mire of prejudice?

They will ask, "What kind of life is it when on each step one meets with ignorance in its most criminal forms?" Indeed, humanity has chained itself with heavy fetters. All through life, even in the cradle, man is subjected to fabrications that have nothing in common with reality. There is often more wisdom in fairy-tales than in the opinions of people. True, it is unavoidable for one to encounter ugly monsters, yet the free will will liberate one from fear and lead beyond all obstacles.

Freedom of spirit is the gate into the Supermundane World. One's entire earthly life can be transformed through the manifestation of the free will. A free man will not dispute with ignoramuses, but will offer them alms in such a way that they will not even notice it, though this small generosity will help them on the way to the Supermundane World. Everyone passes on this way, and the free will is a wise leader. But be certain that the will is truly free.

The Thinker warned, "Do not turn the luminous gift of free will into a kind of madness."

779. Urusvati knows that conducting discourses while taking into consideration the consciousness of one's listener is a difficult art. Neither knowledge, nor straight-knowledge, but a heartfelt attitude will help one to gauge the consciousness of one's interlocutor.

Apollonius of Tyana was reproached for being controversial in his instruction, but the accusations were false. The Teacher never opposed the foundations, but he coordinated the contents of his talks in accordance with the consciousness of the student, for better understanding. The Teacher preferred private conversations, so as to better find the most understandable words. He said that a speech, given for many, cannot be convincing, because discordant consciousnesses can destroy one another.

This method was accepted by other philosophers in ancient Greece. Plato preferred to call one pupil at a time for a walk, and those discourses were especially meaningful. He related information about the Supermundane World quite guardedly. He knew that information not appropriate to the student's consciousness could be harmful, and the harm could even be irreparable.

He tested thoroughly the consciousness of the disciples in most unexpected ways. Everyone's consciousness is individual, and only a loving heart can sense what has been assimilated in the depths of the consciousness.

Especially now, one should discuss the Supermundane cautiously. The consciousness of people is in such turmoil that there could be malicious misinterpretations.

"Just as a sculptor concentrates his attention upon a precious piece of stone, so also does the sculptor of consciousness safeguard the treasured ascent of his student." Thus spoke the Thinker.

780. Urusvati knows that the influences of the Supermundane World cannot be understood by earthly logic. This should be evident, yet even serious researchers usually attempt to explain these communions by physical laws; the result is absurd, and the research is unsuccessful.

Influences from the Supermundane World can be divided into three basic kinds: the first is influence over one individual; the second is influence over an entire group; the third are "touches" of the Supermundane poured out over the entire humanity. Those touches were called the breath from the Highest. One philosopher, wishing to characterize these influences, called them psychic oxygen. Man cannot exist without oxygen; likewise he cannot avoid the breaths of the Supermundane World.

People are mistaken if they think that communion with the Supermundane World can be accomplished only with the help of especially sensitive individuals. Of course, contacts through such people are the most obvious, but in truth, everyone is continuously influenced by the touches of the supermundane dwellers.

It is time to recognize that the Worlds are indivisible. When this is understood, life becomes still richer and more beautiful. It must be remembered, though, that the laws of the Subtle World are subtle. In this way one can understand that the contacts with the Supermundane World are not accidental; nor are they insignificant, as it might seem from an earthly point of view.

It should also be understood that the supermundane touches can be sensed frequently, but only by those of high moral quality.

The Thinker pointed out that the contacts between the Worlds are continuous.

781. Urusvati knows that the beneficent influence of the Supermundane World must be distinguished from the signs of harmful possession. Good influences do not enslave the free will; they open the individual to increased possibilities. Such influence will always be caring and solicitous toward the physical condition of the organism, but possession always ends with something pernicious and destructive for the physical and the subtle bodies.

People usually think that possession takes control of only weak organisms, but the main cause lies in the immoral condition of the possessed one. It can be stated without error that possession enters mainly through the door of immorality, which, whether evident or secret, or just a seed, can invite possession.

It is commonly thought that possession can be cured by strong psychic suggestion, but improvement of the moral qualities is also necessary. Suggestion can eject the possessor for a while, but if the moral condition is raised, the entrance will be closed to the possessor. Biological morality is a firm foundation for successful self-improvement. Thus, no matter what we speak about, we always come back to biology.

The successes of science can raise the level of humanity, but the consciousness of humanity must not be chained by any kind of prejudice. Humanity must be free in order to study the Laws of Nature. Let scientists be true enlighteners.

The Thinker said, "A scientist is Light."

782. Urusvati knows how difficult it is for people to accept the possibility of Armageddon in the Supermundane World. Even those who know about the supermundane life cannot reconcile themselves to the thought that there can be wars in the Subtle World.

Simple logic should make clear to us that battle in the Supermundane World is inevitable. People taken from Earth before their time, filled with almost identical thoughts, gather in one sphere and are bound to continue their earthly activities. And their cruelty, although becoming more subtle, does not lose its force. This leads to heavenly battles, with great consequences both on Earth and in the Supermundane World.

It is not easy to stop these conflicts. Malice drags the combatants down into the lower strata, and you know that while it is not difficult to descend into those strata, to rise up from them is not so easy. Even lofty beings experience painful consequences, when they, out of compassion, descend into the lower strata. Thus, people should remember how easy it is to sink, and how difficult to rise. The lower strata suffocate those who descend from realms of higher vibrations.

All those who preserve malice within themselves should remember that it will act as a poison upon their supermundane path, and that the heart filled with malice cannot easily be cleansed. Therefore everyone on Earth should think about the future life.

The Thinker said, "Live so as not to burden the Supermundane World."

783. Urusvati knows that man is uplifted when he associates with the Beautiful, looks at the Beautiful, listens to the Beautiful, thinks in the ways of the Beautiful. Do not think that this ancient truth has been sufficiently realized by mankind. It is to be regretted that just at present people are more remote from this idea than in many past centuries.

The manifestation of the Beautiful in various realms is usually considered by the worldly "sages" to be not only unnecessary but even untimely, at the same time that they plan the reconstruction of the world. One may ask: How will they bring about a New World without caring about the Beautiful?

In all their philosophizing about the reconstruction of the world, the Beautiful has been given no place. Yet what kind of labor will it be if it is not beautiful? What kind of knowledge can live if it does not contain the Beautiful? What kind of justice can be born if it is bereft of beautiful insights? For all their talk about the essence and the defining of the Beautiful, people do not understand that each grain of the Beautiful turns man into a co-worker of Higher Forces.

Can there be a striving toward the Supermundane World without beautiful wings? Can there be a true creator without a beautiful realization of resplendent flights? It can be understood that without assimilation of the Beautiful there can be no evolution.

The Thinker pointed out, "Live always with a dream about the Beautiful, and you will be given joy and love."

784. Urusvati knows how precious is devotion to the Teacher. But how much disagreement there is

around this simple truth! Some speak about devotion, though by their very nature they do not understand it. Others insist that such devotion limits the free will, and a third group denies even the need for a Teacher.

Many examples can be cited about people who harm themselves by disturbing the harmony with the Highest Ones. Only a few can understand what a blessing the link with the Higher Ones is; only in this way is the communion with the Supermundane World facilitated. It is impossible to imagine how the earthly opportunity is destroyed.. When there is no affirmation of the higher path, one's earthly possibilities are lost.

Do not think that the Teacher can realize His intentions if man resists Him. It is not easy to mend the rent web. Sometimes this mending takes more time than the creation of a new web.

Often people complain about the Teacher, not understanding the reasons for His actions. People suppose that their own earthly decisions better serve the purpose, but they do not understand many things relating to earthly life. Only a few understand the value of Teachership. Perhaps their devotion will help them to become worthy of the Teacher.

The Thinker affirmed, "Learn to be worthy of the Teacher."

785. Urusvati knows the great significance of untiring vigilance. We have often mentioned vigilance, but people pay little attention to this saving quality. For some, being always on vigil is chains, but for others it is wings.

The unwise say, "When danger comes, we will stand watch." But will they perceive danger if their spirit has not developed its keenness of sight? Many qualities are dormant in the consciousness, and one must be able to draw them out of the depths of this treasury.

Fools will appear who will shamelessly deny the necessity of vigilance. They believe that it is not man's work to stand watch and tire himself by such intense concentration. And besides these fools, there are those who do not even understand what vigilance is. Therefore, again and again we must remind people about keenness of eye, concentration, and vigilance.

We have spoken in Our different books about all these qualities, but the complexity of Armageddon compels Us to point out once again the salutary self-defense so needed by humanity. Man hopes to achieve communion with the Supermundane World, but for this he must be vigilant. The spiritually blind will not perceive the beauty of the Higher World, and keenness of sight must be cultivated. It cannot be gained at once. The development of vigilance results from one's desire to safeguard everything High and Beautiful. Because of this striving one will always be on untiring vigil, which leads to Beauty.

The Thinker said, "Remember, always be ready."

786. Urusvati knows how wrong people are to complain about the unexpectedness of supermundane phenomena. They will say, "We waited with all our power of expectation, but nothing happened. And then, when we became exhausted, the manifestation took place." One should say to these inexperienced researchers, "You waited for subtle manifestations with your earthly desires. Do you not understand that the earthly and the Supermundane cannot exist in the same dimension?"

One must cultivate subtlety of the senses within oneself, so that through the earthly din the supermundane manifestations can be heard. One should learn to perceive the Supermundane Light with closed eyes; it is thus that the manifestations of the Subtle World approach. And you will not speak about their unexpectedness, for you will feel their approach with your heart.

Of course, you do not often anticipate the exact nature of an occurrence, but in any case you will know of its approach. Indeed, you will sense the vibrations well in advance. Inexperienced people may think these sensations are signs of illness, for their vibrations are so unusual. But a sensitive observer will be able to adapt himself quickly to the approach of supermundane vibrations and respond to them. Thus is developed true cooperation.

Remember that people are always surrounded by supermundane influences, but usually cannot discern them. Therefore, communion with the Supermundane World must be intensively practiced from an early age, and it should be done joyously, as a beautiful labor.

The Thinker instructed, "Be vigilant, so that at any moment you can perceive the Supermundane Signs."

787. Urusvati knows that one should be able to distinguish between innate human qualities, that is, those already acquired in past lives, and the qualities developed in the present life.

Let us analyze some qualities. First of all, let us pay attention to the inborn ability to feel gratitude. This is not developed easily and requires many tests, earthly as well as supermundane. But if we meet someone who has developed this ability, we can be sure that we will find in him many other positive traits. Such a person is grateful not only for the good bestowed on him, but also for all that is given for the General Good.

It is essential that this good quality be born in the consciousness without any outside forcing. It is one thing when a small child offers thanks because his elders demand it, but it is better if in his consciousness the bright star of gratitude begins to shine. Such gratitude will be beneficial not only for the one who receives it but also for the one who sends it.

Thus let us keenly distinguish all qualities that build bridges to the Supermundane World. An ardent gratitude for all the good, for all the small, for all the great, does not become extinguished, but participates in the weaving of spiritual wings.

The Thinker said, "We shall rejoice when we perceive the quality of gratitude."

788. Urusvati knows the value of the inborn qualities of broad-mindedness and tolerance. These must be stressed especially, for people do not ordinarily think about them. They may complain about intolerance and even see it as a sign of savagery, but at the same time do not want to think about ways to develop tolerance.

Man does not want to examine the foundations upon which tolerance and open-mindedness grow, yet these qualities are akin to compassion. They teach one to look attentively into the consciousness of one's neighbor to understand the causes of his mistakes.

People should be taught, and their moral qualities awakened, but this task is impossible without looking at each person individually. Every one errs in his own way, and the reasons for his errors may be deeply embedded. It is impossible to judge a crowd by its shouting and wailing. Everyone has his own pain and is in need of individual treatment.

People must not forget about broad-mindedness and tolerance, for these bridges will be needed in the Supermundane World. The Supermundane World is needed in each human action. We do not speak about abstract morality, but about the actual building of life. The realization of the Supermundane World must be applied to every action. Only thus can one become a co-worker of the Supermundane World and properly prepare oneself for life.

The Thinker said, "Learn tolerance and it will teach you great patience."

789. Urusvati knows how carefully one must protect the great innate quality of inspiration. We have already mentioned it, but one should turn special attention to this link with the Supermundane World. The very word "inspiration" points to some kind of external guidance. Do not think that such a link can be created instantaneously; it requires many tests over many lives.

People restrict this trait to the realms of science and art for no reason. Man can be a creator in any field. High quality in any kind of labor is in itself an inspiration. Thus, any perfected labor can be welcomed as true creativity.

Precisely at present, during this time of mass development, it is appropriate to mention the close link with the higher energies. An intense dedication to self-improvement will prompt people to understand the nature of inspiration. Pointing out the higher energies is not hypocrisy. People already know about the saturation of space and about infinity, and for them inspiration is a scientific concept.

It has been related that a certain master, whenever he completed a creation, closed his eyes and remained in full silence. Finally, his disciples asked him whether he was resting after his labors or was planning a new work. The master replied, "Neither one nor the other, for in this silence I do not think. But do not call it thoughtlessness, it is beyond thinking. I must find new sight, so as to perceive my work in a new way."

You should also learn to become renewed, to assess more deeply the quality of your labor. Let a fluttering wing from space touch you and bring you new sight and new achievement.

The Thinker ordained, "He who can be renewed from space remains young."

790. Urusvati knows the essence of man's happiness. When his life and work are in harmony with the flow of world evolution, man has no need to reject anything. He is steadfast in his path, perfects himself, and finds new strength for the overcoming of chaos.

Someone will say, "But blessed are the obstacles, so why should a happy man avoid difficulties?" We must not forget that he who walks in harmony with evolution meets with many obstacles, but his attitude toward them is different. He does not fall into despair, but joyously overcomes the waves of chaos. Let us not think that the path of happiness is easy, it can be more difficult than a life of stagnation.

But for a co-worker of evolution there cannot be any loss of strength, for the universal energy will bless him with rejuvenation. He will appear, as the ancients used to say, as an anointed one, for the Supermundane World truly sends universal energy to help the co-worker of evolution.

Every seven years man should examine his activity by comparing it with world events. One can rejoice if one's path is shown to be true and straight. But great envy will follow such a happy traveler. The cunning and the bigoted do not forgive success, but a co-worker of evolution understands the inevitable intrigues woven by the ignorant. He knows that ignorance does not follow the path of evolution. Yet, ignorance senses that its path is crooked and unfit.

The Thinker taught that people should learn how to examine and assess their path.

791. Urusvati knows that fanaticism is a very dangerous psychic condition. A fanatic deprives himself of flexibility. He cannot perfect himself or succeed. A fanatic is as if dead. Fanaticism can be contagious, for weak people fear any kind of advancement; their dark existence rests upon a foundation of dogma.

Regrettably, fanaticism tends to form around any teaching and does not permit the deepening of its foundations. Let us not enumerate the Great Teachings that have suffered because of the savagery of fanaticism. History offers many such dark examples.

But how does one battle fanaticism? It should be understood that any dispute with fanatics will only increase their stubbornness, because they believe that it is precisely they who are the true guardians of the pure teaching. A fanatic responds angrily to any challenging question. A fanatic can only grow more stubborn, and insists that the teaching that he adheres to cannot change. He does not acknowledge that learning is a living process. There can be no stagnation in Eternity; all is in motion—in the striving toward perfection.

Remember that it is impossible to dispute with a corpse. Let the corpse's putrefaction be a transformation into a new existence. Thus, do not dispute with fanatics, pass by the putrescent, and hasten toward victorious knowledge.

The increase in the number of fanatics can be stopped by a manifestation on a cosmic scale. Whether such a shock would occur in the earthly or Supermundane World is of no importance, but in any case, fanaticism is unfit for the Supermundane World.

The Thinker said, "Fanatic, how will you cross the boundary into the Supermundane?"

792. Urusvati knows the harmfulness of the worm of discontent: withering, drying, fading, dying are its products. The foolish ones will say, "But how can one fault discontent if restlessness is ordained?" Answer, "Is it possible that you cannot discern between discontent and the thirst for perfection? Joy is born out of striving for perfection and sorrow out of pitiful discontent."

Many perish in the abyss of senseless discontent. They cut off their paths, both earthly and supermundane. One should rejoice at the fact of being human. This teaches one that under any conditions one can participate in the Great Motion. Just by thinking actively, one is already moving forward on the path. Self-denial leaves no room for discontent. Each light-bearing striving for perfection will already be a victory.

People should realize that the supermundane path cannot be one of discontent. Thorns turn to roses when the wayfarer learns to love the beautiful horizon. Striving to the Supermundane World is forbidden to no one who senses how beautiful it is for those who were able to turn to it. Let passionate joy accompany those who have discovered the path of progress.

The Thinker pointed out that joy is ordained for a happy seeker, but man himself must learn to love the quest.

793. Urusvati knows that some unthinking people complain about the repetitions they find in the Teaching. These complaints are not valid, and only prove that the readers are lightminded. They do not take the trouble to compare these apparent repetitions. Only by an exact comparison will they learn that these are not repetitions, but the development of an idea. Of course, some people need repeated instruction, but in such instances, the instruction should be given in a deeper way, not just by saying the same words again.

We are not afraid of repetition, for the spiral of ascent inevitably passes over former affirmations. True, during the turns of the spiral, the expressed thought is given new, expanded form. Those who criticize stubbornly will always find things to object to, but it is of no importance, for theirs is a personal illusion. The Teaching has in mind all of humanity.

It is necessary to repeat often about the Supermundane World. The entrances into it are hidden from the majority of people. They should be reminded that without the Supermundane World their future can only be a dead end. People who cannot think clearly can only proceed by firm instruction.

The Thinker affirmed that one should not fear to speak often about the Supermundane Paths.

794. Urusvati knows that unlimited divisibility does not contradict the power of attraction to fundamental Unity. Science affirms this, and one can observe it most clearly in the realm of psychic energy.

People should not fear divisibility in life. Often it is precisely what facilitates the manifestation of Unity. People do not admit that dark forces can unconsciously assist Unity, but the clash of the forces can strike an especially powerful spark. It is of no importance whether the hammer that produces the spark is dark or light, but the stronger the blow, the more powerful and curative is the spark.

Divisibility grows particularly during the days of Armageddon. But Unity also grows. The world is striving to the Unity of Cooperation. The world understands how inexorably the new common understanding is approaching. The New World sweeps away the rotten roots. Thus every Teaching must listen for the steps of the New World. Let vigilance manifest itself everywhere, and people will understand what has evolved amidst battles and sufferings.

The Thinker said, "Learn to perceive the veil that is the Great Unity."

795. Urusvati knows that the main cause of discord lies in the individuality of consciousnesses. There are no two grains of sand alike, there are no consciousnesses alike. Such richness of nature could have accelerated evolution, but out of it much evil has been born. It should be remembered that such evil is harmful, not only in the earthly life, but also in the Supermundane World.

Each person can assist in the lessening of evil. For this one must firmly remember about the individuality of consciousnesses, and must not coerce the consciousness of one's fellow man. He can increase friendship and cooperation, but only if he allows for differences of consciousness. Out of such understanding is compassion born. A wise man will show compassion to his neighbor in a way that will not be seen as condescending.

Discord can be smoothed in many small ways. One should not mistake a sensible exchange of opinions as discord. He who sows with kindness will reap more abundantly. We care not only about the earthly life, but even more about the supermundane existence. People must at last recognize that each one is striving toward the Supermundane World and paves his own most suitable path to it.

The Thinker advised, "Help your fellow man to be able to turn in a better and more beautiful way to the Supermundane World."

796. Urusvati knows that an expanded consciousness brings into harmony all surrounding consciousnesses, and even has its influence upon the atmosphere. Thus a kind of magnet is formed that attracts and transforms the surroundings. This condition of broadened consciousness is important not only for Earth, but also for the Supermundane World. True, the expansion of consciousness is not obtained easily. Also, many people confuse the expansion of consciousness with rote learning. They deny the possibility of the influence of psychic energy; material science, for them, is all that is destined for mankind. They cannot understand that science without psychic energy is devoid of life. How can the complex process of broadening the consciousness begin if people close the gates to higher knowledge?

Man must declare to himself, "I want to broaden my consciousness!" Only a free will can create a powerful magnet. "I want and I can." Thus will man open the first gates to the transformation of the World. But the passionate wish must be tempered with patience, for many processes take time. Such a task can be accomplished only by one who has dedicated himself to the service of humanity.

The Thinker affirmed, "Learn to want this. Become citizens of the Supermundane World!"

797. Urusvati knows about the continuity of life. Some may ask, "Why keep repeating about this well-known fact?" But this has been forgotten and rejected by the majority of people on Earth. They believe the absurdity that the passing away from Earth is a cessation of existence. Others think of sleep as an interruption of consciousness. And the vast majority cannot even imagine the river of life, and this is why it is essential to remind them about life's continuity. One can speak about different kinds of life, but the thread of life is unbreakable.

One cannot talk about ethical law if cause and effect are not accepted as a continuous thread. People cannot perfect themselves if they do not realize that they are responsible for their free will. Especially at present, during the raging of Armageddon, it is necessary to help people not only in the earthly life, but also in the Supermundane.

Notice how lightmindedly people regard their supermundane existence. People still believe that the earthly life is the important one, forgetting that it is a brief step in a continuous journey. People, even if only in a primitive way, must ask themselves, "Is this life worthwhile if nothing exists beyond it?" At the same time, people speak about perpetual motion, but this concept of continuity does not lead them to think about the continuity of their own existence. One must repeat this, one must urgently repeat this, otherwise the New World will be just like the old one, decrepit and outworn.

The Thinker warned, "New builders, do not fall into outmoded thinking."

798. Urusvati knows about the deep significance of ancient vows of silence. It can be understood scientifically that in this way people tried to attain concentration of thought, and thus prepare themselves for the supermundane state. Indeed, it must be agreed that every effort toward the deepening of thought is useful, but let us not forget that no forcing of nature is needed for the development of the consciousness.

Man can train his thinking without forcing himself. But also, man is given speech; why should he deprive himself of communication with his surroundings? At present, mentally, without speech, only a limited expression is possible. Man can remove one hand in order to increase the abilities of the other, but is such a forced limitation sensible? Healthy thinking requires a balanced use of all organs. But man must, with all his abilities, strive toward the Beautiful.

Let us regard with respect those in antiquity who took vows of silence. They acted out of desire for self-perfectment, but evolution demands a much broader application of man's forces. Let him actually apply all his abilities, let him live in a continuous state of gaining knowledge. Such intelligent, valiant learning will bestow a real joy of labor.

Knowledge is an inalienable right of humanity. Freedom of learning is participation in evolution. Everyone who opposes freedom of learning is an enemy of evolution. It must be understood to what extent the treasure of knowledge is necessary for the Supermundane World. As an inextinguishable light, it leads the wayfarers on their supermundane path.

The Thinker affirmed, "Let each earthly conquest be an entrance into the Supermundane World."

799. Urusvati knows that the overcoming of an obstacle is a success. The purer the motive, the higher the attainment—this briefly-stated principle is as fitting for the earthly path as for the supermundane one. Unfortunately, people resist the idea that life is a struggle. They are afraid to think about unending struggle. They do not realize that all the worlds are on trial. After reading this affirmation, they will sink into fear.

Each morning man is filled with fear for the future, instead of joy. Man takes that same fear with him into the Supermundane World; such a state impedes self-perfectment. In the Supermundane World, too, man must continue his courageous struggle, for without it he will not find the way to the Higher Ones.

Many obstacles will be encountered in the search for perfection, and the surmounting of these obstacles will be a true perfectment. One's forces are renewed only in struggle. Psychic energy itself is increased on this clear path. It is erroneous to think that the treasure of psychic energy is inalienable; it is in constant ascent or descent. Only the valiant seeker can avoid the sad descent. This counsel must be especially remembered when Armageddon is on the increase.

The Thinker said, "Overcome, and ascend!"

800. Urusvati knows that indifference is like stagnant water; stars cannot be reflected in it, and travelers are careful not to stop near it. Many such comparisons can be made. This deadening indifference is not only harmful for man in earthly life, but even more so in the Supermundane World. With it, one cannot perfect oneself and inevitably sinks into ignorance.

Do not confuse indifference with calmness. Calmness is light-bearing dawn, but indifference is darkness without a glimmer of light. Calmness is a smile of joy, but indifference is a crooked smirk. People often attempt to hide their ignorance under a mask of indifference, but such an ally is dangerous, more infectious than the most deadly disease.

Death does not exist for the enlightened spirit, but indifference is a mark of death, and may cause one to fall into a deep sleep in the Supermundane World. Such a one's heart will not awaken for the luminous flights, and nothing will rouse him from his leaden sleep. The flow of karma becomes sluggish, and a torturous struggle confronts the one who lost his way.

Man should rid himself of indifference. Let him realize his true goal. Let the traveler strive vigilantly and actively into Infinity.

The Thinker said, "Even the animals are not indifferent."

801. Urusvati knows that from time immemorial all the higher Teachers warned about the harm of lightminded criticism. Even so, the majority of humanity is still predisposed to this flaw. In failing to distinguish between a well-founded, just judgment and critical gossiping, people do not realize what irreparable harm they inflict on their neighbors, and on themselves.

People may agree that slander is criminal, but not recognize that they, too, sometimes slander and not even realize the cosmic harm they cause. We speak here not only about physical harm, but also about supermundane harm. You can imagine how the evil of lightminded criticism acts in the Supermundane World, if this viper takes possession of the thinking of just one individual there, where all live by thought and are especially sensitive to mental shocks. A slanderer on Earth spreads harm among a limited number of people, but a supermundane slanderer strikes the multitudes.

It should not be thought that slander sown can easily be uprooted. Regrettably, these poisons have a long life and leave indelible traces in Cosmos. Therefore people should think about the responsibility they bear for their judgments. Proper instruction should contain warnings about ineradicable harm.

The Thinker warned not to dirty the path with lightminded criticism.

802. Urusvati knows that some will argue, "Why mention in a new teaching an old, incurable failing of humanity? Many words have already been spoken, warning about the harm of slander, yet this vice does not decrease, but is spreading widely. Humanity cannot be swayed by words alone." Reply, "When offering a farewell to the traveler, it is necessary to consider his entire load. He should be reminded to take even the most ordinary things, if they will be needed on the journey. But the danger of slander must be pointed out with particular emphasis."

Let us examine why this is so. Although slander is known to be a vice in earthly life, it has an even greater impact in the Supermundane World. But people neglect this study. They think lightmindedly that the Supermundane World is not manifested here on Earth. But every thoughtful investigator knows the many signs of subtle existence that are scattered throughout everyday life. Also, many ignorant people do not want to accept the idea that the supermundane life exists by thought. How can a slanderer survive if his true thoughts become known? His own emanations will herald his slanderous nature even from a great distance. We care not only about the earthly life, but also about the Supermundane.

The Thinker said, "Beware of unfit cargo on a long journey."

803. Urusvati knows that the ancient Thinkers called their earthly life a duel with chaos. A lone, valiant warrior dons his heavy armor and sets out in search of the dragon of chaos. The warrior knows that the dragon lies in wait on all paths, but always in a different disguise. The warrior must draw on all his abilities to recognize the dragon of chaos. But sometimes the warrior falls into idleness and wanders aimlessly, unable to fulfill his destined *podvig*.

It will be asked, "Why did the warrior have to leave the Supermundane Fortress? Couldn't he strike the enemy from its walls, didn't he have a spear and arrows? Weren't there dragons' nests near the Fortress?" But the fact is that the warrior had to seek out the most hidden monsters, in the most distant mountain passes. The more difficult the achievement, the more luminous will it be, and the more victorious the warrior on his return to the Stronghold.

Man should remember that his true Stronghold is not on Earth, and that all his earthly labors should be performed for return to the Supermundane Stronghold. Let him also understand that the quality of his labor must be high; only in quality is labor blessed. Thus can different workers meet and recognize each other by the high quality of their earthly labor.

The Thinker said, "Learn to think about the lofty quality of Be-ness."

804. Urusvati knows that in the Supermundane World thought stands for word; thought is communication and creativeness, and forward motion. Many people believe that it is not necessary to think at all about the Supermundane World, and that one's earthly life is the only purpose of existence. Thus does man fall into harmful error.

One should not think only about the earthly life, nor should one strive only to the Supermundane World. Goalfitness must be preserved in everything; only thus will man learn to create in the earthly life and also find time for striving to the Supermundane World. We live for the future, which is only in the Supermundane World. One's earthly lives are small in comparison with one's supermundane existences.

Picture a man who has entered the Supermundane World and knows only how to communicate by speech; he will find himself in a deplorable situation. He will not easily learn thought-transmission. At first he will, like a mute, repeat words silently to himself. But if those words are not accompanied by clear thoughts, communication will not be possible. Only gradually will the traveler understand how to express thoughts without words, and thus learn to receive thought-transmissions from his new neighbors, and from his instructor.

But why should one wait until one is in the Subtle World to learn the art of thinking, when one can prepare oneself for this advance while in the earthly life? Everyone, under any conditions, can perform his own experiments in mental discourse, and perhaps an answer will come to him.

The Thinker said, "Remember that words are thoughts."

805. Urusvati knows about instantaneous illumination, which is manifested as highest inspiration and insight. Remember that such a psychic state is very rare, for many earthly and supermundane conditions are needed for it. One can yearn for such illumination, but it cannot be forced.

When supermundane conditions are in accord with one's earthly state, the wondrous "Lotus" of illumination can unexpectedly bloom. Man cannot foresee this moment. Often the illumination is ignited unexpectedly, and may even seem out of place, at least according to human understanding. Illumination may be a rare guest, but it is not forbidden to await its visit.

One can begin with brief psychic concentration. Do not think that such efforts are of no use, for precisely in this untiring way can many discoveries be made. Unwise people may often complain that their efforts are fruitless, but where is the scale on which psychic gains can be measured? It is easier to perceive the growth of grass with the naked eye than to observe psychic growth.

Beginners should be reminded that their efforts at concentration will not be in vain. Thus can one prepare for the Supermundane World, where illuminations occur frequently if one has already acquired the habit of thinking about them. Thus everyone can, in all conditions, industriously make his way past the milestones to the future.

The Thinker said, "Do not forcibly pry open the petals of the "Lotus," which will blossom at the destined time."

806. Urusvati knows fiery equilibrium. Much has been said about co-measurement and equilibrium, but such concepts are not utilized because their main foundation has not been understood. Even experienced researchers mistake indifference for equilibrium. Everyone knows that the nature of Be-ness is fiery, but how can one apply this in earthly life? Truly, one can attain fiery equilibrium by living consciously in the earthly and supermundane life.

But one should not think that one need only immerse oneself in the Supermundane World to achieve equilibrium. On the contrary, one should actively apply all one's forces to the earthly existence, but with the understanding that this effort is needed for supermundane achievement. It would seem that this is not difficult to realize, but it is rarely achieved. Too often one tends to live in abstraction or becomes lost in the daily routine.

Do not think that equilibrium is easily achieved. It must be cultivated from one's earliest years, and for this popular books about the Supermundane World are needed. Data about the supermundane life should be collected from the literature of different faiths. Observations from contemporary life must be added to this, for only thus can one correlate the ancient legends with contemporary life.

It is a common mistake for ignorant people to insist

that contemporary life is devoid of psychic manifestations. It can be demonstrated that such occurrences are indeed frequent, but crude ignorance does not notice them. The word "equilibrium" in itself implies all-embracingness.

The Thinker affirmed, "Fiery is our nature. Let us be able to kindle our own sacred fire."

807. Urusvati knows how important great patience is. It is thought that this bulwark of human achievement is based upon knowledge, but the special quality called tolerance is needed even more; therefore one may say that patience is tolerance. This treasured quality must be cultivated.

Tolerance is especially needed in the Supermundane World, for without this quality man builds a pitiable existence for himself. He will reject all whom he meets, for in each one he will find some trait unpleasant to him. Because of this fault he will not be able to notice the most valuable accumulations. Therefore, broad tolerance must be taught to children, even in their earliest years.

They must learn to discern the most valued qualities in others, and not exaggerate unpleasant faults, especially since so many seeming faults appear to be faults only at the time. When their consciousness grows, they will feel ashamed of their intolerance.

Useful books can be written about the harm of intolerance. Many historic examples could be cited in which so-called prestigious authorities failed to recognize the most useful discoveries of their time, and how such narrow-minded leaders became the laughing-stock of future generations. To learn not to reject is a step on the path to great patience.

The Thinker advised His disciples to develop tolerance as the means of broadening consciousness.

808. Urusvati knows the vitality of thought. Thought rushes forward faster than light. It is purified by the spatial fire and, finally, reveals its essence. A good thought, a beautiful thought, appears even more beautiful in the fiery furnace. An evil thought, a harmful thought, manifests itself in even deeper evil. These very different magnets are borne in space and influence the surrounding atmosphere.

Who benefits from a good thought? Who is affected by an evil thought? First of all, the sender himself. Not only in the earthly life, but especially in the Supermundane World, the blows of harm-bearing thoughts fall heavily on the subtle body. Evil thoughts are heavy weights, impeding advance, and the sender of such thoughts does not recognize his own role in generating them. He lightmindedly forgets his poisonous sendings, but they do not forget him. They are drawn to him and will find him anywhere in supermundane space. Similarly, good messages soar and will weave radiant wings for a beautiful flight.

These processes can be explained scientifically, for the energy of thought is subject to scientific investigation. One should accumulate good thoughts; only they will make possible an easy ascent into the Heights. Do not think that evil can easily be burned away. The resultant fiery mark cannot be removed for a long time. Thus remember about your own helpers and harmers in the Supermundane World.

The Thinker said, "World, do not make yourselves ill with hatred."

809. Urusvati knows the healing quality of Great Compassion. People usually suppose that only the Higher Beings possess this quality. But people, in their daily lives, often come in contact with the realm of Compassion.

Truly, mercy, peacefulness, sympathy, kindness, solicitude toward people, are manifestations of various aspects of compassion. Love itself is close to compassion. Is not cooperation kin to compassion? All these good qualities have healing properties.

Psychic energy, sent with good intentions, exerts a healing action. Science should reveal how good intentions heal the nervous system. And let us not forget that he who offers compassion receives beneficial effects in the boomerang-like return of the dispatched energy.

Also, one should keep in mind that such mutual influences are especially evident in the Supermundane World. The dwellers of the Subtle World have no need for verbal expressions of feeling. The feeling itself, quicker than light, reaches the sufferer; and there are not a few sufferers in the Supermundane World who are in need of encouragement. These wandering dwellers did not wish, during their earthly lives, to hear about any future existence. They wander naked and do not even know how to cover themselves. There are many such misfortunes that were caused by ignorance. What a vast field of action is opened before everyone who knows the conditions of the supermundane life! And the compassionate one acquires doubled strength, due to his good feelings.

The Thinker used to say, "Let us reap a crop of goodness."

810. Urusvati knows the joy of achievement. This joy is luminous, but even more luminous is spiritual joy. There is no precise term for the essence of spiritual joy, but it would be the most appropriate to call it fiery joy. With the help of spiritual joy, we can sense the fieriness of all of nature. This understanding will most easily elevate us to the Supermundane World.

Understand the beneficence of fiery joy. It expands the consciousness, and draws all the best accumulations toward itself, as a fiery magnet. The essence of man is transformed and his outworn nature is burned away. It is essential to understand to what extent such regeneration is needed not only in the Supermundane World, but also in earthly life. Then, one would experience exaltation in even the most ordinary surroundings.

Urusvati could be asked how she attained this exaltation. How did the wave of fiery joy fill her spirit and open communion with the Highest Worlds? Urusvati can attest that despondency and irritation are impediments. It is not easy amidst earthly agitations to avoid these companions, but spiritual rapture burns them away.

Anger or irritation must not be thought of as fiery tension. All obstacles fall before fiery exaltation. Everyone can join the Light, but for this there must first of all be a desire for Light.

The Thinker constantly exhorted the disciples, "Let us be joyous, let us be light-bearing."

811. Urusvati knows the "Fiery Lotus." In ancient manuscripts can be found the description of man as a flowering garden; this image has a scientific basis. Actually, when the centers of man radiate they are like varied, wonderful flowers. One heart alone is like a whole flower-bed, because the many centers glow with different colors. But one should not think that such festive luminosity is frequently possible.

Usually, people pay attention to only certain "main" centers, but it is not right to call them the main ones. Man can radiate through many other centers that are no less important. Man's emanations consist of a combination of different radiations, which produce a complex, but blended tone.

Do not think that if the entire garden is not aglow something is wrong. Certain heart centers are ignited only when in communion with the Supermundane World. These centers are called pilgrims into the Supermundane World. It should be understood that the brain centers do not glow all at once. On the contrary, normal thinking utilizes only certain groups of centers, and it would not be good for all the centers to flash out at once. Only during a high state of ecstasy can a harmonious radiation of all the centers be noticed. But such a tension cannot be achieved often, otherwise the physical body would burn up.

The Thinker said, "Treasure man as a divine garden."

812. Urusvati knows that everything that exists is fiery. Eventually, when studying the human nervous system, science will notice the emanations, and will confirm the fiery principle that permeates all.

Much is spoken about auras, but their origins and effects are not understood. In the future, science will understand why radiations are sometimes called the banner of man. But in order to understand this image, the conditions of the Supermundane World must be known. When in the Supermundane World, man carries his banner; he cannot hide its light, and it is no wonder that he then may be either a powerful magnet or an object of loathing. While in the earthly life, man creates indelible effects in the Supermundane. Thus, all the sooner should people think about the quality of their radiations. Each act of good improves one's radiations. People can help themselves by helping their neighbor.

Urusvati knows that the Yoga of today—the link with the Highest—must be accomplished amidst the routine of everyday life. Not hiding from life, but transforming it is required. The fiery essence of the heart is its magnet. Precisely, the heart can open the entrance into Higher Worlds. No special asceticism is needed. Love, labor, and beauty are within the reach of all, under any conditions. Life must be affirmed upon these foundations. Children must be taught that they are the creators of their own happiness. Proper upbringing must precede formal education. Subtle energies are like a wondrous, many-stringed harp.

The Thinker said, "Fiery Banner, illumine the Higher Path!"

813. Urusvati knows the beauty of the Supermundane World. Some may ask, "What if some strata of the Supermundane World are made ugly by the ignorance of their dwellers? Not every newcomer will be able to go beyond these dark strata."

Answer, "Everyone, if not burdened by offences against morality, can fly through the darkened strata and reach the sphere of Harmony."

People are given powerful wings called the will; but it must not be thought that the will can be formed by oneself, forcibly. It must be cultivated, as a precious flower. And man does not know when the "Fiery Lotus" will blossom. Sometimes the lowest, everyday conditions will not be an impediment to a wonderful flowering; thus, man can prepare himself for a most important flight. He will be able to pass by the darkened strata, almost without noticing the ugliness of ignorance. Man is able to ascend to wherever the guiding magnet attracts him.

In ancient initiations the disciple had to pass through a chamber filled with most frightful images. The disciple had to proceed with open eyes, but it was up to him not to notice the surrounding horrors. This test of will preceded entrance into the Chamber of Beauty. Similar tests take place at the entrance to the Supermundane World. The traveler must strengthen his will and learn to focus his thinking toward the final consummation.

The Thinker said, "Be able to fly above all barriers."

814. Urusvati knows the divisibility of psychic energy. One lone fire can kindle a multitude of torches without being exhausted. Similarly, transmissions of psychic energy can reach many hearts. In this must be understood one remarkable factor that is rarely noted. Transmissions in their essence reach their destination unchanged, but the details and means of expression can differ, depending upon the individuality of the recipient. That is why there are sometimes misunderstandings about seeming inconsistencies.

But a diligent researcher could compare a series of psychic transmissions and see for himself that their essence is unalterable, but that the forms of expression can vary. This proves the fiery nature of psychic energy. It evokes from the consciousness of the recipient ways of expression most natural for him. Thus is attested the wise fiery basis of primary energy.

During psychic transmissions one should keep in mind that they may contact unexpected recipients, desirable and undesirable. This prompts one to be cautious. An experienced researcher knows how to restrain his thinking, if it could in any way be harmful.

The exchange of psychic energy is widespread in the earthly, as well as the Supermundane World. Often people think so weakly that instead of clear transmission there is only a poisonous murkiness.

The Thinker said, "Let us send clear and pure thoughts. They will not cause harm on their way."

815. Urusvati knows the ancient teachings about

an easy karma. Man, during his many earthly wanderings, accumulates a heavy load of causes that lead to inevitable consequences. It must not be thought that a burdensome karma is the product only of horrible crimes. It is formed gradually, out of actions of laziness, coarseness, ingratitude, and many aspects of ignorance, but for all this one must pay, and this payment is unavoidable.

Yet the Teaching speaks about easy karma—what does that mean? A free, good will can alleviate the severity of a burdensome karma. But for this, man, in his earthly life, must acknowledge that a long tail of not yet outlived negative acts may be dragging behind him. Man can, thanks to this understanding, patiently endure his misfortunes, and with his own free will and good actions can even lessen them. Thus is molded an easy karma.

Thus, where the ignorant must pay dearly, the expanded consciousness can help to find easier ways. Man, by broadening his consciousness, helps himself to ease his path.

The teaching about easy karma relates to both the earthly life and the Supermundane. In the Subtle World man learns what he is atoning for, and may be astonished that his strong actions are not valued according to his expectations. His small actions are sometimes valued more highly. Man's heart can help him to distinguish.

The Thinker said, "It is our fortune that we are given the opportunity to help determine the payment for our labors."

816. Urusvati knows the power of a deep breath. We have pointed out the benefit of correct breathing before, and much research has been devoted to the subject, but in this book, "Supermundane," one significant fact should be pointed out. In various fields of work, when feeling fatigued, people will interrupt their work or speech by taking a deep breath and thereby receive an influx of new energy. In most cases, they do this out of intuition, without giving thought to the process. How greatly would the power of this process be increased if it were performed consciously!

Remember that this rejuvenating breath is supermundane, for by it man summons Higher Forces. He should understand that for greater effect, he should consciously turn to the Supermundane World and affirm his inner link with the Reservoir of Be-ness.

Some workers, when pausing to take a deep breath, close their eyes. Their intuition is correct, for closing the eyes increases their concentration. We have already said that illumination can be instantaneous. Thus is performed a short pranayama, with the difference that it takes place in view of others. It is in no way lessened because of those present.

Note also that a supermundane breath is single, without repetition. This is significant, for only in a lone breath can be summoned the full power of energy. With rapid repetition, shortness of breath can occur, which harms the work.

The Thinker advised, "Understand the power of a supermundane breath."

817. Urusvati knows the power of the fiery eye. This manifestation of energy may be called magnetism, hypnotism, mesmerism, or, as in antiquity, enchantment or sacred sleep; yet fundamentally it is a fiery manifestation of the primary energy given to everyone, though in different degrees.

But why can some people make use of it easily, while others insist that they are completely deprived of it? With such a declaration, they stifle their own sacred gift. They assume that the eye is given only to see with, and forget that each glance is a transmission of energy. They do not want to understand that the fiery power flares up only when its reality is consciously accepted.

Some people seek the higher link by continually uttering a mantra, at first orally, then mentally. Yet they forget that the most powerful link is through the fire of the heart, an illumination that needs no words or thoughts. It lives in the fiery heart, and nothing can break this sacred bond.

This reality lies at the core of Truth, and one can through one's own efforts develop this power beyond description. For such a one each glance is a transmission and an act of good will. Learning this in a natural way takes time, but each psychic achievement is indefeasible, in the earthly as well as in the Supermundane World.

A refined consciousness expands through its own efforts, and one learns that it is possible to see with eyes open, and also closed. Fiery transmissions have no barriers. Indeed, man can consciously intensify his glance or can weaken it, depending upon the effect desired. Thus every person carries a fiery treasure. It is to be hoped that science will undertake the study of psychic energy.

The Thinker said, "Not the words, not the thoughts, but the fire of the heart will illumine the way of the traveler."

818. Urusvati knows the power of patience. Many cherished human qualities lose their meaning because they are without any realization of the Supermundane World. Imagine a person who, out of ignorance, denies the great Supermundane Reality. What kind of patience can he have, and to what purpose? What kind of devotion can he feel, and for whom or what?

What kind of co-measurement can he know, and with what? What kind of tolerance can he have, and for what? What kind of joy, and about what? What kind of refinement? What kind of discrimination? What kind of self-perfectment, if his horizons are closed? Thus one can think of all the best qualities and see how they will be diminished by being bound to the earthly.

People dream about communication with far-off planets, but forget that they have been given the possibility to communicate with the Supermundane World. Everyone can enhance his ability to learn about the Supermundane World. Everyone, without turning from his earthly labors, can come into contact with the supermundane creativity.

We must insistently advise scientists to turn to the study of the Supermundane World. A researcher can, to various degrees, glimpse his own psychic communications with the Supermundane Spheres.

It may be correct to call the dwellers of the Supermundane Spheres not spirits, but simply inhabitants. In such a way, materialistic science will more easily be reconciled to the idea of studying the Supermundane Spheres. The results of such studies are urgently needed now, when Armageddon penetrates all spheres, and unusual manifestations exist everywhere.

The Thinker asserted, "When the foundation rock is firm the tower will be stable."

819. Urusvati knows the power of the heart. In remote antiquity people understood both the physical and the spiritual power of the heart. The strongest prayers rose from the heart, but in later times the spiritual significance of the heart was minimized and the heart came to be seen as just a physical organ. And soon the attention of people was drawn to the brain, and the heart was thought of as a secondary organ.

People forgot that the heart is the sower, and the brain is the tiller and the reaper. No one would expect a harvest from an unsown field. The heart cannot produce supermundane seeds if the consciousness has lost its understanding of the Supermundane World. It can be understood that the highest degree of power will not be manifested if man does not evoke it consciously.

An understanding of the importance of the heart must develop in the immediate future. The brain should be studied, and its relationship to all aspects of the heart's activity. We do not limit the study of the heart to the point of view of psychic energy. Science should use many approaches, and then a broad understanding will be achieved. Indeed, all brain activity, the entire nervous system, and all secretions of the glands will be studied as channels from the one source, the heart.

Nothing should be demeaned, yet man must remember where lies the center of his being. Let us not disregard the scientific achievements of different nations, ancient as well as modern. Old attainments must not be treated with contempt, because in them can be found glimmers of truth.

The Thinker said, "The heart is a sage; the heart is a prophet; the heart is a supermundane messenger."

820. Urusvati knows the power of equilibrium. In earlier times some people called equilibrium the Middle Path, Golden Path, Scale of Wisdom, Great Rhythm, Supermundane Breath. But ignorant people believed that equilibrium is nothing but indifference. Indeed, even the concept of Nirvana was subject to a variety of misinterpretations. People could not grasp that Nirvana is a state of high harmonious tension. The concept of equilibrium is equally misunderstood.

But it is precisely now that the world needs the Scale of Wisdom.

It must be recognized that violent hatred can capsize the ship of mankind. A wise Helmsman is needed, not only in the earthly world, but also in the Supermundane. But whence will come an understanding of equilibrium if the science of thinking is not studied in the schools? Children should learn to discern where equilibrium and also its sister, justice, are needed.

People mistakenly presume that justice is a relative concept, that everyone has his own justice and his own good. Such a misconception can cause irreparable harm. Justice and good are vaguely understood concepts, and one must look deeply into the essence of consciousness to sense the impregnable Foundations of Be-ness.

One can look into the depths of one's heart only when there is true equilibrium, which is not the same as calmness. Equilibrium bestows insight, and requires the intensification of all one's energies. Thus, let us not forget equilibrium as a true bridge to the Supermundane World.

The Thinker advised, "Weave the wings of equilibrium, then you will not fall into an abyss."

821. Urusvati knows the power of observation. Many times have We affirmed the importance of the broadening of consciousness. Some people think that this highest achievement is unattainable and supernatural, but they are mistaken. The expansion of consciousness is a natural tendency, just as everything is natural in the earthly and in the supermundane life.

Many simple achievements must be examined in order to discern which of them are useful in the broadening of our consciousness. If we look again at these modest helpers, we will find that the cultivation of observation is an important one. Keenness of observation must be cultivated.

Only a few people bring this ability with them from the Supermundane World. In the beginning it can be developed by observing the most ordinary conditions. It is wrong to assume that only the schoolteachers should develop the power of observation. The pupils themselves should understand the value of this ability, which opens all paths, earthly and supermundane.

A little child can see that an unobservant man is like a blind and deaf one. He cannot discern higher manifestations. He stagnates in a magic circle of prejudices. He cannot hasten his advancement and remains like a stagnant pool. Can such a person be a teacher? Can he discern the impressions of the Supermundane World? Can he see the wonderful manifestations of earthly nature? Only a diligent training of observation can transform the ordinary daily way of life.

"Help the blind to recover their sight," advised the Thinker.

822. Urusvati knows the power of vigilance. The deep significance of observation is now known to you. Yet, how can observation be developed without vigilance, without constant watchfulness? These qualities are not acquired at once, they must be cultivated. The more consciously such education proceeds, the sooner will one be able to maintain an untiring vigil. It should be stressed that no quality can be obtained by force. It is necessary to love—by one's own free will—the acquisition of the steps of ascent. Only such a loving conquest will lead one to the open Gates.

Those on the quest should remember that every effort of theirs on Earth is needed also in the Supermundane World. To be pitied is the traveler in the vast supermundane domains who is deprived of the ability to observe and is unskilled in vigilance. The best encounters pass him by. It should be known that in the Supermundane World no one will compel a traveler. He must sense those vibrations similar to his. He will not be lost amidst the varied rhythms, but will strive attentively toward what is closest to him. Thus, out of very simple earthly knowledge are formed supermundane treasures.

We care especially that people should not turn away from earthly purposes, but in every earthly detail recognize the presence of the higher treasure.

The Thinker said, "In each drop of dew is reflected the whole Universe."

823. Urusvati knows the power of joy. Each experience of joy in the good, even the most ordinary, heightens one's vibrations. Thus can be shown how a joyous person is made stronger.

Especially powerful is the joy based upon realization of the Supermundane World. It should be understood that this realization does not mean that one must constantly think and talk about the Supermundane World, but that one's consciousness should become so close to the supermundane consciousness that one's heart would not be able to live otherwise.

For inexperienced people, attempting to force the consciousness creates obstacles, for the consciousness cannot be compelled to embrace the Supermundane. Only gradually can communion with the Subtle World be developed in the consciousness.

A teacher must be able to inform the students, even the youngest, about the power of subtle energies. Let the teacher begin by any means to teach the young to connect with them. For one, astronomy may be the best way, for another cosmography. They should thus start their studies. All the sciences can lead to the

Highest. Only confused thinking can be an impediment to learning. Therefore learn to think; cognize the joy of thinking. Be able, amidst any existence, to strive to the ocean of joy.

The Thinker pointed out that joy in its power is equal to love.

824. Urusvati knows the power of stillness. It is said, "Stillness is stronger than thunder; stillness resounds more than a trumpet; stillness is a bridge to the Supermundane." What is this stillness that is spoken of?

For beginners, external stillness is needed; any sound, even the unimportant ones, can shock and cause pain. But for the one who knows, inner stillness is needed; his ear is open to the Supermundane World. He will abide in an inviolate stillness. But such an attainment does not descend all at once.

A spiritual ear must be open to more than earthly conditions. The aspirant masters the supermundane current and can use it at any time. Nothing can impede his communion with the higher rhythm.

The ignorant will not understand where lies the boundary between outer and inner stillness. They talk just as mistakenly about the great quality of calmness, which for them is like indifference and unconcern. But true calmness is gathered from the depths of inner stillness. It lives upon the trust based on knowledge. Nothing can destroy this stronghold of inner stillness and nothing will unsettle the calmness. Thus can some forever avoid doubt, the viper that will be crushed by the great calmness. Nothing can better arm the traveler to the Supermundane World than calmness. Only through it will be found kindness in all supermundane encounters.

The Thinker said, "Send me the wings of stillness."

825. Urusvati knows the power of victory. A victory should be kind, for then the fires of the heart are beautifully kindled. The less selfishness there is, the more luminous will be the fires.

It will be said, "Not everyone is destined to achieve a glorious victory." No, friends, everyone can gain a glorious victory. Victory is achieved not only upon battlefields. Everyone can overcome his bad habits and thus ignite the fires of the heart. Overcoming one's faults was called in antiquity the opening of the Supermundane Gates. Certainly, on supermundane paths, one's earthly habits can be particularly harmful. Even seemingly harmless habits can enslave one.

A free man is not chained by habits. He will know how to adapt himself to any conditions and will not regret the past, for he has overcome all obstacles and is free. Man himself accumulates petty habits and is not aware that he has become enslaved, precisely by the most petty habits and prejudices. Can one hasten into the Supermundane World with such fetters? Can one freely and in friendship greet new neighbors, when one is engulfed by yesterday's refuse? It must be conceded that the litter of one's life is composed of petty habits. A conqueror does not cling to the past, but freely strives towards new creative labor.

The Thinker said, "Come, victory, and liberate me from my rusty chains."

826. Urusvati knows the power of gratitude. We have already pointed out the great significance of the feeling of gratitude, but humanity does not understand the meaning of this moving force. Therefore, let us repeat about the benefit of gratitude.

It must be understood that it is not so much the one to whom gratitude is offered, but the one who offers it, who benefits. Beautiful fires of the heart are ignited when the feeling of gratitude is born; these fires shine not only in the earthly life, but also in the Supermundane World. Therefore the realization of gratitude stimulates the loftiest vibrations.

Humanity can be divided into the living and the dead, and those deprived of the feeling of gratitude will be as if buried alive. It is necessary to teach children that gratitude—not lip service, but a heartfelt expression—is beneficial. In this way are kindled powerful fires.

The manifestation of light is needed in the Supermundane World, and the ray of gratitude will illumine the way, together with the ray of love. Indeed, gratitude is close to love, and Cooperation is born in that blessed moment of offering. Man has many reasons to render gratitude, and the festival of the spirit will shine forth in the feeling of pure offering.

The Thinker said, "Teacher, teach me gratitude toward all, near and far, visible and invisible."

827. Urusvati knows the power of creative labor. We need not repeat about the value of physical creativeness; this has been sufficiently proved by the process of evolution, but people do not fully understand mental and spiritual creativity.

People will say, "It is not bestowed upon us to become creators." Yet, at the same time, they themselves, not noticing it, create beautifully, psychically, and such creativeness is necessary for their progress in the Supermundane World. Therefore, We affirm the art of the imagination, which facilitates progress in the highest realms.

However, dreaming should be benign, and should not be self-serving. It should not promote ugliness or cruelty.

Let one's imaginings be beautiful. Let them create

a better future for humanity. Let them create heroic images. Let them penetrate into higher, Supermundane Realms. Let them lead one to know the Higher Beings. Only Thus can one's efforts be fruitful. They will strengthen one's consciousness as a creator, and will produce precious vibrations for the Common Good.

Thus every thinking being can participate in the great universal creativeness, and the humblest co-worker can help create a rainbow bridge to the Supermundane World.

The Thinker affirmed, "Create in the heart and fill the World with beautiful harmonies."

828. Urusvati knows the power of a charitable nature—an ancient concept, misunderstood and badly interpreted. People say, "How can there be a desire to do good when man is enemy to man?"

It must not be forgotten how often We have condemned militant evil, and called for the defense of good. But one's free will must teach one to know the difference between defense and attack. People who have defended will understand when it can cease being benevolent.

First of all man should wish well to all of humanity. He should understand that destroyers will be pitiful exceptions, and that the essence of humanity is good. Only with such an awareness can one prepare oneself for the Supermundane World. Nowhere else will there be so many encounters as in the Supermundane World, and the armor of good will is the most reliable armor. But for this, one must prepare oneself, in the heart and in the mind.

One day soon, thoughts, both good and evil, will be photographed. Then physicians will be able to come to medical, scientific conclusions, and demonstrate which thoughts are more beneficial for the human organism.

People should think by the ways of true science. If the heart as yet cannot prompt where truth lies, then scientific deductions will help mankind to approach the Supermundane Ways. That which is predestined must be illumined by all fires.

The Thinker said, "Teacher, teach me to wish good to others."

829. Urusvati knows the power of victory over the past. People revere the historian who is an investigator of truth, and not a slave to preconceived ideas. But there are multitudes of such slaves who impede evolution. Even in ordinary life, the past is a cruel master.

One who is enslaved to the past cannot think about the future, and thus ceases his advancement. Such tragedies take place not only in earthly life; they are particularly terrible in the Supermundane World. There, the slaves to the past take on the burden of all their past existences. They feel oppressed under this load, for they cannot sort out for themselves the complexities of the past. No one taught them to calmly accept the past and apply it toward the future. They do not know that with a sensible attitude toward the past, they could even ease their karma.

But most earthly dwellers cannot deal properly with what happened yesterday or a week ago. Even the smallest past incident becomes for them a cruel persecution. It deadens their every striving toward the future.

Every mistake must be a bridge to new knowledge, not an obstacle. Every erroneous stumbling can be a stepping-stone to the future. There are many mistakes in life; they can all be turned into fiery good if they have not undermined one's courage.

Let us not wail and blame our fate, which is but a logical consequence of human deeds. In the schools, during classes in psychology, a true attitude toward the past should be taught.

The Thinker said, "Let victory over the past open the gates to the Future."

830. Urusvati knows the power of victory over fear. What is fear, this dark enslaver of humanity? The scientist says that fear is a spasm of vibrations caused by a disharmonious lack of understanding. Careful thought will show that fear is born of ignorance. Many definitions of fear could be cited. They all attest that fear weakens the will and thus renders one defenseless. But the most essential aspect is that man himself invites fear, by not understanding the Supermundane World.

Can one give in to terror, knowing about the Supermundane Law? The courageous researcher knows that the human essence is indestructible, and that the strongest paroxysm of vibrations can be overcome by the will. But the necessary tension must be developed. No one can be protected from fear if he does not wish to overcome it himself.

Man should always remember that disharmony can weaken him, and he must consciously protect himself with the shield of will power. We have already spoken about development of the will. It should not be thought that disharmony can be overcome with calmness alone. Any blow implies a counter-blow. Evil returns to its sender. Who would need a sword, if the enemy's arrow could be turned back to its sender, just by the power of will?

"Truly, the conquering one must be on incessant vigil." Thus instructed the Thinker.

831. Urusvati knows the power of victory over self.

People may say, "This battle is beyond the strength of human nature. We do not even know how to begin such a battle." However, each entrance has its own key.

Do not think of yourselves as unprecedented heroes when you begin your attack against the monster of ego! First of all, wage the battle against your "I" and try to replace "I" with "we." It can be seen that such a replacement is not difficult, especially if you recognize that none of your actions can be exclusively yours, for every act is performed by both earthly and supermundane groups. No one can insist that he acts without strong co-workers. Only those who are foolish and ignorant fail to notice how their actions are shaped.

Science affirms how powerful are the supermundane currents. Science already can grasp thought transmissions. It is fitting to replace the "I" with the powerful "we." The man who creates is wrong to think that his creativity is his own. He should think about his visible and invisible co-workers. His labor will be no less valuable if it is shown to be a collaborative achievement. Thus the concept of personal property will be easily transformed into one of property owned in common. Earthly treasures are in man's care, and he will arrive in the Supermundane World not burdened by a heavy load.

The Thinker said, "Man, you can begin the battle with the self at any moment of your life."

832. Urusvati knows the power of victory over slavery. I do not speak here about slave ownership—a kind of slavery that should by now have been abolished, as a shame of humanity. We speak now about inner slavery.

Man carries within himself an inclination toward a most abhorrent slavery. Man is full of enslaving petty habits. Do not think that these habits are harmful only in the earthly life; they are far more harmful in the Supermundane World.

Clumsy and slow is such a wayfarer in the Supermundane World. He alone deprives himself of the more subtle perceptions. He cannot respond to subtle calls. He cannot sense subtle rhythms, for he is deaf and dumb, enslaved. The Teacher cannot communicate with slaves.

It should be remembered that freedom requires a high discipline, and those who manifest disorder and confusion cannot be regarded as free. One may pity those pseudo-free ones who disrupt precious vibrations. They do not understand how widespread and long-lasting is the harm they cause to space. And so, let us weigh which of our habits weaken our free will. Let us understand that we can become builders or destroyers. Manifest understanding of true freedom.

The Thinker pointed out, "Do not be slaves, but manifest beautiful freedom."

833. Urusvati knows the power of victory over carelessness, which causes great harm. People attempt to hide behind ideas that are familiar to them, and thus preserve their lack of concern. For example, people are always ready to hide behind their faith. They will say cunningly, "If we have faith, the rest will follow." In this way, they create for themselves a lazy indifference. They will not be happy to hear that concern and constant striving are required.

How does one tell people that the Supermundane World is full of indomitable striving? What examples could sufficiently demonstrate what indifference leads to in the Supermundane World? One can cite the example of drunkards who lose their way. Such aimless wandering is an apt image.

How can one understand and explain the temporary state of absence of thought that We allow ourselves? This does not indicate a lack of concern, but is for Us a time for renewal of forces. People do not understand that the renewal of energy is an absolute requirement for psychic development. But, even during those moments of absence of thought man does not lose the link with his Guide, nor does his consciousness slumber. On the contrary, it grows keener, ready for new perceptions. Many energies can be either an insurmountable wall or blessed wings. Let the higher energies find man open to receive them.

The Thinker advised, "Do not have friends among careless people."

834. Urusvati knows the power of victory over darkness. What is new in this? The need for enlightenment and the significance of the broadening of consciousness were indicated long ago. Human emanations were recognized in the past, but it must now be added that man can increase his emanations through the power of his will. Of course, this should not be told to novices, who might attempt to strain their wills without expanding their consciousnesses.

One must not forget about the constant, enlightening phenomenon of learning, which is called the torch of victory. Only with it is man able, by the power of his will, to increase his ability to bear light. This will help man in the Supermundane World, and he will become a true light-bearer. He will help himself and his surroundings, a guiding light for the broadening of consciousness. Man should constantly remind himself that he can, through his labor, kindle this inextinguishable, sacred light.

The wayfarer in the Supermundane World should send gratitude to all those who helped him to kindle the salutary torch. Yet, it is not easy to conquer the darkness of ignorance. We shall not tire in asserting the harm of ignorance. Man must never think that the monster of ignorance has been conquered. There is much work for the tiller in the field of knowledge. The condition of Earth itself proclaims the illnesses of humanity.

The Thinker declared, "Light-bearers, increase the strength of your Light."

835. Urusvati knows the gift of equilibrium. Humanity in its ignorance attempts by all means to violate this precious gift. Among the many destroyers let us not forget those two ugly nonentities, despondency and irritation.

Since they are so harmful, why call them nonentities? The reason is simple, because anyone, even a weak man, can conquer them if he wishes. Truly, the causes for irritation and despondency are usually petty. Everyone can feel ashamed of those times when his will was weak.

Likewise, when he is on the way to the Supermundane World man will regret the burden he has imposed on himself. The load cannot be thrown off when crossing into the higher spheres. Particularly burdensome are those small accumulations that on Earth are regarded as harmless. Like a fog they wrap themselves around a darkened consciousness. Man understands with difficulty how unwise he was to disturb the precious equilibrium.

Fools think that equilibrium is something cold and deadening. They cannot understand the intensified vibrations and rhythms of the motion of ascent. Yet, unless they realize on Earth the harm they cause themselves by beclouding their insight, they will wander in the supermundane regions. Therefore let us remind them, whenever possible, about the harm of irritation and despair.

The Thinker said, "He who gives in to irritation and despair cannot think about Infinity."

836. Urusvati knows the gift of insight. People often confuse this gift with goalfitness. They ask, "What difference is there between such close concepts?" Goalfitness can be cultivated amidst earthly conditions, but insight is developed over many lives, and is deepened in the Supermundane World. It is a great asset.

Man correctly understands events from an external point of view. But man can also sense when a path can lead him astray, and though he may not be able to point to the cause of his feeling, his heart knows that something should be avoided. Usually people will call such a feeling intuition, and they will be right, but they have to first admit in their consciousness the existence of intuition.

Such intuitive feelings must not be ridiculed. Man can be illiterate and at the same time bear within himself this gift of intuition. Intuition commonly is regarded as directed into the future, but it is a help to the present and works throughout one's life. Thus let us treasure the accumulations gathered over many lives and during labor in the Supermundane World. Let us not forget that one must labor there too; mental creativeness is by no means as easy as the ignorant think it is.

The Thinker declared, "Manifest insight in everything in your life."

837. Urusvati knows the gift of divisibility of attention. Persistent intensification of the will can increase one's ability to pay attention simultaneously to different objects. Do not think that such a gift is only inherent in some geniuses. Everyone, in the course of different existences, can develop the ability to keenly observe his surroundings and answer different questions. One can write letters to several people at once; thoughts can be sent to all parts of the world, simultaneously. This ability could be called the "threshold" of the spirit's divisibility.

It is necessary, from one's early school years, to develop attentiveness. This is needed for the Supermundane World. Without it the traveler will find himself surrounded by a great variety of new impressions and thus will lose the ability to assimilate them. Without having trained his attentiveness, he drowns in waves of unfamiliar vibrations and sinks into chaos.

It should not be thought that each new dweller in the Subtle World will at once be given a Guide. He must first find within himself the ability to understand mental guidance. True, the language of thought is the same for all, but anyone who has not developed this ability to think cannot achieve an understanding of such help. Therefore We advise you to not neglect thinking about the Supermundane World during your earthly days. Watchful attentiveness can reveal many things not perceptible to the ignorant.

The Thinker advised that one think every day about the future life and intensify attention to the far-off worlds.

838. Urusvati knows the gift of living creativeness. Man creates constantly, consciously or unconsciously, physically or mentally; whether awake or asleep, man continues to create, and in this he fulfills his higher purpose.

Man cannot help but create; when he is creative, he is in contact with the highest energies. Of course, we cannot compare the creativeness of a great thinker to that of a savage; they are incomparable, and yet they will both be in contact with the fundamental energy.

When engaged in creative activity, one is constantly ascending or descending. One can imagine an apparatus—a psychograph—that can register the smallest vibrations of human creativeness. The line it draws will be quite complex. Subsequent to the exaltation of heroism can come pitiful despair or destructive fear, or irritation. The apparatus would register the fall, but could rise again in the rapture of love and joy.

It is impossible to imagine today's man as ever-ascending. Such a constant, ceaseless ascent is possible, not only for a person, but even for an entire group or for all of humanity. However such an expansion and unification of consciousness is still a dream, but every dream is a command to oneself, and the Great Forces will hasten to help the bold spiritual toiler.

Something similar takes place in the Supermundane World, but earthly man should remember his responsibility in the task of world construction. Thus, in the beginning, let us remember that man creates constantly.

The Thinker said, "Who can indicate the limits of human creativeness? Infinity itself is the measure."

839. Urusvati knows the gift of labor. Humanity is beginning to understand labor as having great value. We regard labor as the highest standard, but many still think that it is a curse. Where does such an unjustified idea come from? It is because of a lack of understanding of the Supermundane World.

People do not want to know the first principles of the supermundane life. They do not realize that labor is liberation from the ego, that most harmful impediment to the attainment of supermundane creativity. Labor of high quality permits man to rise above the ego. A creator, at the time of true inspiration, does not think of himself. A worker striving for better quality cannot be enslaved to his ego. Therefore, the gift of labor is liberation from selfhood.

Selfhood can be eradicated by the mind, but are there many who can think in such a lofty way? Labor can help people and protect them from the imperfect conditions of life. People do not use labor enough as a safeguard against falling into the depths of vulgarity.

Searching for higher quality is already a striving into a better future. For good reason the Yoga of Labor was offered to humanity as a direct path to achievement. Let us not be silent about the need for labor, even in early childhood. Family and school must mold the future laborers and creators.

The Thinker said, "Prayerfully let us accept the gift of labor."

840. Urusvati knows the gift of courage. Because of opposing vibrations, an audacious individual can become afraid, but a courageous hero is fearless. Manifesting courage is more than just an earthly attainment. Courage is also developed in the Supermundane World.

A seeker who desires to enter the path of courage receives Help from the Highest. Though he will be exposed to many terrors, he will know that his essence is inviolate, and even the most terrible will not upset his rhythm. With this firm armor the hero proceeds in his earthly life. He can be assured that he has received a great gift.

I can hear the grumbler whisper, "What is new in this? Does not man already know about the benefit of courage?" But he does not know, and the grumbler himself does not attempt to cultivate this valuable quality within himself. One can tirelessly develop the quality of courage in any circumstances of life, and in this striving one can recall long-forgotten accumulations. Active courage is always beautiful, but this is not known by the grumbler, for he does not strive to the beautiful. For him *podvig* is just an empty word. He does not understand why the hero cannot tolerate a vulgar way of life. The grumbler cannot calculate the true benefit of courage; even in his life in the bazaar a little courage would be of value. But the grumbler prefers to vegetate in the soil of timidity, rather than be kindled by *podvig*. After all, *podvig* can be performed in the humblest kind of life. People do not understand that courage is the shortest path.

The Thinker taught that one must proceed into the Supermundane World filled with courage.

841. Urusvati knows the gift of learning. The skeptics will ask, "Can learning be a gift? Is it not an achievement of our free will?" From the point of view of narrow materialism it is so. But refined, exalted thinking understands that learning needs Supermundane Cooperation.

Every thinker can recognize that beyond the mere accumulation of facts is the more elevated level of knowledge, and this is already a higher gift. One cannot refine one's receptivity by earthly reason alone. A true scientist realizes that his knowledge contains some kind of higher threads, which provide an unexpected expansion of what was already learned.

Such an event–when the Higher Guides consider it necessary to interfere for the sake of the Common Good–may be unperceived. But the results would be greater if the scientist consciously recognized and accepted the Higher Guidance; then the Supermundane World could manifest itself in all its glory. The human heart senses expansion, as if ready to receive something Great. Such moments may lead to illumination, but one must learn to accept this current of Beneficence. Forced measures are not needed. One has only to open one's heart and summon in thought the Great Teacher.

The Thinker said, "Teacher, bless me in my learning."

842. Urusvati knows the true meaning of supermundane standards of measurement. Researchers in supermundane science often wonder why earthly dates do not coincide with supermundane ones. This circumstance often promotes doubt in those who are not firm in their resolve. Only by profound study of the conditions of the Supermundane World can one understand that supermundane measures cannot fully coincide with earthly ones.

A man standing on a mountaintop will think and feel differently from someone who is in a deep valley. Supermundane and earthly measures differ even more. In the Supermundane World measures correspond with the essence of those events upon which Our Indications are based. Only a keen observer can perceive the inner connections between events that relate to Our Indications.

Often secondary events can seem insignificant and irrelevant, and only an attentive, keen eye can see a noticeable connection. An unprejudiced scientist will then point out, "Truly, the Supermundane World is close to the earthly one, yet the higher measures must be carefully observed." Thus it can be seen that the supermundane language cannot be the narrow language of Earth.

The heart is always indicated as a focal point of man's essence. Only the heart can listen to and understand the light touches of the Supermundane World. This must be remembered.

The Thinker said, "Teacher, teach me to understand the whisper of the Supermundane."

843. Urusvati knows the true meaning of joy. In ancient India there was a community of physicians who were called "creators of joy." They believed that for successful healing the patient had to be surrounded by joy. They had learned about the healing properties of joy that attract the best vibrations, both mundane and supermundane; by this method, the patient's condition was improved and his cure proceeded successfully.

Physicians of other schools ridiculed the creators of joy. They could not admit that the quality of vibrations assisted the physical healing. Nor could they imagine the spatial power attracted by psychic influences. Such influences should not be commands, but a festival of the spirit. Also, it can be seen that when the physician speaks with joy, the patient more readily trusts him.

Not only the physical substance of this remedy but also its subtle, magnetizing effect on the process of treatment, work in cooperation with the best forces of the patient. Whether near a patient, or in the entire scope of life's creativeness, do not forget the healing quality of joy. Find the resourcefulness to summon joy even during difficult days. Find the strength to create joy, for there are many possibilities in space to kindle bonfires of joy. Truly, joy is the best guide on the supermundane paths.

The Thinker said, "Teacher, help me to unite with the Supermundane Joy."

844. Urusvati knows the true meaning of labor. We affirm labor as the universal value. We call labor the source of healing rhythm. We repeat that labor provides real joy to the worker. We place labor into the foundation of the family and the state. But now We must add one more, the most significant quality of labor–that it gives joy not only to the worker himself, but also to others.

Any labor undoubtedly gives joy to someone. The joy may not be great, but it might also be vast. The manifestation of universal joy is produced by labor.

Let us not forget that in the Supermundane World such joy is incorruptible. It creates gratitude. This unity of vibrations helps the traveler in his supermundane pilgrimage. In this special attention must be given to the fact that the gratitude is not directed to the laborer personally, though these pure feelings will follow him on Earth as well as in the Supermundane World. He will not know those who are grateful to him. The most treasured step on the ladder of ascent is the impersonal, self-healing step upward.

Cooperation is valued when it is strengthened by devotion. Thus let us understand labor as an action of united joy.

The Thinker saw labor as supermundane joy.

845. Urusvati knows the true meaning of friendliness. The luminous emanations of friendliness are a good guide on Earth and also in the Supermundane World. Sincere friendliness is especially needed in the Supermundane World. The energy of thought and the evident emanations exclude any possibility of deceitful intent. In earthly life friendliness creates new possibilities. A friendly glance at one's enemy is not a sign of weakness, but, on the contrary, a sign of advantage.

People should be educated in the realization of the benefit of friendliness. The full value of this quality may not be understood quickly, but undoubtedly an elevation of consciousness will take place. Once again, during this education the harm of hate and revenge should be taught. This is particularly needed now, when malice and hatred are enveloping Earth with a ruinous shroud.

Do not think that these reminders are simply abstract moral precepts. The planet is ill, and people add to its destruction. Therefore, let us gather every grain of friendliness. Let us fill space with transmissions of friendliness. We do not know who will be reached by our sendings of kindness, but they will carry with them a pan-human benefit.

The Thinker advised, "Send out thought of kindness. They will reach their destination."

846. Urusvati understands the true meaning of forgetting. The sages say, "Nothing disappears, everything has a reason." If something has sunk into the depths of consciousness, there is reason for it. If we study that reason, we will find that the forgetting was beneficial.

People also wonder why a memory long-forgotten sometimes emerges unexpectedly from the consciousness. There is a reason for this. Unforeseen vibrations may have awakened the slumbering memory, or the individual may have needed to acknowledge something long ago experienced, or perhaps the Supermundane Guides found it necessary to remind him about his responsibility.

We do not have in mind that careless loss of memory that comes from lack of discipline. We regard this as a dangerous vice. Children should be protected from falling into undisciplined carelessness. People often happily admit to negligent forgetfulness, not realizing the kind of vice they are confessing to.

Forgetting is natural. It collects treasures in the consciousness, and guards them solicitously until their destined time.

In truth, it is impossible for one to remember all the details of one's past. Only in the Supermundane World do the details appear to one, as saviors or accusers. It is impossible to remember, and to accept or reject every detail. For one who strives, forgetting is nothing but the preservation of treasures whose hour will come like a lightning bolt of illumination.

We value the person who knows how to manage accumulated treasures. We are ready to help to summon out of the treasury the needed vibrations.

The Thinker said, "I will also accept forgetting as a gift."

847. Urusvati knows the true meaning of compassion for the less fortunate. Let every act of compassion be a step of your ascent.

A fool beats his exhausted donkey and thus does only harm. But a wise master lets his donkey rest and feeds it, and thus receives benefit. It is the same with the ignorant. It is wrong to rebuke the ignorant in anger, for such abuse is only harmful. But there will be benefit if one makes allowance and finds appropriate words. It is not easy to empathize with the ignorant, but a thoughtful person will understand that when a passage is low, one must stoop to proceed.

Much has been said about compassion, yet every act of compassion requires that one know how to bend to the level of the needy one. Indeed, this affords a glorious ascent. In the Supermundane World, mercy and compassion lead to a speedy ascent. The pilgrim learns to harken to the voices of pain and is imbued with thoughts of healing, which, like wings, bear him aloft.

Man should constantly seek for opportunities to act with compassion. Schools should teach the benefits of compassion, and that negative judgment is fruitless. It can be avoided if one remembers that destruction is, for us, not equal to construction. Let us leave destruction to the wisdom of Cosmos; let us create.

The Thinker said, "Teacher, point out to me the way to ascend in compassion."

848. Urusvati knows the true meaning of inspiration. In many languages, this word clearly refers to influence from without. People love the word inspiration, but often misuse it, not considering its origin.

Even those few who know the origin of the word differ in their understanding of it. Some accept that there is some external personal influence, while others think that an impersonal energy is involved. There is no reason for disagreement, for in every personal action some impersonal energy is at work. It is time for people to recognize the true meaning of the words they utter.

But is it possible to discuss the meaning of inspiration without an understanding of the Supermundane World? No one can acknowledge the cooperation of Higher Forces when he denies their existence.

The word "inspiration" is especially used by artists and scientists. The reason for this is clear since these individuals can more often receive influences from the Supermundane Spheres than ordinary people. The influences would be more frequent if people accepted them consciously, but regrettably the existence of the Supermundane World is generally not acknowledged.

How can recognition of the Supermundane World be expected, when people are so engulfed by hatred and destruction? Even so, the word "inspiration" has not yet been expunged from the dictionary! It can be hoped that teachers will appear in the elementary schools who will explain the great meaning of inspiration. Children should hear about Supermundane Cooperation. This idea will not cause harm, but will touch them like beautiful wings!

The Thinker said, "Teacher, inspire me to better creative work."

849. Urusvati knows the true meaning of enthusiasm. This beautiful concept proves the communion that exists between the Higher Worlds and the forces of the human spirit. Those who deny the existence of the spirit and the soul should not use the word "enthusiasm," yet they love to repeat it, not really understanding its meaning.

They make use of the thoughts and words that fill supermundane space and at the same time deny the existence of the unseen life and the invisible influences existing there. It is not surprising that the concepts known to the ancient world that we are obliged to speak about have become completely distorted.

People of the ancient world created many words of great significance. They knew why these words were needed for humanity, but the centuries have swept away the meaning of many great concepts. Human thought turned to the daily routine and to what people mistakenly thought was progress in life. Ignorance came upon them, stealthily and unexpectedly. Dry reason, instead of a broadening of their horizons, narrowed them down to a state of ignorant negation.

It would seem that scientists should seek and not engage themselves in negativity. Enthusiasm must descend upon the consciousness of a scientist, and he must evaluate its significance. However, by denying the guidance of Supermundane Forces, the scientist weakens himself.

Enough has been said about the conscious creativity that brings clairvoyance and clairaudience, but to achieve these one must first understand what kind of powers he will manifest and what kind of Cooperation is ready to help him. Only then can true enthusiasm be affirmed.

The Thinker advised that even in daily life one should not forget about enthusiasm.

850. Urusvati knows the true meaning of kindheartedness. The beautiful concepts of goodness and kindheartedness should not be demeaned by the ignorant. To them a good-hearted person seems foolish and is not to be trusted. What can be higher than a striving toward beneficence, toward good? It is the wise man who directs all his forces toward good. And when he is in the Supermundane World he will not regret his striving, which, as a magnet of good, will attract to him the best companions on the path.

People in the earthly state dream about cooperation, but in the Supermundane World it is even more keenly experienced. It strengthens the spirit and multiplies the psychic energy. While on Earth, people attempt to raise their consciousness with all kinds of yoga, in order to approach the Higher World. But the Supermundane World demands much greater tension in order to advance. Continuously, without ceasing, the pilgrim in the Supermundane World must move forward—or fall backward, like a stone dropped into an abyss. Goodness offers protection against this, but man must first acquire true goodheartedness. It will help to avoid irritation, violent anger, and malice.

We are not talking about unimportant and impractical matters. The world is so engulfed in hatred that the life preserver of good is indispensable. Man should search for the many forgotten or corrupted concepts. He must learn to apply them in their true meaning. Much good can be found buried in the dust of the ages.

The Thinker insisted, "Put on the armor of goodwill and you will become unconquerable."

851. Urusvati knows the true meaning of grace. Primary energy, grace, psychic energy, fiery energy, prana—there have been many names over the centuries, but the meaning is one. Life-giver, channel of the creative force, impeller to knowledge—thus can people understand grace. But people are far from understanding the foundations of the universe, and will ask, "If the primary energy fills space, why does it not act equally on all of humanity?"

Those who question do not know that there are no two people alike, or that the energy must be acknowledged, invoked, and accepted. An ignorant person is like a patient who demands immediate effect from a remedy. After the first dose he is ready to deny. Thus acts the one who does not acknowledge the primary energy. Likewise, an ignorant person does not understand that one must know how to invoke the energy. The pure will must be tensed so that the fiery magnet is activated. The magnet cannot come to life without the cultivation of the will.

It is also difficult for man to accept grace in earthly life. Like a bird of paradise, grace will beat its wings against its cage, losing its best feathers. He who accepts grace must keep the wonderful bird free, but how to treat it so that it does not become a pitiful prisoner? People have invented many different ways to adapt their everyday lives to the grandeur of the beautiful energy, but often without giving a thought to the meaning of the word grace.

The Thinker rejoiced when he sensed the presence of grace. He said, "I was touched by the fiery bird, the messenger of the Supermundane World."

852. Urusvati knows the true meaning of faith. People speak about blind faith, but We affirm the seeing faith. Faith is knowledge, but knowledge is divided into that of the mind and that of the heart. It is not easy for people to discern the dividing line of this knowledge, but they must understand that knowledge of the heart cannot be acquired if there are no supermundane accumulations.

Truly, it is not possible to advance in the Supermundane World if the fiery magnet of the heart has not been activated. It should be understood that the magnet must be developed to the fullest possible degree in the Supermundane World so that it may shine forth in the earthly life.

Many ways were invented by people to artificially ignite the magnet. But others thought that only spiritual development could add to the development of the magnet—these were closer to the truth. Bodily exercises cannot develop spirituality. Only mental discipline can produce elevated heart-knowledge. But how can one explain to people that every day and every hour are important for supermundane achievement? The mind can impede the heart and deprive it of precious insights.

The Thinker said, "My knowledge is limited, but I have faith."

853. Urusvati knows the true meaning of striving. People often fail to distinguish between the spiritual striving of the heart and the physical tension of the reasoning mind. Unfortunate misunderstandings can bring disastrous results. One can beat one's head against cold stones, but the descent of creative energy will not take place.

You may wonder how one learns to distinguish between the various energies. In order to accept the current of higher tension, it is necessary, first of all, to refine one's consciousness through lofty thinking; thus will come the expansion of consciousness and the kindling of the fire of the heart. This illuminating state can come upon one quite unexpectedly.

More than once have We reminded you that the measures of the Supermundane World are different from the earthly ones. Only by understanding this can one grow accustomed to the Supermundane World. No routine practices or exercises are needed; only thought can elevate man. Only during focused thinking can man feel the presence of the inner fire.

In the ancient teachings can be found indications about the precious talisman that is found in the heart. Truly, it is possible to compare the fire of the heart, kindled by supermundane energy, to a talisman.

People should not think that they must retreat to the life of a hermit in order to properly develop their consciousness. Amidst daily life on Earth can be found beautiful striving, and such *podvig* will be even more wonderful. But the striving must be sharpened, like the arrows of an experienced archer.

Teachers in schools should speak about the power of lofty striving. Moments of silence should be introduced, when children can direct their thoughts to the Beautiful. Such moments may evoke the fiery sparks in their hearts.

The Thinker advised people to gather together, and in silence to direct their thoughts to humanity.

854. Urusvati knows the true meaning of open-mindedness. Humanity can be classified into those who allow and those who deny. The first carry within themselves the seed of the New World; the second produce only cosmic rubbish. However, if one wanted to draw a line demarcating these two types, one would be amazed at how tortuous the line would be.

It is quite astonishing that among the deniers one can find great leaders and scientists. They do not realize that their creativity could increase through liberation from the darkness of self-imposed denial. Only in the Subtle World will they understand how much they have impeded their own progress.

But in earthly life, such deniers are beyond help. Only a strong shock can expand their horizon. Special attention should be given to children, for their consciousness is not yet polluted.

Some think that We offer only moral instruction, but they forget that We are laying the foundation of the Fiery Yoga. For its natural development, a moral foundation of life is necessary. Only a pure heart will not be reduced to ashes by the fiery link with the Highest Forces. It must not be forgotten that people need constant reminders, but they must be given instruction in different forms, according to their capacity and state of mind. Truly, the Teacher must be vigilant and resourceful.

The Thinker advised, "Inspect your own locks, and make sure that you can open them."

855. Urusvati knows the true meaning of friendliness. In his very nature, a Yogi is friendly. He examines every human manifestation thoroughly, and if he finds a particle of good in it, he bases his judgment on that particle. But if the Yogi senses just cosmic rubbish, he will sweep it away, knowing that this kind of decay can be transformed only by fire. A Yogi understands that it is impossible to judge anything correctly by its changing state. It must be examined in its various stages of manifestation, prior to forming any judgment as to its essence.

Understand that this is the basis of friendliness. It is better to err on the side of good than to judge harshly. But the heart of a Yogi will not be deceived; his sensitive vibration will make no mistake in recognizing cosmic rubbish.

Supermundane vibrations can recognize infallibly the decay of a human being. In time it will be possible to utilize these refined vibrations in earthly life too. But one should not expect the appearance of such sophisticated apparatuses any time soon. The coarsened state of humanity is evident, and it is not yet possible to break through the armor of ignorance. Yet, evolution is proceeding.

The Thinker asserted, "Maintain friendliness as a torch in the darkness."

856. Urusvati knows the true meaning of striving. All labor requires concentration in order for the quality of labor to be heightened, but such concentration is external. We wish to remind you about inner striving. Such striving should be familiar to everyone, but in fact it is rarely seen.

Man must familiarize himself with the Supermundane World and show full understanding of the Higher Helpers. But how will he know his treasures, if no one tells him about them? From childhood, people are kept separate from the Supermundane World, and are forbidden to even think about anything "supernatural." They grow up, like the blind in a forest, directionless, until they knock their heads against trees.

Such a big shock is needed for one to be illumined by the inner light. Then one's search begins, and Higher Help becomes possible. In truth, the seeker will notice that his striving enhances the quality of his achievement. Help comes as if by accident, when something is found or someone is met.

Man should free himself, the sooner the better, from his absurd ideas about the accidental nature of events. There is cause in everything, and it is wise to find its source. Striving, like the force of a magnet, increases the power of the seeker. An inner striving will not impede one's labors. On the contrary, as an incessant pulse it affirms the ascent. Man should think about the ceaseless activity of the heart and understand it as an example of incessant striving.

The Thinker said, "A magnetic arrow knows its direction."

857. Urusvati knows the true meaning of rest. We have already said that rest should be a change of labor, but there are other beneficial ways to rest, such as communion with the Supermundane World, enrichment of knowledge, contemplation of the grandeur of nature, and human creativity. Some will call these ways of rest a broadening of consciousness, others a liberation from ego, and others, a victory of the spirit. They will all be right. The rapture of lofty perceptions can transform one's life, if one is able to sustain the valuable inner vibrations.

It is regrettable that people can so rarely make use of these true values. Usually, negative feelings impede recognition of the most beautiful. Rather than take the given opportunities to rest, man sinks into irritation and harms not only himself, but all his surroundings.

The true nature of rest should be explained in the schools. Rest brings health to the spirit and the body. Let the young builders of life find a balance between labor and rest. Let them find the time to think about the Supermundane World. It is possible that they may start with ridicule, but later plain logic will compel them to think more deeply. They may start thinking about astronomy, or chemistry, or any branch of physics, and will stumble upon something as yet unknown to them. Especially now, when people begin to think about energies, it can be expected that inquiring minds will understand the breadth of possibilities that transform life. Unfortunately, people are still too far from freedom of thought. May thought liberate the oppressed slaves!

The Thinker said, "Labor is the liberator, and thought is the guide."

858. Urusvati knows the true meaning of faithfulness. Adamant—thus was called this quality of loyalty in ancient times. Loyalty, steadfastness, and unwavering determination build a stronghold against doubt, wavering, and treason. Radiant faithfulness is a wonderful manifestation. Yes, yes, yes, it is time for people to learn about clear imprints produced by their emanations.

Initial experiments performed in the study of emanations have produced discoveries that have already attracted inquiring minds. At present, when scientific instruments have been refined and enhanced, scientists should without delay continue with further experiments. The significance of the study of emanations is enormous. The New Era is in need of affirmation of subtle energies.

Similarly, medicine will progress when people understand how beneficial positive emanations are, and how harmful are the emanations of malice. The fact is that emanations do not perish, but saturate the surrounding space. People search afar for the cause of epidemics, but they should look within the human organism. The quality of emanation also has great significance in the Supermundane World, where the subtle body brings with it its own, customary emanations. The individual there can be a creative Magnet, but can also be a repulsive monster. It is not easy to rid oneself of ugly accumulations. Therefore it is wise to surround oneself with a salutary light. But, for this, one must first of all accept the Supermundane World and strive to it in full faithfulness.

The Thinker advised, "Remember that loyalty is a reliable shield."

859. Urusvati knows the Ineffable Essence. The divisibility of all that exists is unlimited, yet in each separate part can be found the smallest "something" of the Ineffable Essence. The ancient thinkers, the alchemists, called this "something" "The Treasure of the Mother," "Eye of Jupiter," "The Stronghold of Victory." Now science has come to the realization that this basic particle should be studied.

One may ask how the alchemists, with their imperfect apparatuses, could cognize the finest particles of Be-ness. Indeed, only by way of psychic cognition. We speak about this early example in order to remind you that even perfect apparatuses must have the participation of psychic energy. Science must attempt to solve its difficult problems, but it is time to acknowledge the role that psychic energy must play.

People often boast about their lack of belief, and then indifferently throw together many incompatible concepts.

The Thinker said to those proclaiming their disbelief, "You do not have to believe, but you should know."

860. Urusvati knows the meaning of the expansion of consciousness. There is much confusion and lack of understanding about this concept. Inexperienced researchers think that such expansion comes from without, and that the lucky recipient need only accept with gratitude this highest gift. Such researchers forget the law of free will. They would be distressed to learn that expansion of consciousness comes not from without, but from within. Only the fiery magnet of the heart, ignited by lofty thinking and striving, can attract the highest energies. The power of the highest energies transforms the consciousness and makes it receptive to knowledge of the Laws of Be-ness. People do not value the magnet of the heart and thus diminish their own significance.

It is impossible to believe that the Higher Forces would coerce the free will. On the contrary, the beautiful fact is that man is the initiator of his own ascent. Cooperation will develop depending on the power and purity of his thinking. Thus, man alone prepares his place in the Supermundane World.

The appearance of the Teacher depends on a high level of thinking of the seeker, in whom a low consciousness can act like soggy clothing weighing down the body of a drowning man, making rescue most difficult! Of special importance is the expansion of consciousness leading into the future. A person with a broadened consciousness understands the past as a bridge into the future.

The Thinker said, "Strive to the future, it is calling."

861. Urusvati knows the true meaning of love for the future. It has long been said that life is an uninterruptible current. It can be said that life is a flight into the future. But many people fear the future. Some are sadly reconciled with its inevitability, but only a few love it. It is right to call these few the winged ones. They sense how their invisible wings carry them over the planet. They can discover great truths and can become true scientists. They are confident that none of their discoveries will be lost. They greet each day as a new possibility. They love victory, and stand up against ignorance.

Whence is born in these workers a readiness for incessant labor? Love is a powerful impeller. Love is a magnet and the beginning of achievement. Love for the future is the most powerful impeller and it safeguards the worker from stagnation. Love makes possible the understanding of the Supermundane World.

People often speak about meetings with their dear ones in the Supermundane World. They do not love the future as a fiery victory, but it is good that they dream about the Supermundane World, if only for the dear ones. Yet, how beautiful the Supermundane Path can be for the aspirant who strives to the future! He will lose no time in seeking the solutions to the problems that occupied him in his earthly life, and he will find the Higher Guides.

The Thinker said to children, "Love the future, and your wings will grow."

862. Urusvati knows the true meaning of love for nature. An Agni Yogi loves nature. In its smallest and greatest manifestations he perceives beauty. He feels the grandeur that saturates space. The Yogi knows that for him nature is a window to the far-off worlds and an entrance into the Supermundane World.

It is essential to remind people about the significance of nature, for many do not know how to observe it and do not perceive its importance in their lives. One can see in many children an attraction to nature, and, particularly, to the heavens.

The teacher can observe that there are two kinds of children, and should help those in whom burns the fire leading to the far-off worlds. The existence of these qualities indicates the precious accumulations of former lives. One may expect from such children labor for the common good. This is kindled in them by exaltation before the grandeur of the Universe. But adults often dismiss the most precious traits of little children. Urusvati remembers how her own beautiful vision was ridiculed. Thus, many remarkable manifestations of higher energies are seen by ignorant people as empty nonsense. It is long overdue for true scientists to come to the help of the little children, whose eyes and ears are open.

The Thinker said, "Love Nature and it will teach you to ascend."

863. Urusvati knows the true meaning of assimilation. I have already spoken about containment, tolerance, and understanding, qualities that must be crowned by assimilation. Synthesis can be developed only through assimilation. What is assimilation? With the expansion of consciousness must come the absorption of what has been learned. It becomes, as it were, one's own. With such a treasure the traveler enters radiant into the Supermundane World, for his inner light has been increased.

Such a provident traveler, in most cases, keeps a clear consciousness, and does not need rest through sleep. True, there may be cases of sickness when rest is needed, but even in that condition the assimilated treasure will shorten the period of inactivity. An enlightened seeker strives to the future and on all paths thinks about creativeness. The magnet of his heart will be drawn to the Cosmic Magnet and will propel the heart toward thought-creativeness.

"Beautiful is the attainment of thought-creativity." Thus ordained the Thinker.

864. Urusvati knows the true meaning of compassion. Maitreya, the Lord of Compassion, impressed this pan-human feeling on the future mind. Yet the confusion of the present world is great!

Many physicians will be needed to cure humanity. Psychic epidemics are increasing, together with the bodily ones. Compassion can arm physicians for their urgent battle.

There are some feelings akin to compassion, but only compassion itself is without selfishness. Pity, for example, can be somewhat patronizing, and even charity can have selfish motives, but compassion aids the suffering, taking the entire burden of pain upon itself. It studies the cause of the pain and offers psychic energy to revitalize the ailing psyche.

Psychic illnesses should be understood in a broad sense. People enter upon a path of confusion and thus grow helpless. Much energy for good is needed to support, to not offend, and to express hope in the simplest of words. A sick person can be quite vain and one should not give the impression that his faults are known. Truly, compassion is the most tender and sympathetic feeling. Let us not forget how a subtle feeling helps in the Supermundane World. It reveals the magnet of the heart, and its power makes one invincible.

The Thinker asserted, "Compassion is the crown of the future."

865. Urusvati knows the true meaning of instant illumination. It was said long ago that in a single sigh we are transported into the Supermundane World. A simple statement, yet much perplexity has accumulated around it.

After partaking of a heavy meal people sigh, but are not transported anywhere; nor are they transported into the Supermundane World when they sigh during life's misfortunes. Man sighs when angry or irritated, but only becomes more rooted into the earth.

The process of illumination is very complex and difficult to understand. Very few grasp that many conditions are necessary for illumination to occur. First of all, tranquility of the heart is needed, but this is not an easy state to achieve. Both inwardly and outwardly it strengthens the link with the Highest.

Man is not able to cognize with his mind when and why the beneficent moment will come. The reasoning mind is a poor adviser! Instead of giving help, it can mislead. Only the heart can sense the sacred stillness and in this striving true straight-knowledge is developed.

Developed people can live a life filled with supermundane experiences without being diverted from labor and creativity. The very highest quality will fill the labors of such an enlightened individual. A beautiful illumination descends upon the heart, and man transforms his life into an unending *podvig*.

The Thinker taught, "Hold the entrance pure, so that the Messenger may enter."

866. Urusvati understands the essential cause of harm in malicious speech. It is time to acknowledge the primary energy, and to stop separating moral concerns from the physical side of things. It has long been necessary for humanity to understand the significance of emanations and vibrations, yet, despite all evidence, humanity continues to deny the simplest laws of nature.

Humanity repeatedly hears about the harmful effects of evil thoughts and speech, yet continues to fill the world with such poison, not aware that it causes widespread degeneration and other calamities.

It is time to examine reality with the eye of the true scientist, and, in medical terms to point out the irreparable harm of evil thinking. It is time to speak in the schools about the pernicious harm of the malicious curses that children hear in their homes. But the world has a shortage of teachers and no one warns the children about the consequences of such evil speech.

It is not only drunkenness and narcotics that destroy the organism; evil thinking is no less effective in opening the centers to every possible malady. An evil man is defenseless against pernicious influence. It is not the light of the Supermundane World that surrounds him, but darkness. It is time to understand that evil is a decomposing force, and in evil a healthy generation cannot be born.

The Thinker went to the bazaar, warning, "Hurry, free yourselves of the fetters of evil thinking." The fools only laughed at him.

867. Urusvati knows the true meaning of auto-suggestion. Many regard this concept with disdain, but proper auto-suggestion is a true staff on both earthly and supermundane paths.

People should understand that self-command toward good and the General Welfare will attract Supermundane Help, and victory will come when one commands oneself to overcome the obstacles. Such a victory through self-command shortens the path. It also should be known that in a beneficent command vibrations are created that unite one with the Higher Forces. But even such simple ideas must almost be forced into the human consciousness. Man pictures only dimly his best gift—free will. He does not realize the responsibility this advantage places upon him. How will he make use of free will if he does not understand the power of self-command?

It was said long ago that man should first of all conquer himself, but what kind of victory would it be if man were not imbued with the will to good? Let us remember that auto-suggestion is truly a scientific concept. Everyone, under any conditions, can develop it, and the Supermundane Dwellers will rejoice at seeing new possibilities for cooperation.

The Thinker said, "Friend, light your lamp. Welcome guests will appear."

868. Urusvati knows the true meaning of psycho-life. Even the ignorant, and the dull and obstinate, cannot deny the existence of the psychic world, though they attempt to hide it under absurd names. Of course, it is not to be expected that such people could realize the great significance of the psycho-life, since even more advanced people have not learned to embrace it in all its significance.

Humanity must increasingly be reminded that evolution intensifies the psycho-life, and that it is essential to learn to perceive the vibrations of this higher energy.

Man realizes that psychic energy protects him from illnesses, and from doubts and depression. But, even more than providing such protection, psychic energy can transform one's entire existence. Likewise, psychic energy leads one into the Supermundane World. Affirming the new consciousness, the influence of psychic energy can be observed in all details of daily life, but for this one must respect its existence.

Man is too occupied with the physical aspects of life and deprives himself of the experience of illumination. Man can find at least a moment to mentally tune himself to a higher tonality, but for this it is necessary to understand the importance of the psycho-life.

Again We suggest to the school teachers that they point out the beauty of the psycho-life. But how many teachers can realize its meaning? Humanity must ease the burdensome lives of teachers so that they can clarify for themselves the essence of the psycho-life. Presently, the world is in such confusion that it is important to repeat about the principle of psycho-life.

The Thinker asserted, "The Psychic World knocks at the entrance. Hasten to open the door."

869. Urusvati knows the true nature of thought.

You already have heard about the art of thinking, about the broadening of consciousness, and about the mental command, but now it is necessary to learn about the basic quality of thought. Thinking is the sharpener of psychic energy. It intensifies it and directs it into space. The stronger the thought transmission, the more powerful will be its interaction with the current of primary energy.

Thus, man is a constant conductor of the most powerful energy. An explosion of this energy is like an electrical discharge—the shorter the transmission, the stronger the explosion. Therefore We advocate thinking with brevity, so as to create a series of repeated explosions. Such repetition is the most powerful, but one has to grow accustomed to the brevity of expression. Some people can transmit thought in lengthy sendings, but the result is like a pool of stagnant water instead of a tempestuous torrent.

It should be remembered that the energy of thought is a fiery energy, and thus the comparison with an explosion is fitting. Likewise, it should be known that even the most ordinary mental sendings should be brief ones. Everyone is acquainted with the act of suggestion, and for success one must know how to send the briefest command.

In order to become familiar with the Supermundane World, brevity and clarity of thought are good guides. It is inadvisable to mumble incoherently when you seek a better road. Even children should be taught the importance of brevity and clarity in words and thoughts.

The Thinker said, "Let the explosions of thought merge with the great current of whirlwinds."

870. Urusvati understands the importance of broadness of outlook. A yogi possesses an outlook that is unlimited. A person who shuts himself in the dungeon of negation cannot be a yogi. It is said that the yogic nature is formed gradually over many incarnations, but this does not mean that man in each incarnation should not seek opportunities for ascent.

Everyone must understand that he will meet with so many new conditions in the Supermundane World that only the breadth of his perceptions will help him to grasp the meaning of it all; even when faced with contradictions he will be able to perceive their cause, and instead of denying them will enrich his accumulations.

Man rarely admits that contradictions can be of real benefit to him, but for a yogi, contradictions are merely a challenge for great victory. Young people should begin to understand how a broad outlook provides them with the best wings.

Many examples can be cited of people who gained victory because of their broad outlook. Even when they encountered seemingly insoluble problems, they could find their way thanks to their broad approach. Thus one can think of breadth of perception as the shield of a yogi.

The Thinker pointed out, "Friends, learn to think in a way that is broader than the broadest!"

871. Urusvati knows the true meaning of continuity. Most people fear this natural phenomenon, and invent many explanations to support their desire to believe in interrupted existence. Some of them even believe that sleep is an interruption, forgetting that sleep brings the renewal of rhythm and contact with Higher Forces. Others go still further; they do not want to understand that departure from the earthly state is simply a change in a person's state of being, and hope that so-called death ends life.

The phenomenon of continuity is an aspect of the

beauty of World Creation. It can be understood as a form of tension. One may garb oneself in a new garment, but the seed of the spirit lives in continuity. It not only lives, it also responds to the Cosmic Magnet.

Is humanity in such a low state that it does not realize the beautiful law of ascent? If we cannot dare to hope that man will fully accept the law of World Creation, let him at least harken to the harmonious voice of nature, and admit the existence of the supermundane life. Thus We shall find a point of contact and can restore mankind's consciousness to health.

The Thinker used to say, "Accept continuity, it will lead you to the Gates of Eternity."

872. Urusvati knows the true meaning of influences. Man constantly experiences the effects of many influences, from astro-chemical rays and cosmic currents, to the flow of human thought—everything can uplift or repress the consciousness. It will be asked, "How then can the free will act if man is enslaved by so many different influences?" To such a question you will often have to reply, "The free will determines the main direction of man's activity. If the will directs him to the creativity of good and to the common welfare, man can develop such a strong magnet that the most powerful influences will become his helpers."

Truly, the heart that has learned self-denial can gather around itself a beautiful flower-garden of influences. Thus, once again, science unites with morality.

Especially now, one can observe the poisoning of humanity by an excess of electricity and the intensification of radio waves. We can point to many examples of scientific discoveries that, misused, proved to be poison for humanity, not only physically but also psychically. It is time to think about the Supermundane World and about the significance of psychic energy.

We will not tire of repeating about these foundations of existence. They have been forgotten by humanity or distorted to the point of harmfulness. Lightmindedness is impermissible in situations where the fate of the planet is often decided.

The Thinker said, "Let us evoke good influences, as faithful allies."

873. Urusvati knows the true meaning of renewal. Few are those who rejoice at the renewal of consciousness. Most people fear the least hint of renewal, and each one experiencing such renewal is surrounded by others who becloud it.

Try explaining to someone that his consciousness is outworn and needs renewal, and you will only provoke his animosity. Although he may speak about the motion of all that exists, about the constant development of the foundations—he will nevertheless be frightened by the word "renewal," as if it might knock the ground from under his feet! Thus, one's acceptance of the idea of renewal becomes, as it were, a touchstone by which to measure one's ability to perfect oneself.

The same measure can be applied to test the degree to which one's consciousness is open to the Supermundane World. One who is capable of understanding the Supermundane World will welcome renewal. Such purification of the foundations is necessary for every world viewpoint. Do not think that anything is immovable, for everything moves and develops. Only with such a conviction can one enter joyously into the Supermundane World. Only thus can one advance and renew one's consciousness.

The Thinker said, "Just imagine how the worlds will flourish, if man admits the joy of renewal!"

874. Urusvati knows the true meaning of readiness. A yogi is inflamed with readiness for the creating of good. Under all conditions of life one should be ready for the creating of good. If *podvig* cannot be performed physically, a mental achievement is always possible.

Probably, you will be asked, "What significance can a mental achievement have?" Answer, "In the Supermundane World all achievements are mental, therefore in the earthly life mental achievements have importance. After all, full readiness for *podvig* is born in thought, and it is thus ready to be manifested at the least opportunity."

We value highly the one who is ready for *podvig*. Such a flaming consciousness is like the guiding beacon of a lighthouse. One can imagine how far this fire of readiness shines! It possesses healing qualities and provides help to lost travelers everywhere; therefore let us firmly remember that readiness for *podvig* is an essential part of it.

Can an achievement take place without mental readiness? A strong armor for victory must be created, and magnanimous readiness for *podvig* must burn day and night.

The Thinker advised, "Be ready for *podvig*!"

875. Urusvati knows the true meaning of self-defense. It is said, "Be like an island of defense and ascend the highest rock. Let the supermundane whirlwinds envelope you and blow away the dust of the road."

When the dust of doubt is blown away, you will have the strength to resist all enemies, and you will not be alone. The supermundane breezes will strengthen you and Our Shield will cover you. But the most powerful help will descend only at the moment of your most intense self-defense. Thus, self-defense is a call to Us.

One should not implore and insist. We are not deaf, and the tension of self-defense is already the best call.

It is necessary to repeat about the meaning of self-defense. People have forgotten that they have within themselves an atomic power, which should be turned against all evil. It will not err in finding where evil is, for it does not act for the individual but for the General Good.

The Thinker asserted, "Let self-defense be intensified to the highest degree."

876. Urusvati knows the true meaning of self-affirmation. Some people do not understand the difference between self-importance and self-affirmation, and are surprised to see signs of self-affirmation in the statements of great Teachers. Such people do not know that self-conceit comes from low egoism, whereas self-affirmation is born from self-denial.

Truly, great Teachers utilized self-affirmation for the assertion of the Truth they brought to the world. Such self-sacrificing affirmation can be called *podvig*. It indicates that the Teacher accepted his responsibility fully, and could even use "I" instead of the usual "We." In the Supermundane World, too, one can see such self-affirmation when used to strengthen weak consciousnesses.

An unwavering command is like a salutary arrow. People strongly need an undelayable command. Only a free will can tell when the time for self-affirmation has come. Then the Teacher can affirm the Truth with the seal of His command. And people should learn to recognize the blessing.

The Thinker solemnly indicated, "When you carry an entrusted treasure carry it with the fullest degree of self-affirmation."

877. Urusvati knows the essence of self-knowledge. The ancient saying, "Man, know thyself," has been distorted by weak and lazy minds. They hasten to proclaim it as something superhuman and unattainable. But self-analysis is always possible, under all circumstances.

Test yourself and observe what has been laid deep in your consciousness. If despondency or offence should live long within you and burden your heart, you must consciously eject them. You should know that they cause many illnesses, and impede your spiritual advancement. When you accept this simple explanation, your reason will tell you that it is harmful to succumb to poisonous influences. In the very same way, you will ask yourself about other destructive feelings, and you will summon your free will to expel the enemies, both earthly and supermundane. And if you feel that the *podvig* of self-sacrifice is close to your heart, you will understand that these gates will lead you to luminous victories. Thus, examine your own nature; your heart will not deceive you.

The Thinker said, "Let self-knowledge be a celebration for you."

878. Urusvati knows the true meaning of self-criticism. For some it is like a millstone around the neck, for others it is a gateway to achievements. Let us not behave like slaves under the burden of the millstone, and impede our way into the Supermundane World!

One should not look back and thus stumble on the stony path. Only forward, untiringly forward! Let each mistake be a stepping stone to a new victory.

Let us not misunderstand the high concept of humility, with which one must stand before the grandeur of the Cosmic Laws, before the realization of the Higher World, before the inspiration of the creative Fire. However, climb boldly on the ladder of achievement, and let nothing impede spiritual daring! Science should confirm how much the vibrations of the ascending spirit are needed. The consciousness, out of its depth, prompts man that the way to victory has been ordained for him.

The Thinker said, "Do not set out on a long journey overburdened, but provide yourself with a torch of hope."

879. Urusvati knows the true nature of self-protection, the rhythm that creates the vibrational, protective net. It should not be thought that such a net can be given from outside. It must be created, at least in the beginning, by the individual himself. Free will must lead man to the realization of his need for protection.

The archer shoots his arrow, but the distance it flies can be tripled if the supermundane link is strong. We have already indicated that the highest Help can be given only when a decision is made freely. Only in this way is cooperation developed; in the Supermundane World the law is the same. Our help will not be delayed if there is a strong and conscious desire for cooperation.

Thus, amidst all conditions of life, one must master the art of self-protection as a defense against attacks by one's enemies. One's shield must be ready to accept the arrows of the enemy. It is not an exaggeration to remind about the battle, for it is the threshold to victory.

The Thinker said, "I shall not forget about self-protection, for it will affirm my readiness for battle."

880. Urusvati knows the true meaning of self-control. Ponder upon this idea, which is based on the cooperation of one's psychic centers. You know the harmful effect of everyday disruptions. They are all the more harmful, even destructive, in the psychic realm. It is time for man to firmly realize the existence of the power of the psychic energy that lies within him.

People often speak about psychic energy, but its presence is rarely realized. Likewise, the great need for the utilization of psychic energy in the Supermundane World is rarely understood. The path to realization is not simply given to man. He himself must command his psychic centers to sharpen their activity. The result of such a command may not be seen at once, but the rhythmic beat of the free will, like a pulse, will indicate the life of the heart. Thus, by this continuous pulsation, is created the harmony of the centers.

The Thinker said, "Friends, poor friends, take possession of your treasures!"

881. Urusvati knows the true meaning of personal striving. All of mankind can be divided into the striving ones and the aimless wanderers. Why then do We call it personal striving? Because this quality cannot be evoked externally. It must be sparked from within. It is usually engendered in the Supermundane World, as a seed that sprouts in one's new life.

It may be observed that striving can be directed to good as well as to evil. Regrettably, man is often directed to evil, or, in other words, to ignorance. From an early age, it must be emphasized that ignorance is evil. This ancient truth has still not been assimilated.

Schools still do not offer a clear idea about the need for constant learning. Rarely do teachers know how to instill the joy of learning. The offering of limited information, uninspired by creative thought, will not strengthen striving.

Each act of creativeness can be called magical. I affirm that true striving is creative. All conditions in life offer possibilities for creativity. How beautiful is the torch-light of creativeness for the traveler in Infinity!

The Thinker affirmed, "I will gather the seeds of striving in order to create a Garden of Beauty."

882. Urusvati knows the true meaning of self-assurance. It was said long ago, "Triumph over your self." But it is equally right to say, "Assure yourself." A victory frequently prompts a reverse blow of pride, but self-assurance strengthens one on the path of evolution.

Few people realize to what extent a self-assured consciousness helps one in the Supermundane World. Everyone should accept, in his own way, the importance of self-assurance, which does not, in any way, exclude Higher Guidance. On the contrary, man must freely choose to be permeated with the presence of the Great Teachers, since forcing one to accept a Teacher would be a violation of the free will.

There are very few who can picture existence in the Supermundane World. And those who read about the Supermundane World rarely apply to themselves what they have read. They cannot envision a future life, or imagine wanting a worthy life beyond the limits of Earth. But such dreams, strengthened by receptivity, can be transformed into reality in the Supermundane World. There, thought creates, and in the earthly life thought should build castles of future *podvig*.

When the Thinker was absorbed in reading, or in a mental discourse, and the disciples wanted to urgently question him, he used to tell them, "I am arming myself."

883. Urusvati knows the true meaning of self-torment. Agni Yoga, which leads the way to the Fiery World, warns against all kinds of torment, all kinds of torture. Harmonizing of the fiery centers is painful and requires much care, and when the yoga takes place amidst earthly conditions, each incidence of cruelty becomes unbearable.

We have pointed out before that cruelty is a sign of savagery, and that people should abhor this dark side of mankind. It should be recognized that refined organisms are especially tortured by dark actions. Humanity cannot yet claim to be free of savagery; on the contrary, one can see that the opposite is true. Agni Yoga is directed to the curbing of such savagery.

The last period of Kali Yuga can be a bloody one. One can imagine how thick grow the emanations of blood! The earthly world, just as the Supermundane, is in need of purification and a refining of the centers. Let us be grateful to those heroes who transmit the call for the *podvig* of self-sacrifice.

The Thinker, when asked about the basis of earthly life, answered, "Human, be more humane!"

884. Urusvati knows the true meaning of self-destruction. Certain two-legged ones, thinking only of the physical, earthly world, consider it just another form of homicide. They are unaware of a worse crime—that of psychic destruction. Only very few understand that self-destruction is, in its essence, psychic murder.

Truly, humanity finds itself in a most dangerous condition. People destroy the spirit, and thus deprive themselves of psychic energy. It is hard to imagine how ill humanity is; this plague is spreading over the entire planet. The most populated regions are especially vulnerable to this epidemic of self-destructiveness. People do not think about the image of themselves that they will take into the Supermundane World. Religions have failed to provide a convincing basis for morality, and now are unable to find common ground with science. Instead of a Great Unity, one finds a pitiful disunity. Fragmentation is a sign of weakness. Where then will wandering humanity go? First of all, physicians and teachers are needed. They can warn of the dangers, which indeed are great!

The Thinker said with regret, "Awful is the spectacle of the wandering self-destroyed ones!"

885. Urusvati knows the true meaning of self-healing. "Friend, command yourself to be healthy"—thus did the sages of Hellas sometimes end their letters. In remote antiquity people already knew that beyond all medicinal remedies, beyond the right nutrition, beyond magnetism, beyond prana, everyone has a healer within himself, but they must know how to summon him.

The ability to heal oneself must be developed from early childhood. Man cannot suddenly, when already ill, demand a miracle. Self-healing can take place only if one's spiritual lyre has already been tuned.

Believe Me: One's inner physician will be on alert, and one's consciousness will summon him, but only if one's spirit has learned how to summon the power given to man. In addition, harmony with the Supermundane World must be achieved. Truly, these strings between Earth and the Higher Worlds will resound as a strong, summoning command. He who has cognized the Supermundane World is able to command for the good of mankind. It must not be thought that We speak about some giants of the spirit, for a measure of achievement and restoration of health is given to everyone.

The Thinker said, "Be able to make your inner healer your friend."

886. Urusvati knows the true meaning of self-enlivening. Love life in all its timelessness and endlessness. The worst illness is being tired of life. It awakens all the sleeping enemies of man, who is now perishing from sicknesses in a form of self-destruction that is akin to suicide. Its consequences can be seen in the Supermundane World. By it, man is deprived of independence of action. He wanders about without purpose and loses the opportunity for self-perfectment. Such spiritual degeneration is difficult to outlive.

Man doesn't realize that his earthly depressions, fears, self-pity, and raging malice can cause great calamities! He thinks that his fits of ignorance will pass without trace. Yet, each cause has its consequence, and as long as their free will continues to protect the drifting ones, they should consider the continuity of life.

How many have assimilated this basic truth? Regrettably, only the smallest number keeps in mind about the Supermundane World, without which it is impossible to love and cherish the earthly life. Agni Yoga and Karma Yoga amply stress the importance of labor in earthly life. Many times has it been said, "Love labor, and thus become co-workers of the higher energy."

The Thinker said, "Friends, love both the earthly and supermundane life. Do not fear the Fiery World."

887. Urusvati knows the true meaning of self-preservation. Even narrow, material science allows discussion about the instinct for self-preservation. The study of animals reveals convincing examples. The instinctual behavior of dogs offers evidence of the presence of the Invisible Worlds. Man regrettably has lost this faculty. Life in heavily populated cities, in particular, corrodes the most valuable aspects of human consciousness. And science, by denying the Spiritual World, leads humanity into ever-increasing insensitiveness.

People ridicule belief in the Supermundane World, and therefore it is impossible to tell them how beneficial the instinct for self-preservation will be on their paths in all worlds. Only a few can sense how great is the need to develop this instinct, not only for the earthly, physical life, but especially for the refining of psychic sensitivity. Each manifestation of life must be studied attentively, but for this it must be allowed into the consciousness, otherwise the dog may overtake the man.

Let us not be astonished if the new generations find themselves in a worse situation than the previous ones. They will be stifled by technocracy, and there will be no one to tell them about the art of thinking. It is essential to encourage their best instincts, in order that a faculty for healing self-preservation may develop among them.

At times the Thinker laid his hands upon the head of a disciple, and said, "Is not thy vigilance falling asleep?"

888. Urusvati knows the true meaning of humanity's self-stupefaction. Think about this urgently, think about it! Humanity has never been so greatly poisoned as it is now. People do not want to understand that all kinds of alcoholic drinks, smoking, and so many other poisons, decompose the human nature. They do not want to realize that in the midst of such poisoning a healthy new generation cannot be conceived. People do not acknowledge that they infect space with their poisonous breath, and that by this madness they prepare for themselves a terrible existence in the Supermundane World.

But how can they accept these truths if they deny the very idea of the Supermundane World? It is small consolation that there are institutions dedicated to the restoration of people's health. These are like small islands in a boundless ocean.

We have spoken many times about the poisoning of the planet, but this call remains a cry in the wilderness. People busy themselves with the invention of new harmful substances. And, filled with malice, they do not think about their own poisonous emanations. People, in their mental torpor, not only do not think about others, but even their own instinct of self-preservation is becoming dim. Do not think that Our warnings are exaggerated.

The Thinker said, "Friends, keep on repeating about the restoring of life's health."

889. Urusvati knows the true meaning of self-obscuring. With pity do we turn to the weak-willed ones. They have already gathered many accumulations in the Supermundane World, and could have applied them during their earthly life, but their burdensome daily routine trampled these best flowers of the Supermundane World. The weak will cannot withstand such a calamity; it shatters and falls into shameful cowardice.

Timid drifters are ashamed of the memory of their former accumulations, and thus become harmful negaters, perhaps more harmful than the ignorant. Everyone has met such weak, soul-sick people, whose inner discord brings them to disintegration. When you do encounter them, treat them with compassion. Of course, they are solely responsible for their failings, but it is often family life that crushes their weak will. Understand them as sick people. Do not severely criticize them, for, by doing so you will only antagonize them. They must once again pass through a hard path of learning. May they provide themselves with a firm will in the Supermundane World.

The Thinker said, "Beware of self-obscuring, because darkness is contagious."

890. Urusvati knows the true meaning of self-liberation. One cannot liberate forcibly. A physician can forbid certain habits to a patient, but as soon as the danger has passed, the patient will usually return to his old ways.

Fear, irritation, lies, envy, slander and all other enemies of man must be banished, but without the free will it is impossible to conquer them. It is sometimes said that vices must be outlived, but in trying to prolong this transitory state people use this as an excuse to procrastinate. Therefore it is best to replace the idea of outliving one's faults with a command to liberate oneself. Verily, a firm will can, like a sword, cut away bad habits.

It is especially easy to get rid of these vermin for one who has cognized the Supermundane World. Only with the realization of continuous life can one firmly drive away all harmful thoughts. For the sake of one's unavoidable future, one must intensify one's will for immediate self-liberation.

While crossing into the Supermundane World, one will value the liberation from the dark burden that impedes one's flight. Truly, why torment oneself with small leaps when one can fly beautifully? Why remain behind when one can advance?

The Thinker advised, "Love the beautiful feeling of self-liberation!"

891. Urusvati knows the true meaning of peacemaking. A yogi is peace-loving. A yogi avoids quarrels, and prevents them as best he can. A yogi knows the healing quality of peaceful emanations. A yogi has realized that such emanations prepare for him a warm welcome in the Supermundane World.

How does a yogi come to such a realization? He develops co-measurement and goal-fitness. He understands that malice destroys the bridge of advancement. He has tamed irritation, recognizing it as incompatible with human dignity. A yogi manifests strong striving toward creating peace. Even the smallest pacifying act is a beautiful achievement. It is especially valuable in these times when humanity is destroying itself with hatred. When a word about Good is deemed out of place, the yogi values the thought that protects the weak and persecuted ones. A yogi may not know whom his luminous thoughts will help, but he will not tire of sending them out into space, like a purifying offering: "Let there be good in the World."

The Thinker told a youth who wanted to become a yogi, "First, become a Peacemaker."

892. Urusvati knows the true meaning of self-forgetfulness. People are usually afraid of such concepts as self-forgetfulness and self-denial. They associate them with poverty and rags. But those who work and create know that when striving for higher quality, they forget themselves. A natural renunciation of self-centeredness has taken place. They have liberated themselves from their personality. In the same way one can see that in the Supermundane World man forgets about self, and rises toward beautiful achievements. This step of ascent is mastered without forcing.

Let man sense these wings during his earthly labor. We affirm creative activity as the best means of ascent. People do not often understand the great beauty of self-renunciation. They prefer the self-absorption of earthly life. They do not know how easily a pit of refuse can be transformed into the beginning of a beautiful garden, and make a mistake in thinking that such a transformation is not possible for them. Everyone can be a valiant conqueror of precious realms of thought.

The Thinker said, "At least think, and you will thus acquire wings of self-forgetfulness."

893. Urusvati knows the true meaning of self-destruction. To a yogi all kinds of suicide are alien. A yogi understands the great harm of the premature ending of one's own life. A yogi understands to what extent he can harm not only himself but also his entire surroundings. Each violence against life is a disturbance of harmony, and heavy is the price for any attempt against the rhythm of cosmic order.

It can be noted that, possessed by a blood-lust, humanity grows increasingly mad. However, it is not physical murder alone that is impermissible, but also the psychic arrows sent to others. Also, the despondency that destroys living Prana is contagious. It can be imagined how many suicides, direct and indirect, are taking place!

Yet, earthly scientists are silent about such a poisoning of life. Few studies are being made on the different chemical structure of tears of joy, sorrow, and anger. The radiations and emanations of the body are insufficiently investigated, even though apparatuses exist that could be used for this. But mankind does not wish to think about the Supermundane World and the meaning of such self-destruction.

The Thinker said, "Learn to beware of inflicting harm upon your near and far ones."

894. Urusvati knows the true meaning of self-regeneration. Man should realize that he can regenerate himself, no matter what his condition. However, if he is not cognizant of the Supermundane World he can easily fall into despair and imagine that nothing is left for him, and that he faces inevitable doom.

One can imagine the pitiful state of such a person when he enters the Supermundane World, which he has denied. He has convinced himself of its non-existence, and, despite his conviction, finds himself in strange surroundings, where difficult, painful conditions confront him.

Even in a difficult situation such as this man can regenerate himself, but to do it he must develop a strong will. And let those who have cognized the Supermundane World reassure him that crossing into the Supermundane World is as easy as entering the next room. Let them explain that only he can light up his new home—why wander in darkness, or use someone else's light, if one can have one's own and even help others? But help is an art that must be developed by labors in the earthly life.

Thus man can arm himself with the weapon of Light. Thus uninterrupted self-regeneration can take place; this is one of the most exalted feelings.

The Thinker said, "Friends! You can call self-regeneration self-encouragement."

895. Urusvati knows the true meaning of self-testing. All worlds are being tested. Those who have understood this truth also understand that every particle of the Universe, however small, is continuously being tested.

An intelligent person can discern the tests, whether without or within. He gives himself a task and, as long as the task brings good, he does not fear it, no matter how difficult it may be. At any time, when necessary for the good of humanity, he will willingly put his life at risk.

Throughout history the legends about the Play of the Mother of the World have been known. The courageous self-tester will also reach a level of participation in Her Play. When facing difficult tasks, the only way to approach dangers fearlessly is through self-renunciation. Then the dangers crumble as if under a hero's sword. Truly, the one who tests himself can be called a hero. He prepares for himself a glorious entrance into the Supermundane World, where he will strive at once for new quests. His subtle body will provide him with new opportunities and he will apply them valiantly for his perfectment.

Let us not forget that many supermundane travelers become timid and thus deprive themselves of great achievements.

The Thinker said, "Friend, test yourself on each step of ascent."

896. Urusvati knows the true meaning of self-induced lethargy. We have pointed to the many ways of independent activity that help to develop yogic qualities. However, there are also undermining ways, such as self-induced lethargy, laziness and lassitude, which are harmful not only in the earthly life, but also in the Supermundane World.

The "eagle eye" of the yogi was described long ago. This fiery and ever-alert quality is achieved by a yogi through prolonged contemplation. A yogi strives toward mobility and clarity of thought. A yogi has learned that he must be vigilant in order to advance. Such vigilance must occur even during sleep. It provides, so to speak, a threshold to the Supermundane World.

But a yogi can pass into the subtle state while in full consciousness. It is not necessary to be in a semi-conscious state for this; such a vegetative state will not bring anyone to transformation. Yet, there are many slumbering wanderers who pollute space, and thereby harm all that surrounds them in the Supermundane World.

A yogi knows that self-perfectment is needed not only for him but also for the common good. How can we explain to people that they live for the success of evolution? How can we protect space from pollution?

The Thinker said, "Friend, remember about the 'eagle eye.'"

897. Urusvati knows the true meaning of self-induced stupefaction. One who sleeps can be awakened, but a stupefied one is almost beyond help. Man sinks into a life of daily routine and does not live, but vegetates. Stupefaction crawls into his being like a worm. He is so unhappy that he is unaware of his calamity. He loses his keenness of thinking and is unable to find renewing ways. He loses completely his exalted striving.

But the main calamity awaits him in the Supermundane World. He cannot grasp these new conditions. He cannot perfect himself, because the daily routines he brings with him do not correspond to the new surroundings. He is afflicted with his dullness, and it is difficult to help him, because he did not learn how to attract supermundane forces during his earthly life.

This kind of stupefaction can be seen as one of the most dangerous illnesses, for the brain becomes atrophied and loses its receptivity.

The Thinker asserted, "Warrior, you will not be victorious with a dull spear."

898. Urusvati knows the true meaning of self-adulation. Most people are accustomed to picturing a yogi as an alien creature living in caves, standing on his head, striving only inward, concentrating on himself. Rarely do people picture the yogi as a toiler striving for the good of humanity.

A yogi loves labor and offers himself in self-denial for the betterment of people's lives. Whether a yogi occupies the highest earthly positions or the most modest ones, he continues to strive for higher knowledge.

If someone proclaims himself a yogi, do not believe him. A true yogi will never call himself a yogi or admire himself. Even if, for the sake of good, a yogi affirms himself, he does it not in self-interest, but for the advancement of the people.

A yogi loves labor passionately. He loves self-perfectment. He will not tire of working, for he knows why he follows his earthly path. The Supermundane World is open to the yogi. A yogi does not experience an interruption of life. He proceeds in full consciousness in different bodies and hastens toward higher knowledge.

We do not deny any yoga, but, now particularly, We affirm the Yoga of Labor. Karma Yoga is linked with Jnani and with Bhakti. One cannot labor without knowledge or love. Thus, the yogi brings his life's experiences and offers them to mankind.

The Thinker said, "Friend, love labor. It will forge wings for you."

899. Urusvati knows the true meaning of willfulness. Some people do not understand the difference between willfulness and the free will, though there is a distinct difference. Free will, properly applied, acts according to the law of cosmic rhythm. It produces good, whereas willfulness produces disharmony. One who lapses into willfulness can cause unimaginable calamities.

Ignorance is the mother of willfulness. A person in this miserable state knows nothing about the Supermundane World. He believes that he is, in every way, a self-willed creator of his own fate. When the supermundane laws become known, it will be seen that the path of willfulness is a wrong one. The process of Cosmic Justice cannot be set aside. It would be like a diver trying to find pearls in the depths of the ocean without being properly trained. Willfulness is a bad adviser, and carries destruction with it.

The teachers must tell children about the difference

between the victorious free will and destructive willfulness. Let the children understand how beautiful is the way of free will, when man, through universal law, will be the builder of the Future.

The Thinker warned against the madness of willfulness.

900. Urusvati knows the true meaning of self-distrust. If conceit and willfulness are ruinous for a yogi, then self-distrust is also harmful. People do not understand the border between conceit and self-distrust, but not all psychic boundary lines are evident. Only when in a state of harmony can one discern the differences.

True, cognizing of the Supermundane World also teaches one how to see the harm of one's own self-distrust. Let us picture a person ailing with self-distrust. He will be unhappy in the Subtle World, for he will be unable to sense its reality. He does not trust himself, and will believe the supermundane reality to be a hallucination.

But how can one learn to recognize absolute reality in the earthly world? People, from early age, learn about the relativity of things, and this prevents their looking beyond the boundaries of the earthly, coarse body. However, a yogi learns to have faith in his "third eye." It opens up only gradually, through the exercise of the will.

The yogi should also recognize the Supermundane World, which will be revealed to him as absolute, beyond doubting. A yogi affirms without conceit what he sees, and nothing can shake his conviction. Thus a yogi enters consciously into the Supermundane World, as a welcome and awaited guest.

The schools should find simple words to describe the Supermundane World, as a place where everyone who desires to advance can find beauty.

The Thinker said, "Learn to live simultaneously in both the earthly and Supermundane Worlds."

901. Urusvati knows the true meaning of self-induced anger. A yogi must not succumb to anger. Enough has been said about the harm of the poisons produced by losing one's temper, but no less harmful are the constant precipitations of the anger itself. This is often caused by ignorance, and can start from the least dissatisfaction, growing into a tangle of constant irritation. The best forces become poisoned, and an undeveloped space grows over with weeds, instead of becoming a beautiful garden.

In the Supermundane World anger is pernicious. The emanations of anger turn away the best help. He who becomes ill with anger is drawn to strata that could easily have been avoided; not to mention the contamination of space and the harm that is inflicted on the environment.

It must be recognized that the emanations of anger are powerful and project to great distances, equally in the earthly and Supermundane Worlds. A fit of fury is like black lightning, but a self-induced state of anger is like poisoned food.

The Thinker said, "Don't converse with an angry person."

902. Urusvati knows the true meaning of self-enslavement. People love to talk about freedom from slavery. They care about other people, but forget about their own need for liberation.

What is the slavery of every day, of every hour? Man has bound himself with petty habits. He has ensnared himself in a cobweb of prejudices. How can such a chained captive fight for the freedom of mankind?

Can a yogi bow before the petty demons of daily routine? Can a traveler in the Supermundane World proceed freely under a load of petty, prickly habits? Man so fears to disturb the smallest particle of his daily routine that he does not sense how to approach the renewing of life. It is impossible to affirm freedom, when slavery rules.

The Thinker warned, "Before thinking of the freedom of others, liberate yourself."

903. Urusvati knows the true meaning of self-torture. All Teachings condemn torture and the inflicting of anguish. Only ignorant fanatics allow torture as a remedy in life in spite of the fact that innumerable generations have proved that tortures led humanity to stupefaction, not to perfectment.

The highest yogis did not allow self-torture, for they well knew about the Supermundane World and understood the dark karma that the tormentor weaves for himself. They were in contact with the Supermundane World and knew what scientific and spiritual perfection was possible. Thus man should remember that his self-inflicted cruelties will oppress him instead of bestowing wings.

It would seem that this truth should be known to people, but earthly realities reveal the opposite. Therefore one should speak about the harm of torture, whether physical or psychic. It is time to acknowledge the Supermundane World with all its laws.

The Reminder of the Thinker: "Dark is the one who brings torture; luminous is the one who brings beneficent joy."

904. Urusvati knows the true meaning of self-depletion. Harmony and balance have been ordained, but one who is weary cannot make use of them. Many have perished from overwork, but many also have perished from idleness, from a stupor of the brain; both extremes border on suicide. People perish because of lack of knowledge of supermundane conditions.

To understand the true nature of people, it is necessary to also understand the Supermundane Life. People fall into extremes, not achieving the oft-mentioned harmony. Those who do not know about rhythm and vibrations cannot understand harmony. The ignorant suppose that only yogis can live a life of harmony, and dismiss the essential point that the middle way of harmony was taught to all humanity. They consider the middle way to be a kind of mediocrity, whereas the Supermundane World is founded upon harmony, and every newcomer embraces it as a salutary principle.

If everyone understood more deeply the foundations of the Supermundane World, they would be able to apply them in their earthly life. The schools should teach an understanding of harmony. The manifestation of balance can improve the health of all of life.

The Thinker affirmed, "Man, cognize the power of equilibrium."

905. Urusvati knows the real causes of self-debasement. Of the many negative qualities degrading the dignity of man, ingratitude must be noted. A fool, filled with egoism, shouts, "What I do not see, does not exist; what I do not know, does not exist." Such people cannot cognize the Supermundane World. They do not understand whence can come the needed help and where should be paid the most fervent gratitude.

A stubborn resistance to thinking about the Higher Worlds induces dullness and, even in earthly life, man becomes unappreciative of the surrounding beneficence.

He does not accept that often a small gift brings a big result. An instructor, when teaching his pupils to give thanks for even the smallest gift, acts for the

Good. Thus again we must turn to the Supermundane World.

The Thinker affirmed, "A yogi is never ungrateful."

906. Urusvati knows the real causes of self-debasement. Another trait that degrades man is coarseness. Coarseness is the darkness of ignorance. Coarseness is alien to a yogi. A yogi refines his thinking and thus lives in both worlds.

It can be stated that, unavoidably, a great number of crude manifestations are being brought into the Supermundane World. But these lower spheres of the Supermundane World are not visited by ascending travelers. Only the Higher Teachers, because of their compassion, visit the dwellers of the coarse spheres. Yet even the highest Spirit suffers, when contacting the atmosphere of coarse vibrations.

It is difficult to imagine how contaminated the Earth is with coarseness! People are surrounded by a kind of epidemic. Only a strong will can break through the strata of infection without being affected by it. The consciousness can protect one, but it must be clear. It is not easy to avoid indirect influences of the lower vibrations, but the command of the will can create a shield, and then the Supermundane help can easily reach the pilgrim.

The Thinker warned, "With all your strength eradicate coarseness."

907. Urusvati knows the real causes of self-debasement. Cruelty is a trait that degrades man, and forges for him a cruel karma. A yogi cannot be cruel, for he is in contact with the Supermundane World. He knows how dark are the spheres in which the cruel people dwell. He knows how difficult it is for these dwellers to elevate themselves. He knows that cruelty in earthly life brings no benefit. A yogi manifests the greatest intensity in order to redeem human cruelty with compassion.

A yogi knows that most cruelty is caused by ignorance. The ignorant must be re-educated, but the time required for such education is long since the ignorant do not recognize what is best for them. They do not understand that cruelty is both physical and psychic. The latter is especially abhorrent. Yet how can one speak about psychic cruelty to a person who rejects the very idea of the spirit? The battle against cruelty will be a real *podvig*.

The Thinker reminded, "Cruelty creates a cruel karma."

908. Urusvati knows the real causes of self-debasement. The desire for revenge demeans man. A yogi does not seek revenge for he knows that it acts like a boomerang. The yogi also knows that in the Supermundane World revenge is a crime, and such criminals plunge into the darker spheres. Their vibrations do not permit them to rise and their path toward ascent is a lengthy one.

You know that a Yogi is not without defense. His thought is sharper than a sword and truer than an arrow. Yet a yogi will send such an arrow only when he is convinced that it is not he alone who faces harm, but others too—even humanity.

It should not be thought that the actions of a yogi are ever retributive; it would be better to compare them with those of a solicitous gardener who destroys weeds. True, a yogi may often choose to send an arrow to an unexpected target, and people will not understand the reason for the sudden calamity that results.

I speak again about the arrow of the yogi, for people often tend to imagine a yogi as somehow removed from life and uninvolved with the common good.

Using examples from history, schoolteachers should teach that revenge is unacceptable.

The Thinker said, "Understand clearly how degrading revenge is."

909. Urusvati knows the real causes of self-debasement. Wavering of thought and feeling brings about extreme ugliness. Understand this word in its true sense. Ugliness comes from a loss of clarity and an immersion in chaotic refuse. Ignorant people may fear losing freedom of thought, not understanding that incoherent wavering is not freedom.

A yogi knows the limitlessness of thought, and is full of striving for the good of humanity, for the current of evolution. He has chosen a clear-cut path and it would be unfitting for him to degrade himself by wavering. He acknowledges the laws of the Supermundane World and wishes to choose a short path, for only in this state of tension will he make contact with beauty. He knows that beauty is the Guiding Star, and that it can be cognized only in an understanding of the Supermundane World. There, too, many waverers can be found, and their path is long and tortuous!

The Thinker remarked with kindness, "Do not waver, it will only make your head dizzy."

910. Urusvati knows real causes of self-debasement. Self-flattery and self-admiration are alien to the yogi. Like a winged messenger, a yogi strives into the future. Like a solicitous physician, a yogi foresees the onset of psychic illnesses and hurries to prevent them by his thoughts. Whence comes such indomitable striving into the future? Of course, from the realization of the Supermundane World.

A yogi knows that the duration of earthly life is but a small part of supermundane existence. A yogi has learned how close and simple is the transition into the

Supermundane World; it is performed for the sake of the future and teaches man to comprehend Infinity.

People usually fear the concept of infinity. They prefer, in the lowest routines of their life, to prepare for themselves a gloomy existence in the subtle body. They reject the power of thought and so lose a powerful weapon. They strive to self-deception, forgetting that Truth is the best adornment for a thinker.

The Thinker told His disciples, "Do not worry if a thought dispatched by you did not reach its destination. Perhaps it was attracted to another place, where it will be of greater benefit. Good thoughts are needed everywhere."

911. Urusvati knows the real causes of self-debasement. Absolute power degrades man. Despotic power is a sign of extreme narrow-mindedness, and one who seeks such power is bringing about his downfall. A yogi avoids autocratic power and declares himself a servant of Good. He draws this awareness from his realization of the Supermundane World.

A yogi has great respect for Hierarchy. He knows that there are many Hierarchs above him. But ordinary man faces a difficult step in achieving an understanding of Hierarchy. People do not like what they perceive as subjugation. They consider themselves to have unlimited power, and in their egoism abandon all thoughts of Infinity. In refusing to learn to love the beauty of Infinity they cannot love Hierarchy, unaware that without that love the path of achievement can be easily lost. He who fears Hierarchy is also afraid of the Supermundane World–fear is a poor guide.

No imagined autocratic power can save one from fear. Truly, autocratic power is an eternal sickness of fear. But a yogi, as a Servant of Good, having come to know his Teacher, becomes stronger than any despotic tyrant.

The Thinker said, "Friends, before you are the wondrous steps of ascent."

912. Urusvati knows the real causes of self-debasement. A yogi does not succumb to self-deception. Beginners will ask, "Where is the boundary, where is the foundation, where is the correct decision? What helps a yogi to find true reality and not sink into mirages of the imagination?" You already know what science calls intuition. Some scientists devote much attention to intuition, and do not deny that man, when in a state of nervous stimulation, can come to a correct decision.

Now, let us imagine a yogi, who has intensified his nervous sensitivity and raised his consciousness to reach into the Supermundane World. He will not use conjectures of the mind, but will listen to the voice of his heart, an antenna that receives the waves of direct communication. The stronghold of the yogi is not in the brain, but in the heart.

Science is as yet unable to understand the true value of the heart. The ancient world often referred to the power of the heart, but the rational mind insisted that the brain was preeminent, and thus impeded the surest striving. Until recently the heart was thought of as almost magical, and the conventional scientists stood aloof from such beliefs, so as not to be seen as dreamers. A whole dictionary could be made out of proscribed, but valuable concepts. Let us wish that the scientists become more free.

The Thinker said, "What can be colder than an extinguished hearth? What can be deader than a silenced heart?"

913. Urusvati knows the real causes of self-debasement. Many degrading qualities darken humanity, each of these dark qualities gathers around itself many related ones, big and small. Linked together, they form a chain that can hinder even those of strong will.

The powerful growth of darkness makes more urgent the need to photograph human emanations. By doing this, it will soon be possible to observe remarkable phenomena. Sometimes it will be seen that a bad thought is weakened by an outside influence, and that a good thought can also be darkened by something external. Such manifestations confirm the influence of the Supermundane World.

The lesson of such influence can be affirmed not only by ethicists, but also by biologists. We insist upon scientific research. For many years We have repeated that science is approaching a true way of cognizing the inner powers of man, but in reality very little has been done in this direction. Even the Supermundane World remains for scientists a bugbear of superstition, and We therefore have to act like woodpeckers!

The Thinker advised His disciples to watch themselves, as a way of refining their receptivity.

914. Urusvati knows the High Path. Beginners will come and say, "Point out the way, we are ready." Tell them, "Let it be so, let us try. Know how to develop the power of observation. Know how to understand what you read. Know how to strive without restraint into the future."

The beginners will smile, and say, "Is that all? It is an easy start. We have had the power of observation since our early years, as our teachers attested. Our school recorded our ability to remember our lessons. And finally, who does not dream about the future?" Then the self-praising ones should be corrected. "Who can praise your powers of observation, when you fail to pay attention to the many events happening around you? Are you capable of truly grasping what you read? Can you understand the meaning beyond the letter? And you do not know at all how to strive into the future, for half your consciousness is stuck in the past. Thus, even the initial path is not easy. Besides, you are afraid even to think about the Supermundane World. What kind of future is there without striving to the Higher World?"

The Thinker said, "In ignorance even the difficult seems easy."

915. Urusvati knows the High Path. Love is the key to its entrance. Love is the power of overcoming. Love is the healing spring, the inexhaustible. It is said: Lofty is the Yoga of Love. Some people regard the path of Love as the easiest, but for others it is the most difficult. The heart in which malice and cruelty live cannot love.

Many people are unaware that their storerooms are full of malice, and they cannot overcome their base feelings. They may pretend to heed what they hear about the victory of Love, but their essence is dark, and they will enter the Supermundane World without a torchlight.

The highest vibration of Love cannot be taught if there is no seed of it in the heart. The fire of Love burns powerfully. It should lead to the High Path.

The Thinker taught His disciples to distinguish betwen love and malice by looking into the eyes, "Long ago it was said that the eyes are open wounds. The testimony of such currents of the heart can be trusted."

916. Urusvati affirms the High Path. One must not shout in the bazaar about the Highest. But it is everywhere beneficial to point out the guideposts. Somewhere scientifically; somewhere, like a fairy tale;

somewhere, austerely, and somewhere beautifully. To each one in accordance with his consciousness, to each one in accordance with his understanding.

A yogi is often reproached for speaking in different ways at different times about the same truth. But ignorant people cannot understand that a yogi speaks about different aspects of truth to different people. The tolerance of a yogi should be greatly appreciated when he sows the seeds of good without thinking about the harvest. Karma alone will determine the harvest. Yet nothing is lost in space. Seeds that do not sprout in earthly conditions will produce their shoots in the Supermundane World. Thus it is even more necessary to assimilate the reality of the Supermundane World.

It is difficult to imagine the benefit of good for empty space, but when one knows about the peopling of Infinity, it is easy to perceive the need for good thoughts. A thought penetrates more quickly into immeasurable space than into the house of one's neighbor, and through the magnet of attraction will find its application—so long as one loves the High Path.

The Thinker said, "A solicitous physician will know how to prevent the onset of illness."

917. Urusvati assimilated the High Rhythm. A yogi knows that to harmonize the centers while amidst raging chaos is not easy. A deep inner concentration is needed in order to grasp the higher vibrations. However, even well-wishers can be disruptive.

Two extremes should be noted. On the one hand, there are those who unexpectedly begin to receive Supermundane Messages and, instead of paying attention to and studying them, they regard such manifestations as unimportant and dismiss them. On the other hand there are the credulous ones, who regard each psychic flash as an attainment and initiation.

It is impossible to reconcile such extreme ways of thinking. Such people cannot be spoken to in the same language, or with the same words. One would have to tell them separately about their errors, fully prepared for them to take offense, and instead of good, harm would result. It is better to hint cautiously, and let life itself stop the errant ones. Each of them has at least a glimmer of understanding about the Supermundane World. In time their insights will grow stronger, and the day will come when there will be a possibility of true heart to heart discourse.

The Thinker said, "Friend, of what use is self-perfectment if you cannot recognize the Common Good?"

918. Urusvati knows active Silence, which is what We call the brief silence sent by a yogi prior to the beginning of his labor or speech. Those present would say that he is concentrating, but those who know realize that the yogi is sending a sign into the Supermundane World, asking for cooperation and guidance. Words are not needed for such a transport of the consciousness.

The yogi knows how to send his energy both downward and upward. He does not always know whence the help will come, for his work can reach different realms. An experienced Guide will come if the work is directed to the Common Good. One can discern by the yogi's emanations how the influence of the High Scientists affects him. One may be sure that a moment of tense silence can immediately summon High Help. The silence then ends with a deep sigh.

The Thinker reminded, "In one sigh we are transported into space."

919. Urusvati lives in a state of fiery Illumination. The nature of a yogi is fiery, kindled by constant concentration and elevation of thought. In their daily lives, people glimpse the higher energies, but do not notice them, and the opportunities are thus extinguished. No one has told them that their natural talisman of psychic energy must be ignited, otherwise it can remain unmanifest in its repository.

Likewise, no one has told them that the lightning of the Supermundane World can reanimate them if the spark of their consciousness has forged a magnet. This kind of reciprocity has a decisive importance in the Universe. But no one has warned the one entering upon the path of Yoga that fiery influences can be quite unpleasant.

The earthly and Supermundane fires have much in common, and the one who approaches a fiery *podvig* can understand what will compensate him for his passing pain. He knows that he enters into cooperation with the Higher Forces, and the realization of higher *podvig* raises him above chaos. Then can man be named a conqueror.

The Thinker smiled, "I burn, I burn, yet I am not consumed."

920. Urusvati has mastered the Yoga of thought, which is what We sometimes call Agni Yoga, in order to affirm that thought lies in its foundation. Thought is fiery. Thought is limitless. No one can define the boundaries of the dissemination of thought, which is speedier than light. Thus, it can be understood that thought will be the best link with the Supermundane Worlds. Man's thought should therefore be worthy of illumination by the fire of space.

The greatest pity is when the traveler in the Supermundane World feels that he must be ashamed of his former thoughts. The record of thoughts is ineradicable; it flashes before the eyes of the newly arrived one.

The Yoga of thought could be preferred to the Yoga

demanding physical suffering. A brief pranayama, light diet, and striving of thought gain free entrance. One can accustom oneself to constant pranayama, just as to constant communion with the Supermundane World. Then, the earthly life will not be an obstacle to one's ascent.

The Thinker repeated, "Thought is lightning."

921. Urusvati experienced the transformation of life. Life is dark without the transformation of the spirit. Gloomy is the stagnant life of those two-legged negators who do not realize the cosmic disruption they cause to evolution. When evolution is delayed, or damaged, then powerful energies must be expended again. The karma of negators cannot be stopped; and the cosmic harm inflicted by them must be repaid again. Why disfigure life, when it can be beautifully transformed?

Everyone can create a link with the Supermundane World through the power of thought, and a transformation of the meaning of earthly existence will occur, from within. Why should one wait for an external impulse? One must generate in one's own consciousness an indomitable striving toward the Supermundane World. One must love such thoughts and find the moment to grasp this silver thread of higher knowledge. This knowledge can begin with just a small crumb, but every meager accumulation is already invincible. It can lead to a powerful transformation of one's entire life.

"The transformed life is beautiful." So said the Thinker.

922. Urusvati overcomes currents from afar. We say "overcomes" in order to define the difficulty of this attainment. It is a mistake to think that with the elevation of one's thought, currents and vibrations will

be assimilated more easily. With the heightening of thought, one faces powerful new tasks. That is why the ladder of achievement in Infinity is not easy.

Regrettably, science advances too slowly, and the most significant realms remain unexplored. Astrochemistry is still seen as fantasy, and it is only relatively recently that the attention of observers has been directed to sun spots. The boldest of scientists have even begun admitting the influence of these explosions upon the psychic life of humanity.

Such explosions are obvious manifestations, but myriad less-evident radiations from the far-off worlds constantly act upon man. People often feel unwell or become ill, with no apparent reason. Earthly physicians blame such episodes on the usual physical ailments, without considering the possibility of supermundane causes. They do not study vibrations. They have not heard about prismatic vision. They are not informed about the power of psychic energy.

The most mistaken doctors are the psychiatrists, whose work involves a realm that is still largely a mystery to them. The harm that can be inflicted by such doctors is incalculable. We can all see right now that psychic illnesses are on the increase. The actual conditions that surround Earth should be studied, including the so-called brown gas, which prevents the approach of better vibrations. Truly, such obstacles must be overcome.

The Thinker said, "In surmounting, there is joy."

923. Urusvati has felt the Fire of Space. Glimpses of the fiery elements were already noted in remote antiquity; in all mythologies there is found a deity of Fire, usually of dual nature—destroying and healing.

Even now people argue about the nature of Fire. They do not understand how it is that this powerful element can sometimes be so beneficent. They have no knowledge of the Universal Magnet which can be found in all that exists.

If man's psychic energy is refined and strong, it will find cooperation with the Fire of Space. From such reciprocity will come good, not harm. Moreover, if people knew about the Supermundane World, they would see for themselves that everything is based upon fiery energy.

Urusvati can confirm how often Fire is manifested in life, without causing pain. But to experience this one should approach naturally, and accept the entire scope of manifestations, the smallest and the greatest. They will occur unexpectedly, but will flash up in accordance with the laws of the Supermundane World.

The Thinker said, "Inspiration is in Fire."

924. Urusvati knows the sound of Silence. Great manifestations take place in silence. At the same time, it has been said that Silence can be louder than thunder. One should know the difference between the living silence, full of supermundane harmonies, and the dead silence, when the currents of the Higher Worlds are cut off.

It should be understood that blood pulsations and brain waves have nothing in common with Supermundane soundings. People do not understand that the noise in their ears is not a sign of some kind of achievement. People either deny all such manifestations, or regard them as signs of a lofty achievement. But the soundings of Silence, like powerful chords, ring out, filling all of existence; joy abides in these harmonies.

One should learn to discern the fundamental chords. At times they fill space like a resounding string; at times like many-voiced choirs; at times they resemble a majestic symphony, but sometimes one can hear the song of one Voice. Thus can be heard the Music of the Spheres. Space resounds with a special rhythm at every moment.

The Thinker sometimes, during a discourse, would become silent as if listening, and say, "How beautiful is the sound of the Supermundane World!"

925. Urusvati values the "multihued diamond." This is what we call true knowledge, to which there can be many approaches. A superficial reader will think that We often repeat the very same things, but reveals his inattentiveness by not taking the trouble to compare indications given at different times about the same subject.

One can see that there are no repetitions, but simply different facets to the one Diamond. An experienced observer will see that the different reminders correspond to varying cosmic and psychic conditions. The Teacher knows how cautiously He should touch the consciousness of the disciple. The very same truth, repeated in varied forms, can be more easily remembered, and thus a new path toward achievement can be opened.

Do not hesitate to find the most easily understood words; keep in mind the unsteady consciousnesses of the listeners. Often a complex concept is easily assimilated, whereas the simplest one seems unclear. Then, choose another time, and knock at a different door. It is easy to understand that the entrance through the heart appears to be the simplest, but only one who himself has a resounding heart can find this entrance.

The Thinker directed the attention of the disciples to the Supermundane World. He asserted that one's subtle body will find the most beautiful refracted colors of the Diamond.

926. Urusvati can reconcile adamantine loyalty

with flexibility of thinking. "Always at the ready," says flexibility. "I will not betray," asserts loyalty. To many people, such concepts as flexibility and loyalty seem to be incompatible. Fanatics of loyalty consider flexibility of thinking to be treasonous, and those devoted to flexibility believe that an immovable idol can never lead into the future.

But the Yogi understands the value of both flexibility and the Adamant of loyalty. The Yogi's equilibrium helps him to look forward, clearly and vigilantly. He is sufficiently acquainted with the Supermundane World and knows how necessary flexibility of thinking is in that realm. Yet, the Adamant of loyalty preserves for him his destined place. The elevated nature of a Yogi cannot manifest without the reconciling of such opposites.

People often fear precisely those concepts that are the most important for them to grasp. So many harmful misunderstandings destroy achievements! People will have to understand the idea of Great Unity! But they continue their ignorant disunity, even in the Supermundane World. The Teachers are greatly concerned when They see so much discord and the impossibility of bringing unreasonable people to their senses. True, it is possible to influence them through suggestion, because the will of ordinary people is not very strong, but this kind of influence would be an intrusion. Only voluntary realization of Truth is permissible.

The Thinker said, "Guard the Adamant of loyalty in all ways."

927. Urusvati strives toward the Science of Life. People will think that biology is meant, but, I regret to say, modern biology cannot be called the Science of Life. It is impossible to imagine the study of life without the psychic, spiritual life, and without the Supermundane World, with all its influences upon earthly life. This is why modern biology can be called only a chapter in the Book of Life.

Few people ponder upon the connections between the sciences. However, it is impossible to study astronomy without studying chemistry and astrochemistry, or physics and astrophysics. We have pointed out that the grandeur of the Supermundane World must not be cheapened, but there are few who pay attention to Our warnings, and people continue to demand new things without having fully assimilated the elementary fundamentals of life.

We have spoken often about such lightmindedness, but only a few question their understanding of what was already indicated long ago, or ask themselves whether they have learned to pay attention to the manifestations surrounding them. Just as before, the sky is simply a blue void for them. Just as before, they are deaf and blind, and revelations about the Supermundane World are perceived as frightening phantoms. Man is still unable to trust what his own heart tells him. Physicians cannot be of help to such a person, for they themselves are ignorant of biology in its true, full scope.

The Thinker pointed to the fathomless sky, and taught his disciples to love Infinity.

928. Urusvati opened the gates of Yoga; from early childhood, visions and dreams were impressed upon her mind. Usually children do not pay attention to such manifestations or they begin to be afraid of them, thus breaking the link with the Supermundane World. But the yogic nature collects into the consciousness all received psychic messages.

Often, due to ignorance, people near the child deride and burden the path of natural Yoga. We know the many tests endured by sensitive organisms. Perhaps this struggle is particularly valuable, for one's weapon is sharpened by battle, and is less prone to rust.

People complain at the absence of connection with the Supermundane World, yet often fail to recognize significant phenomena. It is precisely in the earthly life that the supermundane signs burn vividly, and will surely attract the attention of those who can see. Yet man would rather rub his eyes in disbelief than accept having seen something unusual. People are better at driving away than at attracting. We particularly recommend the Fiery Yoga, for it provides a way of natural development. One should learn to accept the fundamental fiery nature of all that exists. Only by learning to love the primary energy can one attract its cooperation.

The Thinker taught the love of Yoga. "It will enrich the earthly pilgrimage."

929. Urusvati is outliving her inherited burden. Humanity should study the foundations of heredity. But this will be possible only when science is liberated from superstition and limitation.

Many accumulations have piled up on man. Heredity of one's personal incarnations, heredity of the clan, heredity of one's people, supermundane heredity, and also the many influences of accidental encounters, which imprint themselves on the psychic nature and change it.

Indeed, scientists of limited mind can observe heredity only within the context of the family; in other words, within the most narrow limitations. They occasionally do observe those inherited traits that may appear even after several generations. But they cannot make the more sensitive observations, because they do not believe in reincarnation or in the Supermundane World.

It is impossible to properly observe man within these narrow, ignorant limitations, but one may hope that science will free itself and will achieve true insights.

Every Yogi understands that he succeeds in throwing off inherited burdens only by elevating his yogic nature. The Yogi knows that contemporary science will mock his achievements, but it is real life that helps the Yogi in his ascent. A Yogi is more of a realist than the foolish negators.

The Thinker reminded, "Liberate science, hasten to remove its fetters."

930. Urusvati does not fear danger. A Yogi knows that people live in constant danger. Since the danger is ever-present, there is no point in fearing it.

People complain about their vulnerability. They have no idea that the Supermundane World is in contact with them. They say, "A dog has an instinct and presentiments, but people have lost these abilities forever." But these complaints are not true. People sense beforehand and foresee a great deal more than they think. Unfortunately their attention is distracted by everyday needs, and the opportunities for observations of subtle phenomena are lost.

When people act correctly because of some unheard command, they think that their own mind made the best decision. They regard their presentiments in the same naive way, and would rather relate them to an upset stomach than to the Supermundane World. It would take a great power to persuade such blind ones to see and understand their surroundings. But why await miracles when all of life is filled with subtle manifestations!

The Thinker smiled, and said, "Is it possible that you would fear each messenger?"

931. Urusvati knows how to guard what has been entrusted to her. Such safeguarding elicits two extreme opinions—that the sacred can be entrusted only to specially tested people, or that the Supermundane Law, the Law of Nature, will find its own best way of dissemination. As usual, extremes are imperfect, and the truth lies in the middle.

Truly, one cannot leave the treasure of a most Sacred Teaching to only a small group of people. But it is also wrong to strew it on the road, where it can be appropriated by hostile entities. This means that one should bestow in accordance with the consciousness of the recipient. But how does one weigh the consciousness of another in order to detect a friend and co-worker? In each case, the proper way to safeguard the entrusted is by listening to the promptings of the heart about what should be given out. This ability is refined through long experience; it is especially valuable when it can be applied in life, and it cannot be exercised without cognition of the Supermundane World. People should think more often about the beautiful application of the Supermundane Laws.

"Thinking of the Beautiful, we attract to ourselves beautiful worlds." So said the Thinker.

932. Urusvati drew the Supermundane World to herself long ago. Through what kind of attraction is such a coming together attained? No pleas or commands can help, no tears or praise can help, if the heart is closed. An ancient psalm proclaims wisely, "My heart is open." He who said it recognized the fundamental magnet.

An open heart is a victory over earthly limitations. Some will say it is too late for us to transform our hearts. They prove their ignorance with such a notion. They do not understand that the word "late" must be banished from their dictionary. Life is limitless and uninterrupted, and it is never too late for any achievement.

Most people cannot imagine that learning is continued when one is in the Supermundane World. The most ignorant people try to avoid Moral Teachings, even here. One can pity the idlers, but they cannot be justified. They must understand how they pollute their own consciousnesses. Only the basest savage refuses to think about the future.

The Thinker said, "Hasten to open your hearts."

933. Urusvati has observed the massing of populations. In earthly history there have always been periods of great population congestion. No one gathers the multitudes, no one leads them, they converge by themselves, and such a mob can cause great calamities. We call such a manifestation swarming.

This can be observed among people and animals. The same thing happens in the Subtle World, where crowds wander aimlessly and disturb the harmony. It is difficult to trace the cause of such wanderings, but it can be found in the varying combinations of planetary currents and radiations. Earthly scientists could observe these psycho-planetary manifestations, but few pay attention to psychic occurrences.

Some observers have believed that the planets may be ill and their emanations poisonous. Of course, science calls such observers mad, and almost included Flammarion among them. But there is observable proof of links between the worlds and the life of humanity. And yet, most scientists do not recognize the filling and overcrowding of space.

Observations of sunspots should be regarded as a

primitive approach. A universe of innumerable luminaries provides innumerable observations. And the combinations of astro-chemical currents can explain the ebb and flow of the Ocean of Life.

The Thinker asked people above all to think freely, and said, "Freedom of thought is the path of progress."

934. Urusvati acknowledged the cosmic nature of man. People often talk about Macrocosm and microcosm, and at the same time, do not see their main foundations. They do not admit the existence of the primary energy, the Supermundane World and the spiritual basis of everything. What kind of Macrocosm could it be without basic foundations? It would be a poor ruin and the microcosm would be a pitifully deformed creature.

Some insightful scientists sense that even in their most brilliant discoveries something is lacking. They understand inwardly that the laws discovered by them are only partial and can be extended to new boundaries. But, since from their early childhood no one ever spoke to them about the law of the spirit, they do not find within themselves the courage to seek unlimited knowledge. Examples can be cited of serious researchers who concealed their broad observations. They were afraid to go beyond the boundaries of their limited science. In secret they read the works of great thinkers but would never admit to their own new paths.

However, if we imagine that all of humanity is transformed from deniers into unrestrained observers, what scientific progress would take place! It can be understood that the legend about "The City of Light" would then become reality.

The Thinker said, "There will come a new scientist, bold and unlimited."

935. Urusvati understood that people can be transformed through better vibrations. It may be asked, "Which people and which vibrations?" This must be explained or there will be misinterpretations. You know well that no one can be forcibly transformed. People must voluntarily desire their transformation, or at least reveal a readiness to receive those vibrations.

Also, the quality of vibrations should be understood. Until now, vibrations were judged rather primitively. Thus, the color blue was believed to be calming, and red irritating, but there are many shades of blue and also many shades of red. Among the reds, there is the ruby-red, very healing and full of higher vibrations. Among the blues, there can be "dead" tints that carry low-spirited vibrations. It is often said that green is good, and yellow is coarse. Such descriptions are primitive. There can be found greens with irritating vibrations, and yellows full of tranquility.

Also one should remember about sound, which can affect each person individually. Of course, in the future science will discover many ways of testing for the best results. Then, people familiar with the Supermundane World will recall the great diversity of emanations, which, while diverse, are grouped harmoniously according to their vibrations.

When the observations of scientists have become sufficiently refined, the same harmony could be developed on Earth. But in order for scientists to be able to investigate those vibrations, a special love must be revealed for the subject.

The Thinker sometimes asserted, "Love at least something, so as not to be left without the light of Love!"

936. Urusvati forefeels and foresees. These two words exist in all human languages, but only few people understand their meaning. On the one side there are the superstitious, and the interpreters of dreams, and on the other, the negators, who, like the superstitious, obstruct intelligent understanding. Only a small number of keen-sighted ones are prepared to study mankind's abilities. Some people reach such a level of absurdity that they even envy the sensitivity of animals. They do not understand that man possesses a higher intuition, but usually does not accept it. And when the consciousness glimpses something that later occurs, this straight-knowledge is seen as accidental.

Indeed, since books about psychology do not mention psychic energy and the life of the Supermundane World, people have difficulty finding the sources of knowledge. You will say that the Supermundane Guides at times can help to find useful books; Urusvati can confirm it. But for such cooperation the heart must be opened and supermundane vibrations assimilated. But this condition is rarely found.

The Thinker said, "Love the science of forefeeling and foreseeing."

937. Urusvati reveres Karma Yoga. All yogas are related to each other; Agni Yoga and Karma Yoga can be regarded as sisters. Agni Yoga leads luminously into the Highest Realm. Karma Yoga ignites the sacred fire of labor.

People rarely revere the life of labor that molds a better karma. People do not think about the quality of their labor. They are unable to acknowledge the joy of creativeness. To them it may seem like chains. They are unable to love daily labor and are unaware of the spiritual ascent that comes from it. No one ever informed them that great wings are created in great labor.

But how can man be expected to understand Karma if he is not aware of the Supermundane World and therefore has never pondered on it? Why would he want to achieve, if he does not know the goal? Agni Yoga will be for him an empty dream he will never have. He will fear Fire and will not understand its beauty. Without beauty he cannot learn to love the Fiery World.

How will you be able to explain to such a man the great labor that will teach him to perceive fiery vibrations? He should at least once in a while sense the inspiring quality of labor, and will thus plant in his heart a beautiful seed of Agni.

The Thinker lamented the inadequate quality of labor.

938. Urusvati thinks correctly about the combining of the elements. Usually, in human thinking, all that exists is divided into harmful and good, but people forget that out of poisonous combinations healing substances can be derived, and by blending beneficial ones harmful combinations can be obtained.

The same happens with people. One can see how a poisonous nature can produce positive combinations, whereas good people can, as a group, be transformed into a most harmful community. The effects of these combinations are clearly seen in the Supermundane World. Inexperienced observers are astonished when they see that those who were enemies on earth can approach one another quite peacefully, and even join together in their quest for perfection. The reason is simple: on Earth they could not understand each other because of surrounding vibrations, but the Subtle World changed the vibrations, and sworn enemies come together. In the same way, faceted stones, when shaken together in a bowl, find the most compact arrangement of contact.

Hints of such transformations can be found in different Teachings; in essence nothing new takes place, but the individual becomes changed because of the combination of the elements. Everything that was dormant in him is stirred up by the least touch of the highest energies.

The Thinker consoled the complaining ones, "We will even transform harm into good."

939. Urusvati knows the difference between the truly striving ones and the cunning pretenders. Often demands for something new are heard. At first one can rejoice, but later it turns out that these strong demands come from people who do not know the fundamentals.

They do not wish to strive to knowledge, and think that they can wilfully leap over the fundamentals and gain something new. They do not understand that the nature of learning is a gradual progression. Do not think that such ignorance is only found in earthly life; exactly the same can happen in the Supermundane World. Some of its inhabitants believe that they can jump over several steps and master something extraordinarily novel. They do not even stop to consider where such a leap will take them!

The consequences could be quite deplorable. Nothing useful would take place; on the contrary, a delay would occur that is harmful from the point of view of Karma. It is sad to see to what extent these people avoid studying the Fundamentals. Even if they had leafed through the Writings sometime in the past, they failed to grasp the meaning of the Teaching.

Many petty, cunning people can present themselves as initiates in order to learn about new things as yet unknown to others, but they do not know how to love to study!

The Thinker often warned, "What is the use of the new to you, until you have learned the fundamentals?

The leaves are at their greenest only when the roots are strong."

940. Urusvati values clarity of thought. Yes, yes, a pure, clear, and commanding thought can be called spatial thought. An arrow must not be blunt; an arrow must not be too long. Likewise a command of thought must be sharp and brief.

Quality of thinking is needed, both for Earth and also for the Supermundane World, where communication is by thought, and an ability to think clearly is especially needed. Imagine a dweller who is used to thinking in tangled and lengthy ways. He will experience great difficulty in communicating with those around him. Also, he would not know how to receive the lightning bolt of a brief message. Worse, he would have to now learn what he could not learn in his earthly life.

It is pitiful to look at such inarticulate ones, for they become tangled in a labyrinth of dark, weak thoughts. Their emanations are weak and will not light up their path. One may say that they present a useless burden to the Subtle World, instead of being luminous co-workers. They will regret that during the days of their earthly existence they did not find the time for the work of mental progress.

The Thinker said, "A great many treasures can be packed into one's luggage."

941. Urusvati loves the sounds of the Supermundane World. The supermundane harmonies are healing and inspiring, but they are often interrupted by the noise of battles, wailing, and the roaring of mad crowds. Much energy is required to transform these earthly moanings into harmonious sounds.

One would think that people would know to what extent earthly sounds fill space and overwhelm it, and would therefore be more considerate about the quality of their sendings.

It is time for scientists to investigate the nature of the atmosphere. If one's psychic energy can create the strongest poisons, then one's emanations will be poisonous. We have spoken many times about the sickness of the planet; it should also be mentioned that the encircling space will also be contaminated. Rather than hope that Prana will transform the poisonous spatial atmosphere into a healthy one, would it not be better for man to abstain from poisoning everything around him?

Man, as a microcosm, bears a great responsibility, and it is time for him to realize that the filling of space with harmful poisons is not in line with evolution. It should not be thought that someone, somewhere, will set right the madness of people, who themselves, in their everyday life, should do good and useful things. Even amidst the poorest of existences, general human advances can be made.

The Thinker warned, "Do not pollute the atmosphere."

942. Urusvati does not tolerate lies. Only the smallest part of humanity struggles against the lie. Some fight against it for moral reasons, whereas others already understand the cosmic harm of the lie. Indeed, since thoughts and words live in space and emit vibrations over immeasurable distances, how many dark and false inventions appear and poison the planet!

The Supermundane World, too, suffers from human lies. And the liars themselves will have to face their own poisonous sendings. They will then understand how gravely they infect space. The cosmic harm of the lie should be taught in schools. The moral teaching will penetrate deeply into the consciousness of students, and the scientific demonstration of its irreparable harm will change their thinking.

Thus the Thinker bade, "Greet those strong ones who fight against the lie."

943. Urusvati, in her search for Truth, strives to the simplest solutions. Harmony lies in simplicity. Complexities do not lead to harmony, which is needed to nourish the planet. Because humanity is far from cooperation with the Supermundane World, do not be surprised that it is necessary to speak daily about the living links with the Subtle World.

It will be impossible to stop the poisoning of Earth if spatial harmony is not found. Harmony should be seen not as something abstract, but as a system of earthly order. It can be observed that great scientists often began with complicated ideas, and then arrived at the simplest. They were true seekers and were impelled to search for the most simple, great, constructive harmony.

You already know that disharmony is destructive, and harmony is constructive. The developing of the Highest Science will lead to the Healing Source. We have pointed out the significance of music, both on Earth and in the Supermundane World. Let youth accept the lofty harmonies which are needed for Earth, and also for the Subtle World.

The Thinker said, "Yes, yes, yes, there exists the blind faith and the seeing faith; be among those who see."

944. Urusvati studies the Supermundane World without personal motives. Many turn to the Supermundane World for personal reasons. Some seek meetings with departed dear ones, others want to gain advantage and success, and others think about the Supermundane World only when in danger or need.

Such limited appeals have nothing to do with study, and are only flashes of egoism.

Not receiving what they want, people turn away and even become deniers. They do not realize that through a narrow door only a small part of nature can be seen. Yet, if you tell such people about the need for broad research, they will not find within themselves the necessary impulse to dedicate themselves to the beautiful process of gaining knowledge. They do not understand that understanding the boundless Supermundane World requires the deepest concentration.

In their egoism, people forget their own desire to study and are even willing to harm their own dear ones if they stand in the way of their desires. These seekers of personal gain cannot imagine that they impose themselves on the Supermundane World. They do not even wish to wait until the necessary favorable conditions have been created. They neither observe nor study, and overlook the most beautiful phenomena. Yet, without study, without striving, it is impossible to even imagine the Supermundane World.

The Thinker pointed out, "Study the Supermundane World scientifically, inspiringly, and untiringly, not for yourself, but for humanity."

945. Urusvati knows the unrepeatability of the manifestations of the Supermundane World. The boundless abundance of the Supermundane World should demonstrate the various aspects of Existence, but for the ordinary scientist it is precisely this fact that keeps him from accepting the investigation of the Supermundane World as science. Long ago We insisted upon scientific foundations, but scientists want their science to be precise. They forget that such precision is relative, and depends on many factors. Scientists

prefer to move slowly along their beaten path and are afraid to look into unknown realms.

We accept scientific logic, but cannot allow scientists to be cowardly. They are afraid of the unknown manifestations of the forces of the Universe. They refuse to understand that the unrepeatability of phenomena should be the very thing that attracts them.

The understanding of Supermundane unrepeatability prompts one to think of the many earthly obstacles. A true researcher will say, "I shall observe the most subtle manifestations. Amidst the many varied conditions, I will probably find the connecting threads that will lead me into the New World." But not all will speak thus, and the Supermundane World will remain a fairytale.

The Thinker admonished His disciples not to fear Infinity.

946. Urusvati has assimilated the continuous supermundane currents. Even an exalted, refined organism does not assimilate such transmissions easily. Let us recall the pain that accompanies sendings of the Subtle World! The earthly armor opposes with all its power the reception of the supermundane voice. Each earthly sound thunders and vibrates as if amplified by a megaphone. The heart is terrified even by the least rustling.

Sacred pains are caused by the incompatibility of earthly and supermundane vibrations. The most natural approach from the Supermundane World seems like an unendurable intrusion, but the strong will overcomes the first stages. Finally, the sacred pains weaken; the rustlings, or even screams, no longer unsettle one, and cooperation with the Supermundane World becomes familiar. Having reached this level of achievement, the researcher can see that the supermundane current works incessantly, but it is man himself who rejects the valuable messages.

Many excuses are invented to explain this away as a matter of chance or because of an ailment. Truly, only a valiant, free will liberates man from superstition and tells him, "Fainthearted one, listen more attentively."

The Thinker reminded His students often, "Listen to each other."

947. Urusvati knows why a Yogi appears unremarkable. People love to embellish their idea of a Yogi with symbolic attributes. But they forget that Yoga is a link with the Highest, and that this privilege must belong to everyone. Thus, the yogic state is a natural condition, but people turn away from it and in doing so reject the basic purpose of their lives. They have rejected their better destiny and will bear the seal of their unnatural condition.

Many examples could be cited of Yogis who remained completely unnoticeable while in the midst of a crowd. They did not wish to be noticed. They did not need the tunic of an initiate to bring benefit to all. Also, remember that the light of the Yogi is in his heart, and that he often deliberately dims his radiations in order not to be seen.

The Thinker reminded His students often that a Yogi, though a bearer of Light, passes unnoticed.

948. Urusvati knows that the Yogi brings joy and health. We confirm that the emanations of a Yogi can be healing and joyful. He actually does bring these gifts. He is connected with the Supermundane World, from which he draws his precious strength.

His heart is full of supermundane harmonies, but he does not impose harmony. It is a joy to borrow from the Supermundane Treasury. One can overcome one's illnesses. Prana comes as a blessing, a panacea that restores one's health. No magical formulas are needed; it is sufficient to immerse oneself in the aura of a purified spirit.

One should not doubt the Supermundane World. Let the entrance be broad and trust be at the threshold. Man must remember the brief command: "Do not doubt!"

"The worm of doubt kills joy and health." Thus did the Thinker urge the doubting ones. "And dark will be your face."

949. Urusvati knows that the Yogi can be called the one who sacrifices. What can be sacrificed by him, who has already renounced all earthly riches? But the treasure of the Yogi is always with him: his labor, his thought, his will and all his great energy. From these sources he can draw untiringly, and what is given is replenished by the supermundane prana.

The Yogi serves as a living link with the Supermundane World; this honorable cooperation is not easy. Chaotic earthly accumulations cause pain and exhaustion beyond measure. But the Yogi is a true sacrificer and knows that the Common Good is not achieved easily. As a sensible manager of his resources, he does not allow overfatigue. He knows that all extremes should be avoided. He will immediately inhale the prana and give rest to his organism. This rest will not be a lengthy one, for the Supermundane World hastens to replenish the loss of energy.

The Thinker said, "We give and thus receive. We sacrifice and thus enrich ourselves."

950. Urusvati knows that the Yogi can be called a sower. He sows good untiringly, not for himself but for humanity. Whence then is gathered the store of good? It cannot increase by earthly means alone. It is sent from the Supermundane World, and the Yogi must be always ready to accept these valuable sendings.

The Supermundane World sends its communications by day and by night. They contain not only general advice, but Instructions for everyday events. Thus one can see how close the Supermundane World is to the earthly one, but only the Yogi can discern the indicated dates and understand the language of the Supermundane World. The sendings are brief, for each moment is filled with them. Therefore people must regard Yogic Service with great respect. Truly, the state of the Yogi is not only exalted, it is also devoted to service for the Common Good.

The Thinker asserted, "Incessantly sow the Good."

951. Urusvati knows that the Yogi can be called a peacemaker. The Yogi radiates peace for the sake of the Common Good. The Yogi ends quarrels. The Yogi does not tire of talking about the Good.

Much patience is needed to overcome human conflicts. What is the source of this invincible patience? It grows from the realization of the Supermundane World. The Yogi knows how each earthly quarrel, each hatred, will resound in the Supermundane World. They increase amidst the subtle energies. Therefore man should not permit himself to sully the Supermundane World. The Yogi not only heals the surrounding space, he also can strike there where the infection has become incurable.

The Yogi's thought is like an arrow, and he will apply all his understanding in accepting responsibility for the purifying of space. Most people will never understand the self-denial of the Yogi, in spite of which he walks valiantly to the luminous goal.

The Thinker used to say, "Ancient is the teaching

about World Peace; the various creeds have assimilated this command. Do not consider it unrealizable."

952. Urusvati knows that the Yogi can be called a builder. Many majestic constructions are created because of the mental command of the Yogi. Many architects have been inspired by the projected thought of the Yogi. Sometimes these sendings were received over great distances, but there also have been personal meetings with Yogis, who never revealed their identity.

Do not believe it if someone calls himself an initiate. The Yogi does not reveal his sacred knowledge. Likewise, the Yogi-builders do not call themselves architects, but say that someone else gave them useful advice.

Truly, upon the face of the planet are rising the milestones of humanity. The mind whispers that in the foundations of many structures lie special thoughts. Invincible magnets attract and purify the attention of the contemplative man. We spoke long ago about these magnets that lie in the foundations. One can trace how the invisible paths form a protective net upon the Earth.

The Thinker taught, "Be builders."

953. Urusvati knows that the Yogi can be called farsighted. Through the grey veil of the earthly everyday life the Yogi distinguishes the contours of the future. People may ask why We call the Yogi farsighted instead of clairvoyant. But We wish to see the Yogi as quite human.

We have no need of fakirs who stand on their heads. We have no need of sorcerers with a halo of clairvoyance, selling their crumbs of prognostication for money. We wish a true Yogi to be a good sower, a servant of the Common Good. This entreaty must be remembered, for people forget the simplest, most urgent advice.

What then is the source from which the Yogi draws his keen insight? Again, from the same Highest Source, and from the Supermundane World. From there, just as from the summit of the mountain, the inevitable events of human life can be seen. There the Yogi sharpens his inner vision. Let us not consider this ability to be supernatural; on the contrary, it is accessible to everyone, but people are too distant from the highest spheres.

The Thinker asserted, "Find the simplest path to the Higher World and learn to love it."

954. Urusvati knows that the Yogi can be called The One Who Hearkens. Truly the Yogi pays attention to each summons of the heart. The Yogi does not respond to cunning curiosity. The Yogi rejects malicious pretense. One should be aware that the heightened vibrations of the Yogi are so refined that he can instantaneously sense the emanations of people!

The Yogi acts in accordance with the instructions of the Supermundane World, but he still maintains his free will. His vibrations are so refined that he is in constant consonance with the Subtle World.

Often the Yogi senses, like lightning bolts, the sendings that come to him. But these are infallible, as much as are those that come so clearly that he can put them into words. Only in exercising his thinking can the Yogi attain subtle vibrations.

One can call thought fiery, because fire lies in the foundation of thinking. Also, understand that attentiveness must be developed from babyhood. Even if it is inborn, the doors must be opened for it. Even if the nature of the Yogi has been already outlined, in his life, like that of a hero, he must be armed for *podvig*.

The Thinker taught, "Without attentiveness the laws of the Universe cannot be studied."

955. Urusvati knows that the Yogi can be called grateful. In the Supermundane World gratitude will always be a valuable quality. Because of his link with the Subtle World, the Yogi understands the significance of gratitude. It has already been said that gratitude is valuable to the one who feels it. At each action of good, the fire of the heart shines brightly and fills the emanations with healing.

Yet people persistently do not want to understand the significance of giving thanks. No one has spoken to the children about the inner meaning of the sendings of good. They can only in their own way grasp the benefit of gratitude. Sometimes they are compelled to repeat some senseless gratitude, whose inner meaning is not even explained to them. What meaning can there be in the senseless repetition of words not even understood? Remember that so-called prayers, uttered without understanding, are of no consequence. People who pray in this way have no bridge into the Supermundane World, and wander lost in the desert, not knowing how to reach the Garden of Beauty.

The Thinker taught, "Learn to understand gratitude. It will build the Abode of Good."

AGNI YOGA SERIES

Leaves of Morya's Garden I (The Call)	1924
Leaves of Morya's Garden II (Illumination)	1925
New Era Community	1926

Signs of Agni Yoga

Agni Yoga	1929
Infinity I	1930
Infinity II	1930
Hierarchy	1931
Heart	1932
Fiery World I	1933
Fiery World II	1934
Fiery World III	1935
Aum	1936
Brotherhood	1937
Supermundane (in 3 volumes)	1938

Agni Yoga Society
www.agniyoga.org

www.ingramcontent.com/pod-product-compliance
Lightning Source LLC
Chambersburg PA
CBHW071557080526
44588CB00010B/940